Public Sentiments

Public

Sentiments

STRUCTURES *of* FEELING

in NINETEENTH-CENTURY

AMERICAN LITERATURE

GLENN HENDLER

THE UNIVERSITY OF NORTH CAROLINA PRESS

CHAPEL HILL *&* LONDON

© 2001

The University of North Carolina Press

All rights reserved

Set in Carter Cone Galliard by Tseng Information Systems, Inc.

Manufactured in the United States of America

The paper in this book meets the guidelines for permanence and durability
of the Committee on Production Guidelines for Book Longevity of the Council
on Library Resources.

Earlier versions of portions of this book were previously published under the
following titles: "The Structure of Sentimental Experience," *Yale Journal of
Criticism* 12, no. 1 (1999): 146–53; "Bloated Bodies and Sober Sentiments:
Masculinity in 1840s Temperance Fiction," in *Sentimental Men: Masculinity and the
Politics of Affect in American Culture,* ed. Mary Chapman and Glenn Hendler
(Berkeley and Los Angeles: University of California Press, 1999): 125–48;
"Pandering in the Public Sphere: Masculinity and the Market in Horatio Alger,"
American Quarterly 48, no. 3 (September 1996): 414–38; "Tom Sawyer's
Masculinity," *Arizona Quarterly* 49, no. 4 (Winter 1993): 33–59; "The Limits of
Sympathy: Louisa May Alcott and the Sentimental Novel," *American Literary
History* 3, no. 4 (Winter 1991): 685–706. All reprinted by permission.

Library of Congress Cataloging-in-Publication Data

Hendler, Glenn, 1962–

Public sentiments: structures of feeling in nineteenth-century American
literature / Glenn Hendler.

    p. cm.

Includes bibliographical references and index.

ISBN 0-8078-2606-5 (alk. paper)—ISBN 0-8078-4921-9 (pbk.: alk. paper)

1. American literature—19th century—History and criticism.   2. Emotions
in literature.   3. Didactic fiction, American—History and criticism.

4. Sentimentalism in literature.   5. Sympathy in literature.   6. Sex role in
literature.   I. Title.

PS217.E47 H46   2001

813'.309353—dc21   00-049441

05   04   03   02   01   5   4   3   2   1

For my mother and my brother,

in memory of my sister and my father

CONTENTS

ACKNOWLEDGMENTS

The first readers of parts of this book were the members of "the dissertation group" at Northwestern, Nina Miller and Nancy Ring. Though only some pieces of what they read remain, and even those have been put into a different frame, I am sure they can recognize their invaluable influence, and I hope they know how much I appreciate it. Bob Fanuzzi, Laurie Milner, Doug Payne, and Matt Roberts were also great colleagues and compatriots during this work's early stages. Thanks for support and intellectual inspiration are also due to Michal Ginsburg, Mimi White, and Nancy Fraser. I had sure-handed guidance from John Brenkman, Gerald Graff, Ken Warren, and especially Michael Warner.

Sustaining me through the years of adjunct work that seem to have become prerequisites for a more stable academic career were friends and colleagues at the University of Western Ontario, including Tom Carmichael, Julie Di Cresce, Jacqueline Jenkins, Sarah King, Marty Kreiswirth, Alison Lee, Jeff Ogborne, and Nicholas Watson. Thanks are due to them, and to others from my time in Canada, which taught me to look with a more distanced eye at politics, culture, and the public sphere in the United States.

As this project has grown and mutated over the years, my debts to friends and colleagues have proliferated, and I worry about leaving someone off this list. But it feels to me like a continuation of an ongoing intellectual conversation, and those who have participated can, I hope, see their contributions in the text itself. Special thanks are due to the members of two writing groups, one at Notre Dame (Doris Bergen, Kathy Biddick, Julia Douthwaite, Barbara Green, Sandra Gustafson, and Christian Moevs) and another in Chicago (Lisa Brawley, Chris Castiglia, Lucy Rinehart, and Sandra Gustafson again). I can only hope that all scholars have at hand such a generous and critical local public for their work.

Thanks as well to Mary Chapman, my coconspirator in the essay collection titled *Sentimental Men,* not only because I could not thank her in those pages, but also because her responses to my ideas have always made my work better. Gordon Hutner helped turn a massive chapter on Alcott into a relatively concise article; though I have now turned it into something else again, his suggestions made it better than it otherwise would have been. Many thanks to Lori Merish for some great conversations and readings. Much appreciation is due to Robert Levine for intellectual help, professional support, and sound advice. Several audiences have responded to talks based on this book; such dialogue not only makes the work better, it also makes it pleasurable. In that regard, especially worth mentioning are audiences at Western Ontario's Centre for the Study of Theory and Criticism and the Centre for American Studies, and colleagues and students who participated in colloquia sponsored by Notre Dame's Gender Studies Program. Also at Notre Dame, I have benefited greatly from conversations with Gail Bederman, Jay Walton, Jeanne Kilde, Mark Behr, John Waters, Laura Winkiel, and especially Gloria-Jean Masciarotte, as well as with graduate students in two courses I taught on "Fictions of the Public Sphere." Thanks to Katherine Eldred for help with classical references. Bruce Burgett helped me more than I deserved; I could not have done it without him. Thanks to Elizabeth Helsinger for inviting me to teach a graduate course on this material at the University of Chicago, and to those students for allowing me another opportunity to test out my ideas. Hi back to Brian, finally. And thanks to my mother, Connie Hendler, for being a supportive and intellectually critical reader. In its later stages, this book owes a great deal to two anonymous readers for the University of North Carolina Press, and especially to Sian Hunter at the Press, who is everything one could ask for in an editor. More informal thanks are due to everyone at the Hopleaf, as well as to Bill Savage, for helping to put the pub in the public sphere.

Work on this book was facilitated by financial support from the Social Sciences and Humanities Research Council of Canada and from the Institute for Scholarship in the Liberal Arts at the University of Notre Dame. I am grateful to these organizations for their support.

Early in this project, my sister died; just as I completed it, I lost my father to cancer. The usual frustrations and satisfactions entailed in the long process of writing a book were thus overshadowed at crucial times by other, very different feelings. Though it may be sentimentality that makes me think so, I feel the absence of Dad and Kim sharply, at unexpected moments, in reading and rereading this book. It is dedicated to the rest of my family—my mother, Connie Hendler, and my brother, David Sloo—in memory of my sister, Kim Hendler, and my father, Glenn Hendler.

Public Sentiments

INTRODUCTION STRUCTURES OF FEELING IN NINETEENTH-CENTURY AMERICA

Public Sentiments is a study of several quite different forms of "cultural work" performed by novels in nineteenth-century America.[1] Some of its chapters analyze novels as adjuncts to social movements, while others examine them as agents of character formation, and others view them as sites on which authors, readers, and cultural arbiters played out ideological and aesthetic conflicts. In its pages appear diverse voices from the nineteenth century, ranging from white working-class drinkers to black nationalist activists, from public librarians to advocates of censorship, from domestic advice writers to feminist speakers, from statisticians to dandies. Its early chapters take a largely historicist approach to text and context, while later chapters deploy psychoanalytic terminology and rest their conclusions somewhat more on close textual readings.

Public Sentiments links novels with the other cultural and political discourses that traverse its pages through a theoretical and historical argument implied in these first two words of its title. Whether the novel under discussion is a work of fiction commissioned by a temperance society, a book published for didactic or commercial reasons, or a text aspiring to higher moral and aesthetic importance, I argue that the nineteenth-century American novel was most often conceived of as a public instrument designed to play in a sentimental key. These key words—"public" and "sentiment"—require extensive and precisely contextualized definitions. Indeed, much of the body of this book is an exploration of what these concepts signified for particular authors, in particular social groups and movements, at particular historical moments, and how these significations shifted even within a particular text or author's career or in the life of a social phenomenon like the Negro Convention movement or an institution like the public library. In this introduction, I want to sketch out in fairly broad strokes the theoretical, methodological, and historical claims that underpin these readings and unpack the terms of my overall argument.

Raymond Williams notes that "sentiment" has existed in English since at least the fourteenth century to denote "physical feeling, and feelings of one's own," and these are still among the principal meanings of the term, whose earlier, etymological origins are in words meaning "to feel." [2] In current usage, "sentiment" primarily connotes private, interior, individual emotions. "Public sentiment" is thus something of an oxymoron. One can describe or express such sentiments, thereby potentially bringing them into public view, but the fact that such expression requires a publicizing act—a publication—only reinforces the commonsense idea that sentiments are, at their origin, nonpublic matters. However, "sentiment" has accrued another, more overtly political, set of meanings, as, for instance, when the *New York Times* reports that the war over Kashmir is helping to "harden public sentiment against Pakistan" in India.[3] This political usage of the word is not without its emotional connotations; the *Times* story, after all, is about nationalistic passions being inflamed by television coverage of a war. However, here the phrase "public sentiment" is roughly coterminous with "public opinion," a collective consensus that is measured—and in important ways constructed—through quantitative instruments like polls.[4] This form of sentiment may be exemplified by someone's personal and individual perspective, as when a television report on a poll is followed by an interview or two with supposedly average citizens who reflect and express the range of opinions documented in the poll. But such sentiment only really exists in its agglomerated, collective, statistical form, not as "feelings of one's own"; it would seem nonsensical to say that a given individual "has a public sentiment."

Williams dates the extension of sentiment to include opinion and not just feeling to the seventeenth century and briefly but suggestively links this conjunction of connotations to the philosophical and literary development of the idea of sensibility. The early history of sensibility and sentiment has been ably analyzed elsewhere, and in any case it mostly predates the nineteenth-century focus of this book.[5] Some key aspects of the phenomenon are important to keep in mind, however. One is that in the eighteenth- and early-nineteenth-century Anglo-American culture of sensibility, feelings were not primarily the sorts of unique, individualized, interior emotions they are in our more psychologized culture.[6] Rather, sentiments required the cultivation of a moral and proper repertoire of feelings, a sensibility.[7] To see this, one need only notice the insistence, in an early American novel such as Hannah Webster Foster's *The Coquette,* that the heroine align her "sentiments" with "reason."[8] A culture in which certain emotions are explicitly valorized over others, measured along a spectrum of rationality, clearly does not conceive of feelings as being indicative of the irreducible uniqueness of the psychologically defined individual.[9] Such affective imperatives persisted well into the nineteenth century. At the end of *Uncle Tom's Cabin,* for example, Harriet Beecher Stowe responds to her own question, "But, what can any individual do?" (to end the horrors of slavery) with her famous, puzzling injunction: "[T]hey can see to it that *they feel right.*"[10] To "feel right" here is to have proper sentiments, an appropriate response to the scenes of suffering and redemption that the reader has witnessed in the course of the novel. Stowe thus tries, as she has throughout the book, to shape the reader's affective response, to structure the forms of identification that the novel evokes.

Feeling Right

Within the evolving "culture of sentiment" that reached its American apotheosis in Stowe's novel, the most highly valorized emotional form was compassion, or what eighteenth- and nineteenth-century writers called "sympathy."[11] One American theorist and advocate of sympathy, the minister Theodore Parker, concisely described it as a recursive emotional exchange: "Feeling, he must make others feel," Parker says of the necessarily sympathetic qualities of a great orator.[12] Specifically, what one must feel is the suffering of others; as Janet Todd writes in *Sensibility: An Introduction,* the purpose of a sentimental work is "the communication of common feeling from sufferer or watcher to reader or audience."[13] Or, as Philip Fisher puts it, "Compassion is, of course, the primary emotional goal of sentimental narration. Compassion exists in relation to suffering and makes of suffering the primary subject matter, perhaps the exclusive subject matter, of sentimental narrative."[14]

Sympathy, by this account, is an emotional response to reading or seeing an expression of another's feelings. It is thus at its core an act of identification. To feel compassion, as opposed to mere pity, one must be able to imagine oneself, at least to some extent, in another's position. Among the major early theorists of this form of sympathy was Adam Smith, who in 1759 described its dynamics in the opening section of *The Theory of Moral Sentiments:*

As we have no immediate experience of what other men feel, we can form no idea of the manner in which they are affected, but by conceiving what we ourselves should feel in the like situation. Though our brother is upon the rack, as long as we ourselves are at our ease, our senses will never inform us of what he suffers. They never did, and never can, carry us beyond our own person, and it is by the imagination only that we can form any conception of what are his sensations. . . . By the imagination we place ourselves in his situation, we conceive ourselves enduring all the same torments, we enter as it were into his body and become in some measure the same person with him, and thence form some idea of his sensations, and even feel something which, though weaker in degree, is not altogether unlike them.[15]

Smith insists that there must be a mediating force between the sympathizer and the sufferer, even if that mediator is the viewer's own imagination. He also implies that sympathy is not simply a natural sensation; it is a sentiment that can and should be cultivated. Jean-Jacques Rousseau's paradigmatic sentimental scenario in his *Discourse on the Origins of Inequality* paints a similarly gruesome but still more complexly mediated scene, imagining the emotions of an imprisoned man watching a beast violently murder and disembowel a child it has just torn from a mother's arms.[16] Here the viewer is meant to identify sympathetically not with the suffering of the child but with the anguish of the mother, who mediates between the observer—kept at a distance and unable to intervene—and what Rousseau depicts as the merely physical pain of the child itself.

The structure of sympathetic identification is similarly mediated and triangulated in fictional nineteenth-century sentimental scenarios. Stowe depicts Eva's death primarily through the eyes of those around her rather then portraying her pain or redemption from a perspective of psychological interiority, and the same can be said of Tom's death, which is mediated first by the perspective of Sambo and Quimbo and then, still more sympathetically, by the appearance of George Harris at his deathbed. Let me cite one perhaps less fraught but no less typical example, from one of the most popular women's sentimental novels of the nineteenth century, Maria Susanna Cummins's 1854 best-seller *The Lamplighter*. Early in the tale, the stepmother of the young orphaned protagonist, Gerty, casually tosses the child's kitten into boiling water, killing it instantly. Cummins may have been asking her reader to pity the cat—briefly—but the scene functions primarily to induce the reader's sympathetic identification with Gerty. The passage focuses on the girl's feelings, not the cat's; it is her ability to love and sympathize with the animal, in contrast with her step-mother's insensibility to the cat's pain, that marks Gerty as an object of sympathy and as the morally developing protagonist of the novel. This sympathy is a form of identification, albeit a mediated one, because readers are asked to feel the same emotions—sorrow, rage, pity for the cat—as does the girl, but mediated through Gerty's perspective.

Sympathy in all of these scenarios is characterized by the conflation of two affective aspects of identification. The reader is asked to feel *like* Gerty, for instance, to compare his or her emotional experiences analogically with those of the protagonist, but in a way that maintains a degree of difference between subject and object of sympathy. At the same time, sympathy de-mands a still closer connection between reader and character; the former is asked to feel *with* the latter, partially to submerge his or her identity and ex-perience in the emotions of the fictional figure in order to transform partial sameness into identity. Recall that Adam Smith went so far as to say that in a sympathetic relation, through imagination "we enter as it were into [the sufferer's] body and become in some measure the same person with him." Even as it produces an affective connection between individual sub-jects, then, sympathy threatens to negate their individuality by confusing the *analogy* it posits between subjects with a fictional and dangerous *coinci-dence* between them.[17] The mediation between a distanced observer and the sufferer is always at risk of collapsing. Put slightly differently, the risk of sympathy is that the idea that one can feel *like* another person feels can be overshadowed by the paradoxically narcissistic and self-negating desire to feel *with* that other, to share the other's experiences as if they were one's own.[18]

A brief excursus into psychoanalytic theory's analysis of sympathy and identification may help to illuminate the logic being played out in these sentimental scenarios. For it is precisely the risk of confusion between analogy and coincidence that makes Freud reject the experience of sympa-thy as a paradigmatic or even healthy example of the kind of intersubjec-tive identification he saw as constitutive of subjectivity. Identification in its most general form can be defined psychoanalytically as a "process whereby the subject assimilates an aspect, property, or attribute of the other and is transformed, wholly or partially, after the model."[19] In Freud's most extended discussion of identification, in *Group Psychology and the Analysis of the Ego,* he tells a story intended to illustrate the essentially psychotic potential of the sympathetic variant of this process of identification. The scene is an encounter between young girls at a boarding school, in which one girl, having received a letter arousing her jealousy, has "a fit of hysterics." "Some of her friends who know about it will catch the fit, as we say, by mental infection," Freud posits. But he insists upon complicating the most obvious interpretation of the situation, in which the other girls' imitation of the first girl's "hysterics" is based upon their sympathy for her suffering. "It would be wrong to suppose that they take on the symptom out of sympathy," Freud argues. "On the contrary, the sympathy only arises out of the identification. . . . One ego has perceived a significant analogy with another upon one point—in our example upon openness to a similar emotion; an identification is thereupon constructed on this point, and under the influence of the pathogenic situation, is displaced on to the symptom which the one ego has produced."[20]

In Freud's account, a sympathetic identification is a mediated, second-order response because it is predicated on the fashioning of a "significant analogy" between two egos. Sentimentalism also represents sympathetic identification as beginning with such a posited analogy. The oft-cited moment in *Uncle Tom's Cabin* when the escaped slave Eliza Harris wins the senator's wife, Mrs. Bird, over to her cause by asking "Have you ever lost a child?" is the classic example of this gesture, in which motherhood and recent loss become the analogous ground on which a cross-racial sympathetic identification can be based. The risk Freud sees is that the affect arising from this analogy can lead "pathogenically" to a misrecognition of the analogy as "coincidence": "The identification by means of the symptom has thus become the mark of a point of coincidence between the two egos." This coincidence, Freud remarks in the abruptly normative conclusion to his analysis, "has to be kept repressed"; otherwise, each incidence of identification threatens a dissolution of the subject's ego.

Sentimental sympathy relies for its power on precisely the outburst of affect that Freud insists on repressing. Eliza's question, "thrust on a new wound," leads Mrs. Bird to "burst into tears," and "every one around her" evinces "signs of hearty sympathy."[21] These characters, like the reader, are meant to make an analogy between their losses and those of Eliza and then to interpret these losses as emotionally equivalent. Stowe enforces this equivalence through direct address to the reader: "And oh! mother that reads this, has there never been in your house a drawer, or a closet, the opening of which has been to you like the opening again of a little grave?"[22] The scenario, again, sets up a figure (Mrs. Bird) designed to mediate between those directly suffering (Eliza's child, under threat, but also Eliza herself, actually experiencing the emotional ravages of slavery) and the reader. It simultaneously promises that the experience of sympathy can efface the emotional differences between the reader, the mediating figure, and the sufferer, that by remembering the death of her own child the "mother that reads this" can answer Stowe's rhetorical question in the affirmative and thereby put herself in the character's place, if not by entering into her body, in Smith's words, at least by emotionally "becom[ing] in some measure the same person" with her.

Sentimentalism's reliance on this fantasy of experiential equivalence is at the root of its affective and political power, but it has always caused unease in some of its readers. Among the gentler early critics of *Uncle Tom's Cabin* was the African American activist, poet, novelist, and orator Frances Ellen Watkins Harper, who penned several poems in praise of both its author and its individual characters. However, in her 1854 poem "The Slave Auction," Harper asserts epistemological limits to the sentimentalists' insistence on affective translatability. Harper bluntly admonishes white readers—those who imagine, like Mrs. Bird, that their loss of a child might give them full understanding of the experience of a slave mother—that they cannot truly "know" the emotional specificity of the slave's suffering:

> Ye who have laid your love to rest,
> And wept above their lifeless clay,
> Know not the anguish of that breast
> Whose lov'd are rudely torn away.

During the 1980s and 1990s, one tendency in the analysis of nineteenth-century American literature and culture has been what Eve Sedgwick calls "a project . . . of rehabilitating the sentimental" from critical neglect and knee-jerk denigration, focusing on sentimentalism's ability both to articulate a protofeminist subject position and to forge emotional solidarity between the predominantly white women who occupied that position and their racial, class, and national others.[23] Another tendency, though, has built on Harper's critique by looking more closely at the cost of that subjectivity for the objects of its sympathy. To critics from a variety of perspectives—but especially those most centrally concerned with questions of race and imperialism — the politics of sympathy is fatally flawed by its drive to turn all differences into equivalences, all analogies into coincidences. The limits of such a politics of affect become apparent when it comes up against any significant cultural or experiential difference between the subject and object of its paradigmatic act of sympathetic identification: if I have to *be* like you and *feel* like you in order for you to feel *for* me, sympathy reaches its limits at the moment you are reminded that I am not quite like you. In other words, any culturally marked or affirmed difference can become an insurmountable obstacle to sympathetic identification.[24] Or still worse, sentimentalism can respond to difference by attempting to negate or suppress it. Analyses of sentimental culture that emphasize such cultural violence include Saidiya Hartman's argument that sentimentalism's putative humanization of black slaves led to more rather than less brutality, as well as Laura Wexler's account of the cultural assimilation of former black slaves and Native Americans in sentimental institutions like the Hampton Normal and Agricultural Institute.[25] As Dana Nelson puts it in her analysis of Harriet Jacobs's strategies of sympathy in *Incidents in the Life of a Slave Girl,* "Sympathy ideally should *bridge* the gap of difference between sisters. Yet it neither can nor should *collapse* the differences that it bridges."[26]

Sentimentalism's power persists to this day both despite and because of sympathy's limits, paradoxes, and potentially violent negations. After all — to use a relatively banal example — Bill Clinton campaigned successfully for the presidency in 1992 by repeating what could be a mantra of sentimentalism: "I feel your pain." Still more banally, the most conventional statement of sympathy in our own sentimental culture is "I know how you feel." Anyone who has attempted to express sympathy for someone else's pain or loss, or who has listened to a series of such expressions of sympathy for his or her own anguish, knows how delicate such phrases are, how carefully chosen the sympathizer's phrases must be in order to seem balanced between claims of knowing and of feeling, between an epistemological and an affective assertion of equivalence. The failure to strike such a balance can be experienced as either an act of indifference or a form of emotional violence paralleling on a personal level the presumption against which Harper warns her readers.[27]

Contemporary historians of sentimentalism tend to focus either on its potential to build bridges between people or its colonizing proclivity to collapse them. In recent years, the critical emphasis has been squarely on the latter tendency, sometimes at the expense of a full understanding of sentimentalism's internal logic. For instance, in a subtle and provocative essay on Stowe, sympathy, and the trope of the "sentimental wound," Marianne Noble makes a statement that she presents as if it were an undeniable fact: "It is fundamentally impossible," she writes, "to bridge the gap separating one person's experience from another's."[28] Such an assertion would astonish and dismay Stowe or any other nineteenth-century adherent to sentimental ideology, which is premised on precisely this possibility. If there can be no communication whatsoever—no bridge—between people's experiences, then the sentimental ideal of "true sympathy" is not merely utopian, it is a lie. To underscore her point, Noble cites Charles Stowe's account of the effectivity of his mother's novel. For him, the language of the novel could "stimulate a sensation of pain that feels so real that . . . '*Uncle Tom's Cabin* made the crack of the slavedriver's whip, and the cries of the tortured black ring in every household in the land.'" Noble responds bluntly, "Of course, it didn't," insisting that such an affective and effective rhetorical act is "fundamentally impossible."[29] Elizabeth Barnes make a similarly blunt assertion about the putative reality of readerly subjectivity in her response to Noble's essay, writing that "the truth is, in the reading experience, nobody's body *really* exists except the reader's."[30] A confrontation with the central premise of sentimentalism—the idea that, through the mediation of textualized sympathy, feelings and experiences can be communicated from one embodied subject to another—seems to make some of the best literary critics of sentimentalism take refuge in an uncharacteristic literalism.[31]

Perhaps contemporary readers are uncomfortable with the nineteenth-century theory of sympathetic identification precisely because of the ways it differs from how we tend to conceive of the experience of reading today. For all the valuable work that has gone into the historical analysis of sentimental culture, it seems to me that we have not yet come to terms with these differences. To the extent that later critics have taken up the suggestions Jane Tompkins made in 1985 in *Sensational Designs* about the distinctions between the sentimental "structure of meanings" and the "modernist literary aesthetic," it has been to make the kinds of claims for the sentimental novel's literary value implied in the title of her concluding chapter: "But Is It Any Good?" Few, though, have explored the implications of Tompkins's assertion that this "structure of meanings . . . fixed these works, for nineteenth-century readers, not in the realm of fairy tale or escapist fantasy, but in the very bedrock of reality."[32] In other words, what a contemporary reader sees as a logical and epistemological impossibility might have been, for Stowe's readers, an equally self-evident fact about reading—indeed, about subjectivity in general. That a novel could make "every household in the land" experience "the crack of the slavedriver's whip" or that reading might be an experience affecting more than a single, discrete, individual body are ideas central to sentimentalism's self-understanding. If readers and authors did not share these ideas to at least some degree, it is unlikely that the sentimental novel could ever have been a popular cultural form, let alone had any degree of political or emotional effectivity.

Even those historians of nineteenth-century sentimentalism who have the most sympathy (so to speak) with its literary/political project have usually defined it relatively narrowly as a feminine literary genre or mode, or a rhetoric that women deployed in protopolitical and political efforts to redraw the boundaries between the public and the domestic, to rewrite domestic ideology in their own interests.[33] To avoid reducing sentimentalism to a form of false consciousness or a merely strategic use of rhetoric, I want to argue that it can be most helpfully described as what Raymond Williams calls a "structure of feeling."[34] The term is a notoriously slippery and deliberately flexible one in Williams's work, but one that seems especially useful for linking a narrative genre with a broader politics of affect. Structures of feeling are, for Williams, "social experiences *in solution,* as distinct from other social semantic formations which have been *precipitated* and are more evidently and more immediately available." He chooses the word "feeling" "to emphasize a distinction from more formal concepts of 'world-view' or 'ideology,'" instead focusing on "specifically affective elements of consciousness," "meanings and values as they are actively lived and felt."[35] It is, in short, a concept tailor-made to describe the way—to return to Tompkins's similar terminology—a "structure of meanings" like that of sentimentalism can become part of the "bedrock of reality" for readers.

Williams writes that "structures of *experience*" might be a better term, but for its inevitable connotations of "the past tense." A structure of feeling is a "practical consciousness of a present kind . . . a social experience which is still *in process,* often indeed not yet recognized as social but taken to be private, idiosyncratic, and even isolating."[36] By "experience" Williams does not mean an unmediated sensation; like Adam Smith, he assumes that "we have no immediate experience of what other men feel."

Rather, "experience" is one name for the mediations that link feelings to social structures and social formations. In other words, Williams wants the concept of a structure of feeling to shift the analysis of social and cultural forms toward an emphasis on the affective processes that make up everyday life, but without losing sight of how even these unevenly developed processes are mediated and structured. It is in art and literature, he says, that such structures are often first made visible: "The idea of a structure of feeling can be specifically related to the evidence of forms and conventions—semantic figures—which, in art and literature, are often among the very first indications that such a new structure is forming. . . . [A]s a matter of cultural theory this is a way of defining forms and conventions in art and literature as inalienable elements of a social material process: not by derivation from other social forms and pre-forms, but a social formation of a specific kind which may in turn be seen as the articulation (often the only fully available articulation) of structures of feeling which as living processes are much more widely experienced."[37]

One advantage of this cultural materialist model is that it reminds us that the always fraught concept of experience need not only refer to an individual act, event, or emotion, to something that requires an imaginary bridge in order to be shared or communicated. As soon as it is experienced, anything—even or perhaps especially an emotion, whether felt directly or vicariously—is in this view "a social material process." In other words, as Joan Scott has influentially argued, "Experience is at once always already an interpretation *and* is in need of interpretation."[38] On this basis, throughout *Public Sentiments* I treat the experience of sympathetic identification as the narrative and affective core of a sentimental structure of feeling. The forms and conventions developed in the sentimental novel—and in the other social and cultural forms I analyze—were articulations of new social formations only then being preliminarily experienced by the audiences brought into being by the deployment of sentimental sympathy in literary form.

Feeling Publicly

The cultural forms that arose within the "culture of sentiment" constructed an affectivity that, as Williams says, appears to be "private, idiosyncratic, and even isolating." Sentimental culture reinforced the sense that sympathy was a purely private relation by representing the experience of sympathy in expressivist rhetoric, and it depended in part on a fantasy of sensory and sensational immediacy, exemplified by Charles Stowe's notion that the sounds of slavery could be heard in millions of households. Theodore Parker's account of the communication of sympathy—"Feeling, he must make others feel"—also seems to confirm the sense that sympathy was an unmediated interpersonal communication of affect. But the demonstrable social and political force of *Uncle Tom's Cabin* may be the best example of Williams's point that, at least when presented in a commodified cultural form like a popular novel, the apparently "private" is articulated as something "social." It is in that articulation—and not, as in a narrowly literal interpretation of Stowe's injunction to "feel right," in the affect itself—that we can locate sentimental culture's politics of affect. Even in Parker's formulation the scene of affective exchange is not one of interpersonal intimacy; it is the relation between an orator and an audience, and oratory is an undeniably public genre.[39]

Throughout this book, then, I argue that sympathy in the nineteenth century was a paradigmatically public sentiment. By using the word "public" here, I mean at the minimum to reiterate that sympathy was not a primarily privatizing emotional exchange between reader, text, and author. Beyond that I mean to invoke—and place this book in the context of—the growing body of critical theory and cultural history influenced by Jürgen Habermas's *Structural Transformation of the Public Sphere*.[40] A brief account of Habermas's argument will help me make clear where *Public Sentiments* follows, puts to the test, and diverges from the broad historical and theoretical rubric he sets out and how I draw out from parts of his text a vocabulary useful for describing the sentimental politics of affect.[41]

Structural Transformation is not usually read as an account of a politics of affect. It presents itself, rather, as both a history and a synchronic theoretical analysis of "a category of bourgeois society" Habermas calls the public sphere, or publicity.[42] In the broadly historical trajectory he outlines, he identifies two "structural transformations" of the public sphere, one of which essentially created bourgeois publicity, the second of which has begun to destroy it. The first transformation established publicity both as the dominant form of legitimation for the democratic capitalist state *and* as a norm that could be used to criticize the state. Previously, the only thing that could be described as "public" was the king or lord's display of what Habermas calls "representative publicness," through which the ruling figure was seen as the embodiment of that group or territory that he or she ruled. For the feudal lord and in feudal law, there was no political distinction between the public and private character of the ruler. Representative publicness was something to be displayed "before" the people, not represented "for" or in the name of the people.[43]

The first structural transformation of publicity occurred when the ascendant bourgeoisie began to set up as norms the principles of openness and accountability, a discourse of rights and freedom of expression, the value of debate and discussion leading toward agreement or consensus — in short, all the positive principles that we still commonly associate with the word "public." The liberal public sphere could emerge when public opinion became a regulative principle, one that should and did shape and restrict the actions of the state. By "public opinion," Habermas does not mean to refer to either the generally accepted and expressed prejudices of so-called common sense or the aleatory whims now traceable through daily CNN tracking polls; these he refers to as "mere opinion." Public opinion must be formed in the course of rational discussion that takes place in a sphere that is not a subset of the state. Neither should public opinion be characterizable as the expression of any particular private interest, especially not economic interests, which is why the public sphere comes into existence to mediate between state and society, and why it is not entirely reducible to what is referred to as "civil society," which incorporates the economic market. Habermas can thus claim that "a portion of the public sphere is constituted in every conversation in which private persons come together to form a public," so long as they are acting neither as representatives of the state nor as "professional people conducting their private affairs." In short, bourgeois publicity is predicated on a fiction of abstracted, disinterested, and disembodied subjectivities interacting in a sphere where "the best argument," rather than coercion, carries the day.

The fictionality of this sphere and the putative disembodiment of the subjects occupying it do not mitigate its material and ideological ramifications. Such a public sphere as a concept is grounded in the existence of actual spaces in which such "rational-critical debate" can be practiced. In the most materially historical thread of his argument, Habermas discusses a set of institutions that emerged in full force in the eighteenth century: cafés, reading clubs, subscription libraries, and, in some countries, newspapers. What was significant about these institutions was that in them interpretation could take place with a degree of freedom from the political strictures of the state as well as from the economic imperatives of the market. Literature and the discussion of literature have a crucial and exemplary status in this strand of Habermas's argument. A novel, as a commodity that "pretended to exist for its own sake" — or, perhaps more important, that existed for the purpose of being interpreted and discussed — could instantiate the public sphere in much the same way as did a private conversation about public issues.[44] Literature "was claimed as the ready topic of a discussion through which" bourgeois subjectivity "communicated with itself."[45] Insofar as literature was designed to be openly criticized and actively interpreted, and insofar as it made a claim to at least a limited autonomy from both the state and particular private interests, it exemplified the openness and the rational-critical basis of the political public. In a sense, literature itself — along with the structures that allowed for its distribution and reception — became one of the "institutions of the public sphere."

This last phrase, drawn from a section heading in Habermas's book, provides the title for the first section of *Public Sentiments*.[46] Each of the section's three chapters puts this aspect of Habermas's argument to the test in an American context by locating fictional forms as institutions of the public sphere themselves, as well as in relation to the organized social spaces that structured the novels' production, distribution, and reception. The first chapter examines novels and stories written in support of the Washingtonian temperance societies that sprang up all over the country in the 1840s. The Washingtonians were among the first to accept that fiction could be a part of a social movement, and writers including Walt Whitman and T. S. Arthur devoted their efforts to furthering the cause of organized abstinence from alcohol. The Washingtonian use of fiction functions in my argument partly as a paradigmatic case of the novel's use as a public instrument. The narratives, disseminated through the medium of print that Habermas asserts was essential to the formation of the bourgeois public sphere, enlisted the readers' identification with fictional protagonists to align them with the cause of personal and social reform. Some aspects of the Washingtonian phenomenon, however, put the Habermasian model to the test. The movement's working-class basis puts into question Habermas's claim that the public sphere was always an essentially bourgeois formation, that public spheres emerging from other economic and cultural sectors were variants "suppressed in the historical process."[47] Still more important for my argument's emphasis on public *sentiments,* the Washingtonians expanded and reproduced their public sphere through dramatic displays of male emotionality; according to contemporaneous accounts, their large and public meetings were distinguished by scenes in which masses of men would together burst into tears in response to a particularly affecting story of drunken iniquity and redemption. These narratives and the responses they provoked, along with Washingtonian novels written by Whitman and Arthur, thus challenge the emphasis on rationality in the Habermasian account of the public sphere, even as they exemplify certain aspects of that account.

In an essay written in response to the translation of Habermas's book into English, Michael Schudson tests the applicability of the Habermasian model to an American historical context, coming to comparable conclusions about the model's focus on rationality. "Was there ever a public sphere?" he asks in his title; "if so, when?" To answer his own questions, Schudson first scrutinizes political participation quantitatively, reaching the familiar conclusion that during the heyday of mass party politics, from 1840 to 1900, electoral and party activity reached an unprecedented and still unsurpassed peak. He then examines the quality of that participation, measuring it against Habermas's notion of "rational-critical discourse." "It does not appear," he concludes, "that in any general sense rational-critical discussion characterized American politics in the colonial era," and "political discourse did not become markedly more rational and critical" in the nineteenth century.[48]

The emphasis on publicly displayed affect in the Washingtonian movement certainly jibes with this generalization. However, like many historians who have searched for a public sphere in nineteenth-century America, Schudson may not have looked in the right places. Perhaps no American institution better fit the Habermasian model than the Negro Convention movement that flourished among free blacks—under repressive conditions—from the 1830s through the Civil War and beyond. Chapter 2 examines this movement as an institution of the public sphere, one that produced voluminous accounts of markedly rational and critical debates among black advocates of abolition, voting rights, and temperance, and in some cases active resistance and black emigration. In the more radical wing of this movement stood the main subject of my chapter, Martin Delany, who engaged in virtually every public activity open to a black man in the decades before the Civil War. I examine his career, his political writings, and his choice in the late 1850s to turn to the novel as the genre in which he could best articulate his black nationalist sentiments to his public. *Blake;*

or, the Huts of America is perhaps not the most overt statement of Delany's political philosophy, but it is the text in which the rational-critical discourse of his involvement in social movements, in the press, and in other forms of activism comes most directly into dialogue with the sentimental politics of affect that characterizes the novel as a genre. Through a reading of this novel, and especially of its implicit definitions of citizenship and civility, I discuss the ways in which various forms of sentiment pervade Delany's nonfictional political writings, as well as the ways in which he builds into the novel itself a notion of print, narrative, and affect as instruments for producing and affecting public discourse.

Both the Washingtonian temperance movement and the Negro Convention movement might best be described not as publics but as "counterpublics." This latter term developed, in a sense, as a reaction to a reference Habermas makes in the preface to his book to "the *plebeian* public sphere as a variant that in a sense was suppressed in the historical process."[49] German critics Oscar Negt and Alexander Kluge respond to this assertion in their book *Public Sphere and Experience* by delineating a set of alternative publics that they claim exist in potential and actual form in the working-class's "social experience."[50] When in this book I use the term "counterpublic," it most broadly denotes an appeal to a public marked by status attributes other than those possessed by members of the hegemonic bourgeois public, that is, a public of noncitizens or of those excluded from any of the perquisites of citizenship. By the middle of the nineteenth century in the United States, property-owning, native-born white males possessed basic citizenship rights and at least some access to the public sphere. Thus, when the Washingtonians refused on principle to lobby the state for changes in liquor laws, or when the Negro Convention movement failed in its efforts to prevent states from rolling back voting rights for free blacks, the concept of a counterpublic seems especially appropriate. But it is important to keep in mind that this term does not necessarily designate a fundamental difference, in principle or practice, between these publics and the others analyzed in this book.[51] After all, in Habermas's account the paradigmatic public sphere of the European bourgeoisie begins with exclusion from state power and for that reason maintains a critical distance from it; thus it can, at one point in its history, be legitimately described as a counterpublic itself.

The third and last chapter of my opening section locates a set of novels by Horatio Alger in a public sphere institution that is not in any strong sense of the term a counterpublic sphere, though it is not just an instrument of state power either. I am referring to the public library, where the morality of Alger's novels was debated and discussed in various forums, including an 1879 library convention. At stake in these debates about the role of popular fiction in the formation of the character of boys and young men was, above all, the relationship between the public sphere and the economic market. In Habermas's account of the novel's role in the development of the public sphere, the market played an enabling but not a defining role. The material book itself was made widely available in the form of a commodity, but its reception and interpretation occurred ostensibly free of economic constraints. It is important to Habermas that the logic of commodification did not yet penetrate either the content of the book or what he calls the "psychological" relationship between reader, text, and author.[52] Only later, during the second transformation of the public sphere, did the rise of mass culture, advertising, and "manufactured publicity and nonpublic opinion" begin to make the audience itself into a commodity that would ultimately be bought and sold by television networks and advertisers.[53]

rise of mass culture = second transformation of the public sphere

Those librarians, ministers, and critics who were critical of Alger claimed that his books were too fully implicated in the economic market to be appropriate purchases for a public library. In making this claim they were struggling—sometimes explicitly—to fix the meaning of the word "public" in the phrase "public library." Late-nineteenth-century cultural analysts were anxious about trends similar to those that Habermas decries as threatening to his ideal type of the public sphere, such as the tendency to put forms of subjectivity—in this case boys' masculinity—on the market to be "read" and targeted by authors and publishers. My analysis puts the worries of these cultural arbiters into a conversation with Alger's own notion of the public sphere. Public space and public character were central concepts in his formula. Contrary to the understanding of his novels as narrating a trajectory "from rags to riches," by my reading Alger was far more emphatic that his boys rise from obscurity to a position of some public note. By the end of his novels his protagonists have almost invariably performed a heroic act in a public place, appeared in the newspapers, or won a degree of public acclaim for their honesty and virtue. Publicity was a crucial aspect of his heroes' character; its nuances and contradictions across several of his novels are explored in Chapter 3.

The chapter on Alger also takes up a debate mentioned earlier in this introduction by countering theories and histories of nineteenth-century sentimentality and domesticity that describe these modes as "private" and place the domestic sphere in binary opposition to an economic realm defined as public. The fact that both Alger and his critics strive to define the public sphere as distinct from the economic market points to the problem with this conceptualization, which is quite simply that under capitalism the economic realm is in important ways private, not public. Habermas makes this point emphatically, noting that in early conceptualizations of the public sphere "professional people conducting their private affairs" were theoretically excluded from its boundaries. As in American republicanism, where the citizen acting in public was meant to disavow all private interests and act as an "abstract" citizen, in forms of bourgeois publicity in general the subject is ostensibly abstract, putting aside particularizing status attributes, interests, and desires.

Such abstraction was enabled, as Michael Warner has demonstrated, by a special way of thinking about publication and especially print. Merging arguments from Habermas with ideas from Benedict Anderson's discussion of "print capitalism," Warner argues that print became the vehicle for an "authoritative mediation." Rather than viewing their published words as expressions of opinions that readers should link directly to their authors, writers often wrote anonymously or pseudonymously in order to validate their opinions by detaching them from their persons. Warner terms this dynamic a "principle of negativity," showing that in this model "[w]hat you say will carry force not because of who you are but despite who you are. Implicit in this principle is a utopian universality that would allow people to transcend the given realities of their bodies and their status."[54]

As I argue above, such self-abstraction is always imaginary, what Warner calls a "fantasy of publicity." It is first of all a fantasy in a relatively straightforward sense; as Warner puts it, "the ability to abstract oneself in public discussion has always been an unequally distributed resource."[55] In other words, only those with certain attributes — in the American context these have included whiteness, maleness, property ownership, and native birth — could perform the abstraction or "disincorporation" essential to the validation of their public discourse; thus self-abstraction is in actual practice linked to specific traits even as it disavows the public relevance of particularity. But the dynamic by which this differential was legitimated involved a more complex fantasy as well. Warner continues: "Access to the public came in the whiteness and maleness that were then denied as

(margin note) Warner's "mass subject"

forms of positivity, since the white male qua public person was only abstract rather than white and male." The differential was established not only by forms of legal exclusion from, say, voting rights; it also lay in "cultural/symbolic definitions" of race and gender, which established that "[s]elf-abstraction from male bodies confirms masculinity" while "[s]elf-abstraction from female bodies denies femininity."[56] Just as the experience of sympathy depended upon a fantasy that differences could be effaced by defining human identity affectively, publicity depended on a fictional erasure of status attributes.

The "just as" in that last sentence marks more than a casual analogy; it indicates a homology that is at the core of Habermas's argument and that helps to link the two sections of *Public Sentiments*. Habermas argues for the mutual constitution of, on the one hand, psychological and affective categories like sympathy and sentiment, and, on the other hand, social and political categories like the public sphere and the citizen. He has been roundly and rightly criticized for underemphasizing the dominative dynamic underpinning both sides of this homology, for ignoring the way bourgeois publicity's actual exclusiveness *and* its theoretical inclusiveness legitimated the political and cultural hegemony of white, male, propertied citizens at the expense of those marked as subaltern.[57] Indeed, one hazard of taking up this account of the public/private distinction is that it risks reinscribing the very dichotomies it is designed to deconstruct. In other words, in accounting for the way the public sphere came to be ideologically identified as hegemonically masculine, *Public Sentiments* risks glossing over the important feminist scholarship that has focused on women's important role in constructing not only the domestic ideology that delimited it, but the definition of publicity itself.[58] At least since Linda Kerber's 1988 review essay, "Separate Spheres, Female Worlds, Women's Place," literary critics and historians have been conscious that "political systems [in my context, the bourgeois public sphere] and systems of gender relations [here, the form of public/private distinction epitomized in nineteenth-century domestic ideology] are reciprocal social constructions."[59] And as Eve Sedgwick has concisely put it, "The immense productiveness of the public/private crux in feminist thought has come, not from the confirmation of an original hypothesized homology that male:female::public:private, but from the wealth of its deconstructive deformations."[60] The same is true of the other binarisms that *Public Sentiments* maps unevenly upon the distinction between public masculinity and private femininity, including the antinomies of politics and domesticity, rationality and sentimentality, authenticity and theatricality.

And yet five of the six chapters in this book deal almost exclusively with public sentiments expressed and written by men. In part my decision to focus on masculine material is meant as a corrective to the long-standing tendency in scholarship on nineteenth-century American literature and culture to associate femininity with sentimentality, a corrective that is continuous with the volume I coedited with Mary Chapman, *Sentimental Men: Masculinity and the Politics of Affect in American Culture*. But the decision is also an acknowledgment that structuring all the "deconstructive deformations" we can identify in nineteenth-century systems of politics and gender were hegemonic gender ideologies, powerful discourses that made the gendering of the public/private distinction a norm to be reckoned with even if it was neither a seamless practical reality nor the single coherent ideology indicated by the phrases that have been used to describe it: "domestic ideology," "the cult of true womanhood," and the doctrine of "separate spheres." Thus, as I show in Chapter 1, even though the Washingtonian temperance movement deployed men's tears to articulate a particular form of masculine public identity, its rhetoric metaphorized sentimental sympathy as maternal, thereby at least provisionally reinscribing the association between sympathy and femininity that its interpellation of readers and auditors as "sentimental men" would appear to deconstruct.[61]

Habermas himself certainly pays insufficient attention to the gendering of public spheres, and none at all to the racial structuration that is essential for any understanding of the American articulation of publicity and privacy.[62] At moments, though, he is acutely conscious of some of the ideological contradictions inherent in bourgeois publicity, providing at least some understanding of the dynamic by which these exclusions were legitimated. Following Marx's argument in "On the Jewish Question," he points out that the bourgeois public sphere was based on the "fictitious identity" of two roles that only bourgeois individuals were able fully to inhabit: "the role of property owners and the role of human beings pure and simple."[63] The mediation between these two roles takes place first of all in the intimate realm, most notably the family. Those who were most able socially and psychologically to construct their subjectivity as private and domestic were also those best equipped to participate in the cultural and political world. The bourgeois public sphere thus resolved potential contradictions between publicity and privacy by defining the public as made up of formally equal, privatized individuals gathered together for social ends.

Once again, culture played a critical role in this ideological mediation. Habermas emphasizes throughout his account that the privatized identities of participants in the public sphere were secured through the medium of literature. As he puts it, the bourgeois public "from the outset was a reading public."[64] Literature, especially the novel, mediated between private personality and public sociality because it enacted the division of public and private in each reader merely by evoking his or her identification. In "the psychological novel"—by which he clearly means eighteenth-century novels of sentiment, since his examples run from Richardson to Sterne— "[t]he relations between author, work, and public" became

> intimate mutual relationships between privatized individuals who were psychologically interested in what was "human," in self-knowledge, and in empathy. Richardson wept over the actors in his novels as much as his readers did; author and reader themselves became actors who "talked heart to heart." . . . On the one hand, the empathetic reader recreated within himself the private relationships displayed before him in literature; from his experience of real familiarity (*Intimität*), he gave life to the fictional one, and in the latter he prepared himself for the former. On the other hand, from the outset the familiarity (*Intimität*) whose vehicle was the written word, the subjectivity that had become fit to print, had in fact become the literature appealing to a wide public of readers. The privatized individuals coming together to form a public also reflected critically and in public on what they had read.

Through this procedure, Habermas concludes, these individuals "formed the public sphere of a rational-critical debate in the world of letters within which the subjectivity originating in the interiority of the conjugal family, by communicating with itself, attained clarity about itself."[65] Again, Habermas confirms the importance of fiction in the development of the public sphere by arguing that the shape, boundaries, and makeup of the public sphere are at stake in the way people read, in the forms of identification evoked in works of fiction. As Bruce Burgett puts it in an analysis of early American literature strongly inflected by the Habermasian account of the public sphere, "[T]he sentimental literary culture of the period relied upon readers' affective, passionate, and embodied responses to fictive characters and situations in order to produce political effects."[66]

This is the point at which a history and theory of the public sphere usefully converge with the discussion of the sentimental structure of feeling with which this introduction began. The experience of sympathetic identification characteristic of the sentimental novel, an act that often took place in the intimate realm of the nuclear family, functioned as psychological preparation for readers' participation not only in the reading public, but also in the political public. The novel was thus not just part of an institution of the public sphere, providing an occasion for "rational-critical discussion," it was also an instrument of subject formation, producing, through acts of identification, a publicly oriented form of subjectivity. This conjunction of the psychic and the public, the emotional and the political, is what I have been referring to as the sentimental politics of affect.

At this point Habermas's argument makes claims that could be contested empirically by scholars in disciplines including history, sociology, political science, and social psychology, not to mention my own discipline of literary and cultural studies. My point here is somewhat more modest, though not minor. In each chapter of *Public Sentiments* I demonstrate that nineteenth-century American writers, critics, and other cultural arbiters operated under the assumption that novels had public implications in one or both of the senses that Habermas discusses, and that they embedded these assumptions into their novels. For some of them, the novel was itself, or was part of, an institution of the public sphere, and its reception instanciated public discourse in much the same way as did a temperance meeting, a librarians' conference, or a convention building support for black emigration. This way of conceiving of the novel's public implications is, again, the focus of the first three chapters of this book. Though many of the novels discussed in the second half of the book can also be positioned in relation to public-sphere institutions, my emphasis in those three chapters is on the novel as an instrument of subject formation. Here I build on Habermas's claim that the bourgeois public sphere is predicated on the development of a subjectivity he describes as "a privateness oriented to an audience." [67]

Habermas uses this almost oxymoronic phrase to describe the link forged in the eighteenth century between the domestic, the literary, and the public spheres. "In the intimate sphere of the conjugal family," he argues, "privatized individuals viewed themselves as independent even from the private sphere of their domestic activity—as persons capable of entering into 'purely human' relations with one another. The literary form of these at the time was the letter . . . through letter writing the individual unfolded himself in his subjectivity."[68]

In this period, which he refers to as "the age of sentimentality," letters were a primary site for affective exchange: "[T]hey practically were to be wept." In this sort of emotional transaction, which could be an intersubjective exchange or a self-relation—and most often was both simultaneously —developed an early form of the psychological subject, which we might call "sentimental subjectivity." It is sentimental because its very notion of "the human" is defined in emotional terms as a form of sympathetic identification. "[P]sychological interest," Habermas writes, "increased in the dual relation to both one's self and the other: self-observation entered a union partly curious, partly sympathetic with the emotional stirrings of the other I."[69]

Sympathy, in this account, proliferated in the other written genres designed to elicit it, and its proliferation culminated in the formation of a distinctive form of subjectivity constituted through these interpellations and identifications: "The diary became a letter addressed to the sender, and the first person narrative became a conversation with one's self addressed to another person. These were experiments with the subjectivity discovered in the close relationships of the conjugal family." As such, even the most apparently private and intimate forms of writing—or rather, especially such forms—were central to the history of publicity: "Subjectivity, as the innermost core of the private, was always already oriented to an audience (*Publikum*)."[70]

Habermas's account of the constitution of this audience-oriented subjectivity remains somewhat sketchy. He does not go very far toward explaining the means by which subjects are interpellated as public citizens, nor does he explain how they come to identify with a particular subject position. The formation and performance of audience-oriented subjectivity is the focus of the section of *Public Sentiments* entitled "Performing Publicity." I identify and analyze performative, theatrical forms of character that pervade novels as different as Louisa May Alcott's *Work,* Nathaniel Parker Willis's *Paul Fane,* Fanny Fern's *Ruth Hall,* Henry James's *The Bostonians, The Princess Casamassima,* and *The Tragic Muse,* Mark Twain's *Adventures of Tom Sawyer,* and William Dean Howells's *A Boy's Town.* Audience-oriented subjectivity exists thematically in the novels themselves, of course; one would be hard-pressed to deny the theatricality of the dandy figure in Willis's or James's novels, or of Twain's Tom Sawyer. More important, though, is the way the novels use this thematic element and characterization to produce such a subjectivity in their relation to their own audiences—in other words, how they construct their reading publics.

Here, again, is where Habermas's arguments about the public sphere and its audience-oriented subjectivity reconverge with the points I made earlier about sympathy and the sentimental structure of feeling. All of these disparate texts constitute their readerships—interpellate them as sentimental subjects—through various reformulations of sympathetic identification. Sympathy, however central it was to nineteenth-century notions of publicity and subjectivity, was not conceived of in a consistent way across time, across cultural boundaries, or even within the works of an individual author. Each of the genres and novels I discuss defines sympathy in ways that necessitate revisions of the conventions of narration, character formation, and plot that characterize the genres to which they belong. For instance, in Chapter 4 I analyze Louisa May Alcott's revision of the sentimental women's genre in her novel *Work: A Story of Experience*. In this novel, Alcott struggles to reconcile domestic ideology's definitions of feminine agency and psychology with the form of feminist, proto-socialist individuality she attributes to her protagonist, Christie Devon. In other words, Christie is repeatedly impelled to go public with her sentiments. When Christie participates in the quintessential sentimental practice of mourning, it leads her to work toward social activist ends. When she renounces a career on the stage, it nonetheless teaches her performative skills that serve her well when she becomes a speaker on behalf of working women. In *Work*, Alcott deploys all the apparently personal, privatizing, psychologized emotions that pervade nineteenth-century women's fiction but rearticulates them as public sentiments.

When I argue that these authors rearticulate the conventions of genre, character, or narrative form, I am not claiming that they "subvert" or "undermine" these conventions. More often than not they perform a more subtly immanent critique, carrying the internal workings of a convention to places it otherwise might never have traveled, but not rejecting the form outright. Thus Alcott carries what I call "the logic of sympathy" to the point where her heroine's sentiments lead her to form a multigenerational, interracial collective of women and to become a social activist, all without straying from the domesticating rhetoric characteristic of the women's sentimental genre. In Chapter 5 my focus shifts from genre to character, and from femininity to masculinity, as I analyze the peculiarly performative figure of the dandy as he appears in novels by Fanny Fern, Nathaniel Parker Willis, and Henry James. As all these authors portray him, the dandy is constantly performing for publics that may be as small as one person or as large as a nation, but that are always portrayed in theatrical terms, as an audience, and always seem necessary for the confirmation of the dandy's very identity. In particular, Willis's fascinating and underexamined *Paul Fane* explores the dandy's subjectivity, developing a strikingly modern concept of "personality" while simultaneously deconstructing many of the oppositions on which current psychological notions of personality are based. As my chapter title states, "publicity is personal" for the eponymous protagonist of Willis's novel: there are no fundamental distinctions to be drawn between interiority and exteriority, between intimacy and publicity. The dandies in Fern's and James's novels—both of which, I demonstrate, can be directly linked to Nathaniel Parker Willis—perform masculine character in similarly complex and contradictory ways. Each novel positions its dandy figure in relation to norms of masculinity and portrays him as performing for a public that it portrays as importantly *national* in character. Even when positing personality and intimacy as constitutive of gendered character, nineteenth-century American novels portray these traits as oriented toward an audience.

Chapter 6 brings together the focus in Chapter 4 on gender and genre with Chapter 5's analysis of gender and personality. The "bad-boy book" became an identifiable literary subgenre after the Civil War with the publication of semi-autobiographical novels by Thomas Bailey Aldrich, Mark Twain, William Dean Howells, and Charles Dudley Warner. In these novels successful, well-published middle-aged white men look back upon their boyhoods as ambiguous precedents for their adult masculinity and public status. They set up boyhood as a presocial state of atavistic "savagery," nearly devoid of the virtuous traits that make up their adult personalities. They most emphatically deny that their previous "bad-boy" selves were capable of any emotionally intersubjective sympathy, describing scenes of casual cruelty and of their manipulation of the sympathies of others. The only trait possessed by the bad boy that anticipates his future public success as author and public figure is a propensity for theatrical flamboyance, a personality that can without ambiguity be described as audience-oriented subjectivity. Tom Sawyer's dramatic appearance at his own funeral is only the most notorious and obvious example of the bad boy's theatrical nature, a character trait that implicates him in the same affective economy of sympathy that he repeatedly disavows.

In this final chapter, as in the others, I analyze the identificatory dynamic in which the characters—and, by extension, the novel's audience—are implicated. Implicit in that "by extension" is the overall argument of *Public Sentiments,* and in particular another link between the two sections of the book. The first three chapters emphasize the social formation of publicity, the means by which institutions of the public sphere constituted spaces in which citizens could carve out public identities and act in the social world. The next three chapters emphasize the psychological formation of publicity, the means by which subjects performed their public identities through the very categories that seem to distance and differentiate them from the public sphere: particularities like race and gender, categories like personality and intimacy, forms of affect like sympathy.

Public Sentiments as a whole is meant to complicate the distinction between the social and the psychological that structures the book's division into two sections, to take seriously the homology bourgeois publicity constructs between these two categories. Each chapter on an institution of the public sphere demonstrates the ways in which that institution was suffused with sentimentality, from the way Washingtonian meetings dissolved into tears to the way Martin Delany articulated his black nationalism through a rhetoric of maternal sympathy. And each chapter analyzing a performance of publicity demonstrates that even putatively privatizing ideological categories were articulated in a publicizing rhetoric and imbricated with public institutions, from the way *Work*'s heroine expresses her private sympathies by joining a social movement to the way *Paul Fane*'s protagonist supports his personal aesthetic preferences with appeals to an explicitly national public. These fictions vary in the way they relate the social and the psychological, but in every case the structure of feeling they articulate is a set of public sentiments.

I

Institutions *of the* Public Sphere

CHAPTER I SENTIMENTAL EXPERIENCE
WHITE MANHOOD IN 1840S TEMPERANCE NARRATIVES

It is hard to imagine a more public display of sentiment than a Washingtonian temperance gathering. In the early 1840s the Washington Temperance Society brought together hardened drunkards, mostly artisans and mechanics, to sob convulsively before dozens and often hundreds of their peers.[1] These gatherings opened not with the prayers and sermonizing that had typified earlier temperance drives, but with one or two featured lecturers telling the stories of their own drunken pasts and their conversions to teetotalism. Rather than asking their listeners to condemn these men for their indulgence or their horrible treatment of their families, the Washingtonians wanted their audience to empathize with the inebriates' plight and to display that compassion through tears. The *Boston Mercantile Journal* wrote of an assemblage run by the celebrated Washingtonian John H. W. Hawkins: "We believe more tears were never shed by an audience in one evening than flowed last night. . . . Old gray haired men sobbed like children, and the noble and honorable bowed their heads and wept."[2] By the end of the evening these tears had led many to undergo a physical and emotional conversion experience, manifested by their decision to sign, again in full public view, a standardized pledge of total abstinence from alcohol.

Tears were not only the medium through which these men's conversions took place; they were also the means by which the Washingtonian movement reproduced itself. After the initial storytelling, the gathering was given over to men in the audience spontaneously standing up to describe their own alcohol-induced depravities. Like the professional speakers, they dwelt at length upon their abuse of mothers, wives, and children, as well as on the horrible deeds they had committed to keep themselves supplied with alcohol. Some followed the lead of John Bartholomew Gough, another popular Washingtonian, by graphically describing the physical sensations and hallucinations of delirium tremens. Many concluded with an account of the act of sympathetic kindness from another man that had brought them to the meeting and attested to the power of such sympathy by walking to the front of the hall and signing the temperance pledge. Each performance of masculinity thus reenacted and recommenced a set of emotional and narrative conventions, a sentimental formula that the Washingtonians called an "experience meeting."

In 1842 these public displays of sentiment attracted enthusiastic attention from three prominent figures representing different versions of nineteenth-century masculinity. Early in that year Timothy Shay Arthur, soon to be a regular contributor of sentimental tales to *Godey's Lady's Book* and a decade later the best-selling author of *Ten Nights in a Bar-Room*, published *Temperance Tales; or, Six Nights with the Washingtonians,* a linked series of short stories based on experience narratives he had heard at some of the earliest Washingtonian meetings held in Baltimore.[3] In February, Illinois lawyer and legislator Abraham Lincoln delivered an address to the Washington Temperance Society of Springfield, Illinois, and afterward helped lead reformers and converts in a grand parade.[4] And in November Walt Whitman followed up a series of pro-Washingtonian editorials in the *New York Aurora* with the publication of a novel, *Franklin Evans; or, The Inebriate,* which appeared as a special edition of the *New World.*[5] Whitman continued to evince his interest in temperance two months later with the publication in the *New York Washingtonian and Organ* of an installment of *The Madman,* which was apparently intended to be a second temperance novel.[6] Though they use different forms and genres, each man repeats the same story—that of the seemingly irredeemable drunkard restored to respectable manhood through the medium of a voluntary association—and promulgates the same affective politics, in which the sentimental experience of sympathy is both personally and socially transformative so long as it is mediated by such a voluntary association.

In other words, these texts advocated, participated in, and further developed the political logic of temperance, which Michael Warner has aptly characterized as "a civil society phenomenon, arguably the largest and most sustained social movement in modernity."[7] Beginning as a group of six Baltimore drinking buddies who wrote and signed the pledge in May 1840, the Washingtonians claimed that over 200,000 had signed up by the end of 1841 and that their membership passed the one million mark during 1842. Even though this figure was probably exaggerated, the fact that in March 1842 thirty-eight separate Washingtonian organizations existed in

New York City alone, several with over a thousand names on their membership lists, indicates that the movement's new tactics were remarkably successful, especially since mainstream temperance groups had for years been losing members and momentum.[8]

To the extent that literary history has noticed the temperance movement in general and the Washingtonians in particular, it has usually been to draw out the "foreground" of Whitman's earliest literary productions, or more broadly to note the way tropes from the temperance narrative pervade fiction and poetry of the antebellum period, especially literature of reform movements.[9] More is at stake, however, in analyzing the cultural products of the Washingtonian phenomenon than providing a historical context for a minor, though widely read, genre. The Washingtonian narrative in both its oral and printed manifestations is an unlikely but significant progenitor of a variety of popular cultural forms that rely on the affectively transformative effects of sympathetic identification, including much of the sentimental and sensational fiction that dominated the literary marketplace in succeeding decades. In that sense Washingtonians' display of the reformed and transformed drunkard is an exemplary moment in the history of public sentiment.

By beginning with the Washingtonian experience narrative, I mean to propose a revision in literary and historical interpretations of the gendering of affect in nineteenth-century American culture. The widespread popularity and emotional power of these narratives are evidence that analyses of nineteenth-century sentimentality have too quickly categorized it as a form of feminization and a force of privatization. Feminine sentimentality, by the conventional argument, is defined in opposition to masculine rationality, and the two correspond to interdependent but distinct domestic and public spheres.[10] Applications of this homology to literary and cultural histories of the antebellum period have made possible important new understandings of the political functions of sentimentality in the period, notably the revisionary recovery and critique of women's writings from the cautionary seduction narratives of the early republican years to the best-selling domestic fiction of the 1850s and beyond. Analyses that align sentimentality with domestic ideology have also produced powerful historical accounts of the formation and hegemony of the American middle-class.[11] And it has become clear that domestic ideology and literary sentimentalism—what Elizabeth Barnes aptly calls "the politics of sympathy"—are essential concepts for understanding the shift from republican to liberal forms of citizenship and embodiment in the early national and antebellum period.[12]

Understanding the political and cultural forms developed by the Washingtonians requires that this model be complicated still further. After all, they were able to deploy an expressively emotional form of sentiment as a way of making heterosocial alliances—bringing more women into the temperance movement than ever before—while at the same time their tearful male sentiment served to refigure and buttress the homosocial bonds that underlay the masculine character of the public sphere. Their use of sentimental conventions seems to have extended the appeal of the temperance movement beyond its traditional genteel constituency; contrary to interpretations of sentimentality as a purely bourgeois phenomenon, Washingtonian meetings were noted at the time for drawing in working-class drinkers in unprecedented numbers. Moreover, their representations of the bloated, red-faced, lustful, uncontrolled male inebriate, both in literature and in experience meetings, made him the most vividly embodied figure in early-nineteenth-century fiction and public life, except perhaps for the black slave with whom he was often compared. The drunkard's conversion, through tearful narration, into a sentimental, sympathetic, responsible white man demonstrates that the boundaries between sentimentality as a characteristically feminine form of embodiment and publicity as a legitimating form of disinterested masculine abstraction were more porous than we usually assume.[13]

The sentimental masculinity visible in the forms and conventions developed by the Washingtonians is not an anomaly visible only against a normative background in which sentimentality was simply gendered female. Rather, it is evidence of a more complexly gendered sentimentality, one that requires a rethinking of our understanding of the nineteenth-century politics of affect. The experience narrative, I will argue, is best read as an anticipation of new social formations only then being preliminarily experienced by the white working-class men and artisans who made up the movement. Experience meetings, oral Washingtonian narratives, and the temperance novels by Arthur and Whitman were all attempts to articulate sympathy, which might otherwise be seen as a private emotion and individual experience, as something social—or to use a more historically and theoretically specific term, as something *public*. These social practices were not just expressions of preexisting identities; as we will see, they constructed whiteness and masculinity as part of a structure of feeling constitutive both of the public sphere in which they took place and of the embodied subjects who populated that sphere. This chapter thus analyzes the specific identificatory mechanisms the Washingtonians and their fictionalizers used to constitute both their public sphere and its corresponding form of subjectivity, the forms of sympathy at the narrative and affective core of the sentimental structure of feeling that is the subject of this book. The chapter focuses most closely on the ways in which the Washingtonians tried to institutionalize these identifications in the form of a social movement.

Sober Sentiments

Washingtonianism was the first massively popular movement organized explicitly around the experience of sympathy. Its proselytizers differentiated their organization from earlier temperance movements on precisely this basis. Most notably, the Washington Temperance Societies were the first such groups to believe that habitual drunkards could be redeemed. Previous activists had largely agreed with the blunt assessment put forward by a founder of the American Temperance Society, Justin Edwards: "Keep the temperate people temperate; the drunkards will soon die, and the land be free." [14] In contrast, Abraham Lincoln argued in his address to the Springfield Washingtonians that such a callous stance was "so repugnant to humanity, so uncharitable, so cold-blooded and feelingless, that it never did, nor never can enlist the enthusiasm of a popular cause. We could not love the man who taught it—we could not hear him with patience." [15] By Lincoln's account, not only was the earlier temperance position inadequately "charitable" to be effective in the conversion of a drunkard, it also prevented the temperance advocate from receiving "love" in return and therefore limited the potential scope of temperance as a "popular cause." The rejection of all limitations on sympathy, as well as the insistence that such compassion be reciprocal, was typical of the newer movement's rhetoric, and both arguments recur in the fiction. Whitman's novel, for instance, contains several subplots that emphasize not the dangers of drinking, but the risks of failing to extend sympathy and humanity to a drunkard.

As such, the Washingtonian temperance crusade exemplified the tendency of sentimental politics, in Philip Fisher's words, to "experiment with the extension of full and complete humanity to classes of figures from whom it has been socially withheld." Here sympathy is not extended to its "typical objects . . . the prisoner, the madman, the child, the very old, the animal, and the slave."[16] Instead the Washingtonians brought crowds of ethnic and working-class drinkers into the movement, thereby alienating many of the ministers and middle-class men who made up the core of earlier temperance drives.[17] Older temperance regulars also resisted the new activists' insistence that sentiment, rather than reason or religion, was to be their primary weapon against intemperance.[18] A drunkard could be redeemed, the Washingtonians argued, if he could be induced to exercise his sympathy while listening to the story of a reformed drunkard. This sympathy was designed to produce an emotional equivalence between speaker and audience; as Lincoln said, "[O]ut of the abundance of their hearts their tongues give utterance. . . . And when such is the temper of the advocate, and such of the audience, no good cause can be unsuccessful."[19] Interpellated by such emotionally egalitarian rhetoric, the debased alcoholic subject becomes the protagonist of a new narrative whose telos is the restoration of his masculinity: "The drunkard found himself unexpectedly an object of interest," one observer wrote. "He was no longer an outcast. There were some who still looked upon him as a man."[20]

The affective exchanges that are both the plot and the purpose of the story are designed to replicate themselves, diegetically and extradiegetically, in the resolution of the protagonist's narrative problems and in the concomitant moral and physical transformation of the listener or reader, whose responses set the narrative circuit in motion once again. Thus Washingtonian speeches elicited spontaneous public confessions from their auditors, stories in which the drunkard was not just "an object of interest," but narrator and protagonist as well. This activity was modeled in the opening speeches; both Gough and Hawkins concluded their standard conversion narratives with scenes in which they found themselves in front of a crowd, almost involuntarily describing their harrowing experiences with alcohol. Listeners were quick to follow their lead, narrating their life stories up to the present moment of redemption. Narratives and emotions are figured as objects that should be freely exchanged: "Let us have your experience," calls out the organizer of a meeting in *Six Nights* at the end of one chapter, and a new narrator begins a new story.[21]

Whitman's *Franklin Evans* reproduces the affective logic of the experience meeting without actually representing such a gathering in the story. First of all, Whitman exhorts his reader to move into an intimate and sympathetic proximity with his first-person narrator: "Reader! perhaps you despise me," he writes. "Perhaps, if I were by you at this moment, I should behold the curled lip of scorn, and the look of deep contempt. Oh, pause stern reverencer of duty, and have pity for a fellow-creature's weakness" (179). The narrator also displays a marked willingness to allow other characters to tell their own stories, stories that are made to serve a role like that of the spontaneous narration of the experience meeting. Whitman underscores the homologous functions of these different levels of narration when, late in the novel, Franklin Evans's benefactor tells him a story about a young man who is saved from a life of intemperance by the sentimental sight of his young sister's death. After finishing his tale he confesses that "he had indeed been relating a story, the hero of which was himself" (200). A paragraph later, Franklin has signed a temperance pledge. The Washingtonian strategy of narration parallels Franklin's experience as an auditor with the reader's experience, for the novel itself begins with two lengthy paragraphs referring to a "stranger" in the third person, only to reveal in the third paragraph: "Reader, I was that youth" (129).

The power of the experience narrative derived from the egalitarian equivalence it established between its participants as well as its spontaneity and direct emotional appeal, the sense that "those unlettered men . . . spoke from the heart to the heart," as one contemporary writer put it.[22] As such, its nearest relative as a narrative form was the nascent genre of sentimental women's fiction, which was similarly centered on the enactment or performance of sympathetic identification, an exchange of affective experience between author, character, and reader. Writers like Catharine Maria Sedgwick and Sarah Josepha Hale had already established many of the conventions that later best-sellers by Maria Susanna Cummins and Susan Warner would follow, depicting the trials and tribulations of young women of the same gender, age, race, and class of the readers they intended to address. As I argue in my analysis of women's fiction in Chapter 4, sentimental writers did not simply presume that their mostly female readers would sympathize with their protagonists; the heroines themselves are characterized primarily by their own capacity to sympathize. Readers, along with the heroine, are witness not only to suffering itself but to numerous examples of the power of sympathy to relieve that suffering. They are then asked, often explicitly, to extend the chain of sympathetic identifications into the real world. That extension of sympathy is typical not only of those sentimental novels like *Uncle Tom's Cabin* whose concerns reach beyond the domestic sphere; even those novels overtly intended to reinforce women's domestic role deploy the same logic in trying to make their readers into more loving and sympathetic wives and mothers. In that sense sentimentality, at least in its literary manifestations, is a structure of feeling that is always oriented toward the public.

Both defenders and critics of women's fiction characterized this publication of sympathy as a kind of affective contagion, communicated by the immediacy with which suffering was depicted.[23] Women readers had long been associated with a sometimes excessive propensity to sympathize and an insufficiently mediated relation to the narratives that absorbed them. Whether these ostensibly feminine characteristics were viewed as the source of woman's moral superiority or as the sign of her inadequate rationality, sympathetic absorption in narrative was by the 1840s already seen as a—perhaps *the*—quintessentially feminine characteristic. It is all the more surprising, then, that the Washingtonians built a mass movement around a compulsively repeated primal scene of tearful, sympathetic identification with another *man*'s suffering.[24] Descriptions of experience meetings make them sound like collective scenes of sentimental reading, with the pale, solitary, emotionally responsive woman reader replaced by a mass of tipsy but tearful red-nosed auditors. "The simple tale of the ruined inebriate," one observer stated, "interrupted by a silence that told of emotions too big for utterance, would awaken general sympathy, and dissolve a large portion of the audience in tears."[25] Like the female reader "forgetting herself" in her novel, listeners lose their individuality in the flow of sympathetic identification with the reformed inebriate. Another writer reported that after an experience speech the audience's "hearts were melted, tears glistened, and that human mass became knit together by a common spell."[26] Despite its male focus, then, the Washingtonian experience narrative possessed a prototypically sentimental structure.[27]

Bloated Bodies

In all its narrative manifestations, sentimentality is more than an exchange of ideas and emotions; it is a form of embodiment, a "bodily bond" that links character and reader to each other and to the social body. Shirley Samuels describes female sentimentalism as "a project about imagining the nation's bodies and the national body," and Karen Sánchez-Eppler argues that "[i]n sentimental fiction bodily signs are adamantly and repeatedly presented as the preferred and most potent mechanisms both for communicating meaning and for marking the fact of its transmission."[28] The "bodily signs" most often used as the means of this communication in sentimental fiction are, of course, tears, and these signs function similarly in the Washingtonian narrative apparatus. Tears are consistently cited as evidence of each step of the restorative process: the drunkard cries when he is first approached by the kindly Washingtonian; he cries again as he narrates his tale to the larger audience; the audience cries in response; and the fictionalized retelling of the experience inevitably concludes with tears that practically flow off the page onto the reader.

According to Karen Sánchez-Eppler, the "feminist-abolitionist discourse" she analyzes deployed sentimentality in order "to transform the body from a site of oppression into the grounds of resisting that oppression."[29] The logic of abstract personhood characteristic of republican and constitutional discourse was so capable of disconnecting the citizen from his body that "it did not seem absurd for the founding fathers to reckon slaves as 'three-fifths of a person' " without imagining that such a division would entail "amputations."[30] In contrast, Sánchez-Eppler argues, feminist-abolitionist discourse insisted on "acknowledging the corporeality of personhood," in part by making bodily signs like tears the goal of the narrative and the sign of moral humanity.[31] Washingtonian discourse was equally insistent upon representing corporeality, but it formulated the sentimental relation between the (male) person and his body differently. However fundamentally it relies on bodily signs, the experience narrative has as its goal the diminution and metaphorical dissolution of the body that serves as its "object of interest." Ultimately the embodied subject of the narrative is replaced by a person who aspires to the disembodied abstraction that is the prerequisite and privilege of white male citizenship.[32]

Of course, men's bodies do not literally disappear in this transaction; in fact, the physical manliness of Washingtonians was constantly reiterated in narratives and newspaper accounts of their meetings. Such descriptions may have focused on the men's virility in part to counteract the conception, still prevalent among working-class men, that strong spirits strengthened the body and abstinence led to effeminacy.[33] But contemporaneous accounts of the best experience speakers also linked their visible masculinity to their ability to reduce a sympathetic crowd to tears; manliness is depicted as an effective form of sentimental rhetoric. In 1841 the *Boston Daily Mail* described the speaker John Hawkins as "a man of forty-four years of age—of fine manly form—[who] said he had been more than twenty years a confirmed inebriate. He spoke . . . [in a] free and easy, off-hand, direct, bang-up style; at times in a simple conversational manner, then earnest and vehement, then pathetic, then humorous—but always manly and reasonable."[34]

Hawkins's "fine manly form" and "direct, bang-up style" had their desired effect on his listeners; the article goes on to describe the "fountains of generous feeling" that "gushed forth in tears" in the lecture hall. Gough's appearances were even more melodramatically masculine. Carried away in his own performance, he would stride across the stage acting out the violent acts to which Demon Rum had driven him or his intemperate acquaintances, pantomiming "a man laying his child on an open fire or clutching his wife's throat with a death grip."[35] Gough's audiences, according to a writer in the *New York Observer,* "were under the spell of this young charmer . . . alternately elevated by the grand, thrilled with the horrible, dissolved with the tender, enchanted with the beautiful."[36]

The seductive physical immediacy projected in these speakers' styles was underscored in the stories they told, which focused obsessively on the bodies and faces of their protagonists. The drunkard was described as red, blotched, bleary-eyed, and, most consistently, "bloated." Gough, for instance, repeated in many of his speeches the tale of a drunkard's return home after a long binge; his mother's greeting at the door is "Son, you are bloated." Michael Moon notes that vivid descriptions of the body often appeared in anti-onanism writings of the period; in temperance discourse such words similarly designated a person's excessive devotion to bodily appetites that were often simultaneously alcoholic and erotic.[37] Whitman's use of the trope of bloating is typical: before his first wife wastes away due to his neglect, Franklin Evans speaks of her "hot tears that fell upon my bloated face"; he mentions one drunkard's "red and swollen eyes" and says of another that "his face was bloated, his eyes inflamed, and he leaned back in that state of drowsy drunkenness which it is so disgusting to behold" (175, 153). Overall, Evans is depicted as a murderous personification of an overactive libido; in the course of the novel he manages to acquire two wives and one mistress, all of whom die as a result of his drinking.

The alcoholic body in Washingtonian discourse is, then, clearly sexualized.[38] Its manliness is marked racially as well. Typically, at one especially low stage in the narration of a drunkard's descent into absolute abjection he is described as a man so far from normative masculine identity that he has lost his whiteness, at least insofar as whiteness is a visible condition of the skin. The narratives repeatedly decry the physical discolorations that alcoholism produces, remarking on the "unnatural redness" of one drinker's face, while another's is "flushed with a deep red" that contrasts vividly with the "pale" and "colorless" face of his worried daughter.[39] At one of the worst points in Franklin Evans's life, when he describes himself as "a miserable object," the clearest sign of his fall is his skin color: "My face, I felt, was all dirty and brown, and my eyes bleared and swollen. What use had I for life?" (186). After his rescue from "the forces of the Red Fiend" a former drunkard is invariably whitened, not only by the cleansing baths that usually accompany his being taken in by the Washingtonians, but also by the restoration of his face's "natural" color (237).

Such color coding, the passage from red and brown to white, might be legible in other than racial terms if not for the consistency with which temperance tales make reference to both Native Americans and black slaves. Stories of Native American alcoholism typically serve to illustrate the social and especially national repercussions of alcoholism. An otherwise gratuitous narrative inserted early in Whitman's novel is introduced by a man who "can conceive of no more awful and horrible, and at the same time more effective lesson, than that which may be learned from the consequences of the burning fire-water upon the habits and happiness of the poor Indians" (133). The man goes on to say that a "whole people—the inhabitants of a mighty continent—are crushed by it, and debased into a condition lower than the beasts of the field. Is it not a pitiful thought? . . . They found themselves deprived not only of their lands and what property they hitherto owned, but of everything that made them noble and grand as a nation!" (45). After this moralizing preface the ensuing narrative makes no mention of alcohol. However, the story does serve the purpose of attributing to Native American men a pure masculinity against which white men can measure themselves: at a climactic moment, a young man exclaims, "Wind-Foot is not a girl. The son of a chief can die without wetting his cheek by tears" (53). Conjoined with the elegy for Indian nationhood, the story produces, as in James Fenimore Cooper, a cross-racial emotional identification while simultaneously placing the equivalence between white men and native men implied by that sympathy into an irretrievable past.[40]

Temperance fiction's pervasive deployment of the figure of the slave is more ambivalent and complex, but it also entails a powerful, though temporary, bodily identification with a racial "other." Arthur's narrator, for instance, describes his first experience meeting as a crowd of "mostly mechanics and working men. . . . We pushed our way close up to the speaker's stand, and then turned to survey the countenances of the assembly. It was a sight to move the heart. . . . Men who had been slaves, some for a long series of years, to the most degrading vice. But now they stood up as freemen, and there was scarcely a face, marred sadly as some were, that had not an expression of serious, manly determination and confidence."[41] The drunkard's liberation from his excessive embodiment was a passage not only to manhood, but also from slavery to freedom.[42] Alcoholism in temperance discourse is regularly figured as a bondage either to "King Alcohol" or to the body itself, and the other group besides sentimental women that was regularly portrayed as excessively and oppressively embodied was black slaves.[43] Indeed, that embodiment was, according to Sánchez-Eppler, one basis for the always conflicted alliance between feminists and abolitionists, as feminist-abolitionist discourse worked to change the body from a site of oppression into a basis for liberation. The same connection extends to the figure of the drunkard, making available a metaphorical equivalence between alcoholism and slavery.

As a rhetorical device, the comparison between alcoholism and slavery could be articulated in various ways. In his history of the antebellum black temperance movement, Donald Yacovone describes a shift from the 1820s and 1830s, when black temperance was seen by its advocates as part of a movement for universal moral reform, to the 1840s, when "temperance and abolitionism had become virtually synonymous." He cites two exemplary phrases from Frederick Douglass's speech to the World Temperance Convention: one where Douglass declares that "I am a temperance man because I am an anti-slavery man," and another in which he represents slaveholding itself as a form of intoxication and addiction, proclaiming that "Mankind has been drunk" and that if it were sober "we could get a public opinion sufficiently strong to break the relation of master and slave."[44] A sober public, it seems, would be rational, democratic, and free.

While Washingtonian discourse posits a similar equivalence, it narrates the connection in reverse. Again the Washingtonian body follows a trajectory opposite that of the bodies in feminist-abolitionist discourse, whose embodiment is an assertion of their gendered personhood. Not only does the Washingtonian body move toward the abstracted masculinity described earlier; at the same time it takes on a newly valorized whiteness visible in its contrast with both the "unnatural" bloated redness of the drunkard's body and with the slave's inability to own his body and exercise his will over it. The contrast between these two deployments of sympathy and embodiment is evident even at moments when white Washingtonians explicitly connect the two. Somewhat later in his career Gough invoked a scene from *Uncle Tom's Cabin* as a parallel example of the transformative power of sympathy, but with a significant difference in emphasis. Gough compared the treatment the drunkard receives from the world with the moment in the novel "when Ophelia shrank back from little Topsy [and] 'the girl felt it.' You shrink back from the drunkard, and he feels it. The finger of scorn pointed at him, stings the seared heart as if a burning brand were pressed upon the quivering flesh."[45] Rather than figuring sympathy itself as a form of embodiment, Gough represented its *withdrawal* as a painful physical sensation that makes the drunkard, like Topsy, excruciatingly aware of his body. Though the project of Washingtonianism was typically articulated in gendered terms—an attempt, as Whitman says in *Franklin Evans,* to abolish "those pestilent places, where the mind and the body are both rendered effeminate together" (239)—and although it defined itself as a working-class movement in contradistinction to other branches of temperance, it was equally a "racial project" that constituted working-class masculinity as a form of whiteness.[46]

Washingtonian sentimentality is thus more than a persuasive rhetoric; it discursively constructs its male subjects in a way that articulates racialized, classed, and gendered forms of identity together into an affective whole, a sentimental structure of feeling. White working-class masculinity can be viewed as sentimental in this discourse because its defining opposite, alcoholism's involuntary servitude, is depicted as an inability to sympathize. As one of Arthur's speaker/narrators describes his intemperate state, "All natural affection seemed gone from my bosom. I loved only myself, and sought only the lowest sensual gratifications."[47] It is this lack of "natural affection" that allows the drunkard to abuse and abandon his wife and children, as well as to lose his self-possession to the extent that he sees himself as a slave. It is the restoration of such affections that Washingtonian sentiment enables. Two pages later, the same speaker describes a Washingtonian speaking to him "in a kind sympathizing tone. . . . This melted me right down. For years a kind word had never been spoken to me."[48] Sentimental personhood is thus restored both by the reciprocal sympathy of the experience meeting and by its concomitant dissolution of the hardened, sinful body of the drunkard. The male bodies in these stories are transformed first into grotesque, bloated, red and brown monsters; then, through the power of Washingtonian sympathy, they are "melted down" into their properly white "manly forms"—pale, respectable, docile bodies.

For the Washingtonians, then, the male body was the site of the audience's transformative identification. The narrative trajectory of the body in the experience narrative was from an excessive physicality toward a more contained and controllable sentimental personhood. Even as readers or listeners wept over the death of a child or wife, they identified with the tearful feeling of regret expressed by the vividly embodied, lively, and perversely interesting perpetrator of the crime, rather than with the pale, sickly victims, whose narrative function was to waste away, or even with the virtuous reformed drunkard, whose interest only lasted as long as he narrated his depravities. Of course, the reader's sympathy with the alcoholic's violent desire was meant to be prelude to an identification with his more respectable later self, but the Washingtonian narrative was notoriously ambivalent about how to maintain an affective connection with a figure whose main characteristic was his lack of exciting affect. Critics of the movement often argued that the real appeal of these stories was in the sensational depravities they depicted, noting quite accurately that they rarely focused at all on the less eventful later life of the sober convert.[49]

Whitman acknowledges this tension in *Franklin Evans* in the midst of the weirdest, most gothic, and most explicitly racialized episode of the novel. When Evans tries to escape his depraved past by moving to Virginia, his hypermasculinity displays itself in its most destructive manner, leading to the abject "disgust with myself" that is prerequisite to a Washingtonian transformation. He has won the affections of a beautiful light-skinned slave woman, whom he has freed, married, and then promptly begun to neglect in favor of a visiting white widow. He then describes how his inattention drives his wife to murder the white woman. Immediately after narrating these events, but before his conversion to teetotalism, he opens a chapter by rhapsodizing: "How refreshing it is to pause in the whirl and tempest of life, and cast back our minds over past years! I think there is even a kind of satisfaction in deliberately and calmly reviewing actions that we feel were foolish or evil. It pleases us to know that we have the learning of experience. The very contrast, perhaps, between what we are, and what we were, is gratifying. . . . The formal narration of them, to be sure, is far from agreeable to me—but in my own self-communion upon the subject, I find a species of entertainment" (219).

As his use of the word "experience" signals, Whitman is here describing—and perhaps struggling to legitimate—the reformative strategy of Washingtonian narrative form.[50] As a reader of his own life history, Franklin finds "entertainment" in accounts of his own virile sexuality, even as he sheds tears over the victims of his voracious, "bloated" body and asks his readers to applaud that body's transformation into a more respectable masculine form. He also claims, as Gough implies in his graphic descriptions of delirium tremens, that the conversion to teetotalism represents a complete bodily metamorphosis, asking rhetorically, "What if the whole system must undergo a change, violent as that which we conceive of the mutation of form in some insects? What if a process comparable to flaying alive, have to be endured?" (179). The function of the experience narrative, as well as Whitman's novel, is to enact such a physical and affective transformation, first constructing a mammoth and monstrous figure of "discolored" masculinity, only to dissolve that body in tears, leaving a sober, respectable white man in its place. As if to dramatize to the fullest the Washingtonian reversal of feminist-abolitionist discourse's narrative politics of sympathy, both the white mistress and the black wife of Franklin Evans die in the process of this dissolution, the former from a deliberately inflicted, wasting illness, the latter by her own hand.

Counterpublic Sentiments

Discussing a different moment in the history of sentimentality, Eve Kosofsky Sedgwick asks: "[I]f the sentimental as we have been taught, coincides topically with the feminine, with the place of women, then why should the foregrounded *male* physique be in an indicative relation to it?" Her claim is that gradually after 1880 "the exemplary instance of the sentimental ceases to be a woman per se, but instead becomes the body of a man who . . . physically dramatizes, *embodies* for an audience that both desires and cathartically identifies with him, a struggle of masculine identity with emotions or physical stigmata stereotyped as feminine."[51] So far I have demonstrated that the dynamic Sedgwick analyzes here was in operation in American popular culture earlier than she claims. Sentimentality in the nineteenth century was never as feminine nor as private an affective structure as we assume it was. As early as the 1840s, when the ideology of gendered separate spheres was being forcefully inscribed in American culture, sentiment and male embodiment were already being deployed together as part of a public discourse of political reform and masculine self-fashioning that was also a racial project.

The final section of this chapter is meant to draw out the implications of this argument for the interrelation between the cultural public sphere and the political public sphere. Washingtonian sentimentality strove for more than the reformation of individual moral character or the restoration of broken families. The movement's critique was aimed less at private behavior than at the social formations that reproduced behavior. At the same time, it was not a political movement in any simple sense; indeed, a distinguishing feature of Washingtonianism was its commitment to "moral suasion," or noncoercive social reform through voluntary association, rather than to legal prohibition. In other words, the Washingtonian public sphere was seen by its participants as importantly distinct from the political public sphere and especially from the state. In much of the fiction, "talking about politics" is considered just as degrading as drinking itself, in part, of course, because party political activism usually involved a great deal of drinking. Political campaigns at least since George Washington's had budgeted money to "treat" prospective voters to alcohol. As Arthur says, "Elections . . . were carried by drinking. An electioneering campaign resembled, in some respect, the Bacchanalian orgies of old, rather than a general rational movement of the people, preparatory to an expression of their honest sentiments at the polls."[52] The Washingtonian movement so emphatically avoided electoral politics that many of its members opposed prohibition legislation; one reason for the group's factionalization later in the 1840s, in fact, was the ongoing debate between prohibitionists and those devoted to moral suasion.[53]

Although it used individual bodies as its instruments and eschewed electoral and legislative politics, the Washingtonian movement's remedy for social ills was a transformation of the public sphere. Indeed, one thing that was meant to distinguish these scenarios of men crying from a potentially feminizing sentimentality was their overtly public nature, which both implicitly and explicitly marginalized women. The publicity of the experience narrative and the abstinence pledge, the Washingtonians argued, provided the regenerate man with a collective source of emotional support; it also drove home the threat of collective public censure were he to backslide.[54] No less important, though, was the way an act of public speech reinforced gender distinctions that the sentimental responses of the crowd might otherwise have thrown into question. Women provided at least half the audience at most experience meetings, and they were encouraged to sign the pledge; Washingtonianism was noted even at the time for involving an unprecedented number of women in temperance activity through auxiliary Martha Washington societies.[55] Women figured in the narratives as well, of course, though most often as passive victims of alcoholic male brutality. But women were not allowed to speak in the experience meetings themselves; they could neither lecture from the podium nor narrate their experiences from the floor.[56] The narrative and affective exchange of the experience meeting was meant to be a transaction between men.

Even as the Washingtonians emphasized their homosocial exclusivity, they fit Sedgwick's description of sentimental male embodiment as "a struggle of masculine identity with emotions . . . stereotyped as feminine." Writers and speakers constantly described Washingtonian sympathy as maternal: "We don't slight the drunkard; we love him, we nurse him, as a mother does her infant learning to walk."[57] Articulating this maternal sympathy as a form of public masculinity was not as easy as writing rules to exclude women speakers. In "The Widow's Son," one of the embedded tales in *Six Nights,* Arthur expostulates at length about the proper relation between these two sets of values, embodied in the relationship between a widowed woman and her son, Alfred, an aspiring lawyer. "A mother who truly loves her son, has perceptions of right and wrong, far above his rational discriminations," Arthur writes, and at first these perceptions, combined with the young man's rationality, are sufficient to keep him from drink.[58] "He did not, of course, as a man, lay aside his rationality, and allow himself to be blindly influenced. He only sought the aid of a woman's perceptions to enable him to see a doubtful point in a truly rational light. . . . She was cautious not to make him feel restraint—nor to destroy his rational freedom; but, rather, to guard him by counsels that did not seem, and were not felt as such."[59] But eventually the young man loses touch with his mother's sense of right and wrong, and she is horrified by "the discovery that her pure-minded, noble-spirited boy had fallen from the calm, rational dignity of manhood by a weak self-indulgence" that has cost him his reputation as a lawyer.[60] The story depicts at length the various ways in which Alfred is tempted to drink, including an argument presented by a rival attorney that "seems rational" to him, and conversations in which the young man's friends claim that it is "manly" to drink. Each time, the thought of his suffering mother descending further into poverty is almost enough to recall him to sobriety, but then a new challenge to his "manhood" makes him fall back off the wagon.

One of these challenges comes in the form of a political campaign; Alfred "sink[s] lower and lower" to the point of running for office. For Arthur, the problem goes beyond the fact that this activity gives the young man more opportunity to drink. Even though his campaign is described relatively positively as a form of "active service" that allows him to "rise above" the memory of what he has lost due to alcoholism, the loss of the election, combined with his reaching the limits of his finances, brings him to the point of vowing abstinence from alcohol.[61] Politics is not the public realm that will lead him to redemption, however, for this private vow depends on a faith in self that does not fit in with the Washingtonian formula for public redemption. So Alfred relapses again until he encounters a more authentic public sphere in the form of a Washingtonian meeting. As in most Washingtonian stories, it is only this experience meeting that permanently cures the young man of his drinking, leading him to financial success, a happy marriage, and a reconciliation with his mother.

The Washingtonian theory of moral suasion, then, was based neither on individual will nor on political force, and it depended on more than a balance between the power of maternal sympathy and the force of manly rationality.[62] To be effective, both of these individual faculties had to be made collective and, most important, public. Washingtonian publicity exemplifies in many respects the Habermasian concept of the public sphere. As I explain at greater length in the Introduction, the bourgeois public sphere is a theoretically open and accessible realm of civil society in which private individuals gather for "rational-critical" discussion of social issues. To guarantee its openness, the public sphere aggressively asserts its independence, first from the state and the church, and later (and less emphatically) from the market; its operations should be dictated neither by reasons of state nor by purely private interests. Such a public realm is necessarily a fiction rather than a real space or group of people; in Benedict Anderson's terms, it is an "imagined community" like the nation. The "idea and ideology" of the public is typically mediated through the technology of print, especially in the form of newspapers, and instantiated in nonstate institutions of civil society ranging from British coffeehouses in the eighteenth century to American voluntary associations in the nineteenth.[63]

When a Habermasian model of the public sphere is deployed in an

American context, it is most often in relation to early republican institutions and ideology, as in Linda Kerber's *Women of the Republic* and Michael Warner's *Letters of the Republic*. Labor historians such as David Montgomery and Eric Foner have noted, however, that nineteenth-century working-class movements tended to use republican rhetoric long after it had ceased to play a role in the dominant liberal ideology. In that context it is perhaps less surprising that the wing of the temperance movement noted for its working-class and artisanal constituency would fit such a schema. More problematic for any use of the Habermasian notion of publicity is the criticism of theorists and historians like Nancy Fraser, Mary Ryan, Susan Davis, and Michael Schudson, who have argued that Habermas's emphasis on rational-critical discourse as the medium for public deliberation is both historically inaccurate and implicitly masculinist.[64] By this argument, Habermas virtually precludes consideration of the performative, theatrical, and spectacular forms that political discourse took in the Jacksonian era, such as election demagoguery, parades, and riots, and similarly militates against consideration of women's participation in the public sphere through, for instance, the sentimental rhetoric of domesticity.[65]

The central role of sentiment in Washingtonian publicity underscores the critique that Habermas's model misrepresents the nineteenth-century American politics of affect as a calm, rational-critical discourse. However, even Habermas argues that one essential proto-political process through which the imagined community of the bourgeois public was formed was an implicitly sentimental form of readerly identification. Such identifications were oriented toward the public both by the generic form of the novel and by institutions such as reading groups, printed reviews, and coffee clubs, in which the novel was legitimized and canonized. But they are still recognizably sentimental, and even the "rational-critical" discussion that took place in these institutions was set in motion by readers' affective responses to what Habermas calls "the psychological novel." These individuals thereby "formed the public sphere of a rational-critical debate in the world of letters within which the subjectivity originating in the interiority of the conjugal family, by communicating with itself, attained clarity about itself."[66]

The Washingtonian movement used remarkably similar procedures to figure and form its public — or rather, since it was defined in some tension with the hegemonic bourgeois public sphere, what theorists after Habermas have called a "counterpublic." Like the bourgeois public, the Washingtonian counterpublic constituted itself in relation to "the conjugal family," drawing extensively on domestic ideology. The trajectory of its narratives leads almost invariably toward the reconstitution of the family, even if that family unit has been ravaged by alcohol; again, this emphasis is paralleled in feminine and middle-class sentimental fiction, as is the constitution of the public by a circuit of publicly mediated sympathetic identifications.[67] The Washingtonian public, however, was primarily working class or artisanal rather than middle class and entrepreneurial, with its leisure activities and spaces far less rigorously divided from the workplace and less closely tied to the domestic sphere than were the increasingly gender- and class-segregated leisure spaces of the bourgeoisie.[68] Thus the Washingtonians organized "fairs, picnics, concerts, balls, and processions" in the 1840s, as well as coffeeshops, temperance restaurants, reading rooms, and meeting places furnished with cold water. According to Ian Tyrrell, a single issue of the Washingtonian weekly *New York Crystal Fount* "often listed a half-dozen temperance concerts; one such meeting in December 1842 attracted over 4,000 persons, although attendances of around six hundred were more common at such functions."[69]

The ubiquity of stories about Washingtonians in the newspapers of the early 1840s, as well as the fact that Whitman's novel was published as a special issue of a New York weekly, underscores the centrality of print as the medium that brought even this oral narrative form and voluntary association to the attention of a wider public. As if they were not getting enough coverage from mainstream newspapers, Washingtonians also founded innumerable new publications themselves. Not all were based in major cities as the *Crystal Fount* was; as late as 1846, for example, Jackson, Michigan, was the site of publication of the *Michigan Washingtonian*.[70] The Washingtonians were especially fond of positing an alternative nation by sponsoring Fourth of July picnics "complete with games, feasts, toasts (in cold water), and bombastic orations on the 'second declaration of independence,'" from "King Alcohol."[71]

The experience meeting and other social forms produced in the Washingtonian movement were, then, all moves toward the construction of a counterpublic sphere, but to argue the same thing about the temperance novels of Whitman and Arthur is to contradict claims that pervade the theory of the novel from Ian Watt to Nancy Armstrong: claims that the modern novel, especially in the early stages of its development, is quintessentially middle class precisely because of its individuating and privatizing narrative form, construction of character, and relation to its readers.[72] And it is true that the fictional narratives are far less likely than newspaper stories to represent the movement's alternative institutions. Indeed, they tend to deal with the conversion itself and anything afterward in an almost perfunctory manner, concluding that there is nothing more to tell once the drunkard has been cured, no narrative of sober life as engaging, as provocative of sentiment, as the iniquities of the inebriate.

The narratives' usual failure to thematize the institutions of Washingtonian publicity is, I would argue, a result of the fact that the novels themselves are meant to instantiate that publicity. The novels do not need to represent these alternative institutions because they are such institutions themselves. Of course, all fiction aimed at social reform depends to some degree on the idea that publication is a public act in this sense. It is important to remember that such a use of the novel was a relatively new phenomenon, especially within the temperance movement; it was not until 1836 that the American Temperance Union voted to approve the use of fiction to further the cause. Accordingly, the prefaces of both Arthur's and Whitman's texts, amidst standard claims to be built on "a basis of real incidents" and not to be "a work of fiction," announce themselves as "powerful auxiliaries in the promotion of [a] noble cause" and remind readers that the "New and Popular Reform now in the course of progress over the land, will find no trifling help from a TALE OF THE TIMES."[73] In other words, for these authors the novel is what Michael Warner calls Charles Brockden Brown's *Arthur Mervyn:* "[A]n exemplary public instrument."[74] And even when it is focusing on ostensibly domestic and private events like family reconciliation, Washingtonian fiction is far more explicitly and directly oriented toward the public than are either the novels Habermas cites or subsequent sentimental fiction. As one small example, Arthur's "The Widow's Son" ends happily when a newspaper prints a paragraph entitled "A Pleasing Scene," which recounts the lawyer Alfred's recovery from alcoholism and his return to the "vigor, depth, and brilliancy of mind that distinguished his best efforts at the Bar, more than ten years ago."[75] Alfred's lover, Florence, who had rejected him years earlier due to his drinking, reads this paragraph, and the couple is thereby reconciled. Even romance and marriage, in the Washingtonians' world, are mediated through the publicity of print.

Both Whitman and Arthur emphasize the affective core of the reform movement to which their texts contribute; public opinion takes the form of public *sentiment*. As Arthur says, the guarantee of the "truth" of his tale is that "[at] every step of his progress in these tales, the writer has felt with the actors—sympathising with them in their heart-aching sorrows, and rejoicing with them when the morning has broken after a long night of affliction."[76] Such sentiments are designed to transcend the individual subject; they become public and specifically national in scope. Arthur concludes his introduction with the hope that "the whole country can now attest their power to move the heart," and Whitman even remarks on the distribution of his text in "the cheap and popular form you see . . . wafted by every mail to all parts of this vast republic" in such a way as to affect "the mighty and deep public opinion" of Americans.[77]

Seeming to target individual moral transformation, Washingtonian sentiment in fact aimed at a total reformation of American society and nationality. The group's often grandiose rhetoric of social transformation was in part a reflection of the millennialist character of most antebellum reform movements.[78] Those who lived through the period saw the relatively secular Washingtonian tide as a part of this phenomenon; one observer recalled that "[t]he 'Washingtonian' movement had swept over our land like a moral tornado, giving sight to the blind, healing to the broken-hearted, deliverance to the captives, a year of Jubilee. Miracles of healing had been wrought, and many hoped that the millennium had dawned!"[79] Whitman's representation of this Jubilee demonstrates that the Washingtonian millennium integrated sentimental and national rhetorics into its transformation of the public sphere. Near its conclusion *Franklin Evans* contains a chapter in which its eponymous protagonist dreams that he is wandering through a "mighty and prosperous empire." In typical Whitmanesque fashion, this nation—identified as America by the ubiquitous display of "the Star-Flag-emblem of Liberty"—is uncontained by national borders: "And how countless were the inhabitants of that country! On I went, and still on, and they swarmed thicker than before. It was almost without boundary, it seemed to me—with its far-stretching territories, and its States away up in the regions of the frozen north, and reaching down to the hottest sands of the torrid south—and with the two distant oceans for its side limits" (220).

Evans has arrived in this phantasmatic nation on "some general holyday," which turns out to be the celebration of the last drunkard's signing of the temperance pledge. He looks on in pleasure at the spectacle, which includes a parade: "First came a host of men in the prime of life, with healthy faces and stalwart forms, and every appearance of vigor [who] had once been under the dominion of the Tempter, but were now redeemed. . . . Then I saw a myriad of youths, with blooming cheeks and bright eyes. . . . Not the least beautiful part of the procession, was composed of bands of women and young girls" (221). This pleasurable display of gendered bodies is succeeded by a banner depicting the victory of feminine sentiment over masculine embodiment, showing "the figure of a fair female, robed in pure white. Under her feet were the senseless remains of a hideous monster, in whose grapple thousands and millions had fallen, but who was now powerless and dead" (222).

Finally this display of "public joy" reorganizes itself around "the Last Vassal," who signs the pledge. In the process, however, the crowd has been refigured: "Far around, on every side, countless multitudes of nothing but human heads were to be seen, in one compact body" (222). The man signs the pledge, and "the people are regenerated!" (223). Introduced by Evans's paean to the pleasures of looking back on his "experience," this dream sequence stands in for the experience meeting never actually depicted in the novel. In its imaging of an imperialist nation apparently engaged in perpetual public display, it also clearly represents the utopian outcome of Washingtonian publicity, as the display of virile, desiring bodies is supplanted by the affective unity of a single public body whose "rational sentiments" are signaled by the fact that its only visible feature is its multiplicity of heads.

Describing the body around which this celebration is organized with the peculiar archaism and Old World associations of the word "Vassal," however, again points up the unstable valence of the rhetorical equivalence between alcoholism and slavery, for this time it is directly linked to an explicitly proslavery discourse.[80] Imagined by a man who has escaped the seductive temptations of the northern city only to be more fatally tempted by the conflicted pleasures of miscegenated southern desire, who has just narrated the story of his black wife's murder of his white mistress, and who has a few pages earlier almost gratuitously apostrophized the virtues of southern slavery—which he calls a "merely nominal oppression" when compared to "the stern reality of starvation and despotism" in Europe— this version of the Washingtonian counterpublic is subtly but significantly racialized (202). Its central figure, like the novel's protagonist, has publicly performed an odd version of the blackface minstrelsy that was a popular form of temperance entertainment among the Washingtonians, playing

"The Last Slave of Appetite" before an audience only recently and tentatively able to identify with the position of white masculinity to which he aspires.[81] "I joy that I occupy my position before you now, as I do!" he exclaims, in an oddly recursive act of interpellation. And now he has emerged "regenerated" from his downward spiral, free from the bodily bonds that are figured as unambiguously parallel to those binding black slaves: " 'This day,' continued he, 'I throw off the chains, and take upon myself the pleasant bondage of good' " (222).

Even in its most phantasmatic and utopian incarnation, the Washingtonian counterpublic depended upon the status attributes that were prerequisite to full participation in the bourgeois public sphere of antebellum America: whiteness, maleness, self-possession. In themselves none of these attributes are made unambiguously appealing in temperance narratives, whether they are depicted as a "pleasant bondage" or especially when they are characterized as pure negations, as the absence of color, of sentiment, of bodiliness, of affect. What this public fantasy offered the ethnic drinkers who were the Washingtonians' newest recruits was the capacity for abstracting and unmarking the bodily particularities that constituted their racial and gender attributes.[82] Washingtonian whiteness and masculinity are constructed through a dialectic of identification and disavowal; the drunkard, and those who sympathize with him, become white men by dissolving their bodies in tears. The temperance story provides a narrative form for that process, restructuring the ambiguous affective responses embodied in the figure of the alcoholic and transforming them into a more legible sentimental experience.

CHAPTER 2   CIVILITY & CITIZENSHIP
MARTIN DELANY'S BLACK PUBLIC SPHERE

Martin R. Delany was a vocal temperance advocate for much of his life, probably beginning with his appointment as recording secretary of Pittsburgh's Temperance Society of the People of Color in the late 1830s.[1] Indeed, he was involved in virtually every institution of the public sphere accessible to a black man in the middle decades of the nineteenth century, including the press, the scientific community, Freemasonry, the U.S. military, state politics, and the novel. But race—and Delany's particular performative experience of his blackness—shaped his orientation toward the social, political, and literary institutions of the hegemonic national public sphere, making his constructions of public masculinity significantly different from those of the white men discussed in Chapter 1. In this chapter I focus simultaneously on Delany's orientation toward and representation of the dominant white public sphere and on his astonishingly various forms of engagement in the antebellum black public sphere, notably his vocal advocacy of black emigration from the United States and his participation in the Negro Convention movement.[2]

My analysis emphasizes the period from 1854 to 1861, from Delany's rise to a degree of national prominence through the serialization of his only novel, *Blake; or, the Huts of America.* Some components of his conceptualization of the public sphere were, however, evident from even earlier in his career. One such element is at the origin of what has been variously described as his nascent Pan-Africanism or his black nationalism.[3] The classical education Delany acquired in Pittsburgh, a city with a notably cohesive and organized black community, led him to develop an interest in Egypt as an African origin of the Greek and Roman civilizations he was studying at the local African Methodist Episcopal (AME) Church school. Along with Molliston Clark, a slightly older man who was then studying for the ministry and would later be the editor of the AME *Christian Recorder,* Delany founded a group dedicated to the discussion of these and related cultural matters. In the spirit of their Egyptian interests, they called it the Theban Literary Society, which Delany biographer Dorothy Sterling says was patterned on Benjamin Franklin's Junto. Though it always maintained an interest in the African achievements its members located in ancient Egypt, the organization later changed its name to the Young Men's Literary and Moral Reform Society and joined in the fight against illiteracy. With the society's shift in emphasis, Delany became its first librarian.[4]

While in his mid-twenties, at roughly the same time he got involved in temperance activity, the literary society, and the library, Delany was affected by another expression of public sentiment characteristic of the antebellum period: the antiblack riot. Biographer Victor Ullman describes how one Saturday in 1839 when white riots were in the air, Delany's mentor, John B. Vashon, "distributed arms to some of Delany's stalwart young members of the Philanthropic Society," another organization in which Delany was an officer, and which functioned as "a highly efficient fugitive slave organization that made Pittsburgh almost as safe a haven as the ultimate Canadian destination."[5] Delany led a delegation to the courthouse, where he politely but firmly informed a judge that any further white violence would lead to black retaliation. This bold move led to the newly elected mayor of Pittsburgh, Dr. Jonas R. McClintock, to consult directly with Delany. The result of their encounter was that the mayor authorized a unique institutional solution to the problem: an ad hoc police force consisting of pairs of armed men, one black and one white, that would patrol the city when such riots threatened. That night, though two or three houses were torched, the patrols mostly managed to suppress the mob of several hundred white men that had gathered. According to Ullman, "[It] was the last planned anti-Negro riot in Pittsburgh."[6] Such relative social peace was unusual for an era when race riots were frequent and brutal in other cities.[7]

The patrols had an ambivalent relation to the state, represented in this instance by the local government. The black men's initial impetus was toward an independent vigilantism, a relatively straightforward and symmetrical reversal of the logic of the white mob. Ultimately, however, they turned over any white troublemakers they apprehended to a militia in which the mayor was an officer, the Duquesne Grays, thus engaging the state on their behalf. And although the incident clearly demonstrated that Delany was a man of some public prominence in Pittsburgh, he was also painfully aware that only a year earlier the state of Pennsylvania had disenfranchised its property-owning free blacks by adding the word "white" to the state constitution, thus stripping him of the sine qua non of citizenship. It is this kind of ambivalence that I will argue characterized Delany's various formulations of a black public sphere throughout his writings and activities.[8] Even as he constituted organizations best described as counter-cultural or counterpublic,[9] even as he imagined alternative black nations located in Canada, Central America, the Caribbean, and finally Africa itself, Delany struggled to maintain a dialectical relationship to the state, the nation, and the hegemonic public institutions he was encountering. In other words, he constructed through his writings and activities a complex notion of political subjectivity, of citizenship.

Statistical Citizenship

In the conclusion to his most extended work of political thought, *The Condition, Elevation, Emigration and Destiny of the Colored People of the United States, Politically Considered*, Delany makes what may be the most obviously and yet strategically disingenuous statement of his contradictory career.[10] "The writer is no 'Public Man,' in the sense in which this is understood among our people," he writes, "but simply an humble individual."[11] Anyone, then or now, who has read anything by or about Delany would recognize that what connects his many divergent activities—as physician, scientist, emigrationist activist, newspaper editor, novelist, Freemason, African explorer, ethnologist, recruiter for the Union army, the first black major in the U.S. military, Reconstruction appointee and political candidate in South Carolina—was his continuous devotion to fashioning himself as a "Public Man." To the extent that Delany's assertion is not to be dismissed as a mere bow to contemporary conventions of authorial self-effacement, it forces us to ask what he could possibly have meant by the term "public man," or perhaps more important, what he thought his "people" understood by the term.[12] In other words, it raises the question of what kind of political subjectivity he imagined and constructed through his writings and activities, how he conceived of citizenship.

Condition is the text in which Delany is most explicitly engaged in such theorization, but in this chapter I trace his evolving notion of citizenship through three other events in his public life. The first is the August 1854 National Emigration Convention of Colored People held in Cleveland, over which he presided as chair. The 1854 convention is generally considered a high point of Delany's emigrationist activism; it was also the culmination of his long history of engagement with this particular form of political organization. The second is Delany's appearance at the International Statistical Congress, which took place in London in July 1860 and was the occasion of a minor international incident. And the third is his one novel, *Blake; or, the Huts of America*. The novel fairly neatly bridges the other two events, as he seems to have begun work on it in 1852 or 1853, although its first partial serialization in the *Anglo-African Magazine* did not begin until 1859.

The core of my argument is that Delany's notion of citizenship was, like all such notions, defined and delimited by what he saw as the boundaries between civility and incivility. A number of different and partially contradictory concepts are embedded in these terms, but two sets of connotations are primarily in play in Delany's thought and activities. On the one hand are those associated with the phrase "civil society," the kinds of nonstate institutions that Tocqueville famously referred to as the "voluntary associations" characteristic of democracy in America and within which Delany developed most of his political ideas. This concept of civil society is closely linked to the notions of the public sphere and counterpublics discussed in the Introduction and Chapter 1; however, the concept of civility also carries with it a set of associations with manners, behavior, politeness, and civilization. It is thus both a broader concept than the public sphere and one that incorporates institutions normally considered definitionally nonpublic, such as the family.[13] As we will see, Delany's own notion of civility plays with both of these sets of connotations in suggestive ways.[14]

The Negro Convention movement was one of the most important institutions free blacks used as a way of participating in the political public during a period when they had little or no access to the mechanisms of government.[15] From 1830 until the outbreak of the Civil War, free blacks met at both state and national gatherings to debate issues, pass resolutions, and raise money for various causes. While they consistently condemned slavery, the conventions were never only abolitionist platforms. Like many institutions and organizations in the antebellum period, they quickly became a sphere in which social, moral, and political reform were both debated and rhetorically effected. As historian Howard Holman Bell describes them, "Generally speaking, antebellum conventions were socially experimental—or simply reformist in nature. Devoted to propaganda and education toward a specific goal, they used the available methods for making their ideas known: debate on the assembly floor, resolutions expressing the stand taken by the delegates, public addresses from the convention, and petitions to state legislatures and to Congress. By these various means the public became indoctrinated on the issues involved."[16]

In the thirty-year antebellum history of Negro Conventions, their emphases shifted according to the perceived needs of the moment. At one point they might focus their attention on education and try to raise money for the foundation of a black college; at another they might resolve that temperance was the key to racial uplift; and in other years or other states they might emphasize economic self-help or efforts to gain or regain the franchise. One recurring concern at the conventions was how to publicize their debates and decisions, which led their members to propose and raise funds for a variety of newspapers and other publications.[17] Editors of black journals jockeyed to position themselves as the founders of what some believed would be the national press organ of the black people, but by 1848 a convention held in Cleveland voted to declare that Frederick Douglass's *North Star* had, de facto, taken on that role.

This was a somewhat ironic victory for Douglass, since only a year before, at the Troy convention, he had argued against the establishment of any such national organ. As Bell describes Douglass's earlier opinion, "[S]uch an arrangement would soon result in its being the press of a clique, rather than that of the Negro public."[18] To some—including eventually Delany, who left his own Pittsburgh-based newspaper, the *Mystery,* to become coeditor of the *North Star* in 1847—at risk in Douglass's rise to prominence was precisely the claim of an individual, a newspaper, or an organization to represent the black public. As in many of the debates at the conventions, what was at stake in discussions of the black press was the legitimacy of the conventions' claims to represent what Delany refers to in *Condition* as "our people"—specifically, northern free blacks. Even the formal procedures by which the conventions secured representative legitimacy varied; as Bell says, "There was no consistent pattern followed in choosing delegates to the various assemblies. In most cases the ideal was the election of local representatives to state or national conventions, but in few cases was the rule followed rigidly."[19]

Robert S. Levine has aptly characterized the conflicts between Delany and Douglass as concerning "the politics of representative identity."[20] In Levine's account and in the debates themselves, Delany's objections to Douglass's leadership arouse the suspicion that what he really wanted was to occupy that representative position himself. This may have been so, but these controversies over power and prestige also staged one of the conflicts that Habermas argues was constitutive of the bourgeois public sphere in early modern Europe. In his account, one productive ideological tension motivating the transformation of the public sphere from its prebourgeois form of "representative publicness" to its modern form was a conflict over the relative openness of political representation, the public's irreducibility to what he, like Douglass, calls a "clique." In Habermas's words, a new system of representation arose to replace that in which a monarch or lord represented himself "not for but 'before' the people." "However exclusive the public might be in any given instance, it could never close itself off entirely and become consolidated as a clique; for it always understood and found itself immersed within a more inclusive public of all private people. . . . Wherever the public established itself institutionally as a stable group of discussants, it did not equate itself with *the* public but at most claimed to act as its mouthpiece, in its name, perhaps even as its educator—the new form of bourgeois representation."[21]

The Negro Convention movement is in many ways a perfect example of such a public institution, as speakers at conventions regularly claimed to represent their public as both "mouthpiece" and "educator." From Delany's perspective, however, even though the Negro Conventions claimed to be inclusive, open to debate, and organized to allow for democratic participation, their claim to represent the black public as a whole was illegitimate because they had excluded the topic of voluntary black emigration from the United States. Delany agreed wholeheartedly with the conventions' repeated denunciations of those who advocated Liberian colonization, insisting that "Liberia is not an Independent Republic: in fact, *it is not* an independent nation at all; but a poor *miserable mockery—a burlesque* on a government."[22] But over the years he had become a leader in developing an emigrationist position ideologically distinct from the colonizationists.[23] The tension between these positions came to a head in the months before the Rochester convention of 1853, which was clearly to be dominated by anti-emigrationists like Douglass. Delany publicly refused to attend and immediately thereafter called for a "National Emigration Convention of Colored Men."

In Levine's analysis of this convention call, he discusses the irony, also noted by Douglass, that Delany's response to the exclusion of his position from the national convention was to call for a still more exclusionary convention, limited to supporters of emigration.[24] And indeed, the first event of the convention, after the election of officials, was the Committee on Credentials' proposal of an emigrationist catechism, which simply read: "1st. Are you in favor of Emigration? 2d. Do you subscribe to the objects and sentiments contained in the Call for a National Emigration Convention, and will you do all in your power to carry out the same?"[25] However, Delany almost immediately thereafter suggested an exception to this rule. He put forward a motion offering newspaper editor William Howard Day "the privileges of the Convention . . . whether or not he altogether agreed in sentiment on minor points."[26] Day was not a committed emigrationist, but as implied by the title of his periodical, *The Aliened American,* he shared with Delany a belief that free blacks in the United States were "aliened," excluded from both political and civil society. Here civil society is defined in *national* terms; we will shortly see how Delany counterposed a *trans*national model of civility to the one that "aliened" him.

Delany's several-hour-long speech to the convention on the "Political Destiny of the Colored Race on the American Continent" was his most rigorous exploration of the form of this alienation from citizenship. Reprinted in full in the convention proceedings and later as a supplement to Delany's authorized biography, the speech opens with Delany addressing his audience as "fellow-countrymen." "We have not addressed you as *citizens,*" he proclaims, "a term desired and even cherished by us—because such you have never been."[27] He then gives an etymological history of the concept of citizenship, rooting U.S. definitions of the term in those of Rome, where, Delany claims, "[a]ll who were deprived of citizenship— that is, the right of enjoying positions of honor and trust—were termed . . . public and private *enemies,* and foreigners, or *aliens* to the country."[28] This, Delany argues, represents the "condition, precisely, of the black and colored inhabitants of the United States."[29] No people, by his definition, possess what he calls "the *sovereign principle* which composes the *true basis* of his liberty" unless they constitute "an essential part of the *ruling element* of the country in which they live. . . . The liberty of no man is secure, who controls not his own political destiny. What is true of an individual, is true of a family; and that which is true of a family, is also true concerning a whole people."[30]

As Delany's own analysis reveals, the difference between the institutions he and other free blacks patronized and those that Tocqueville claimed were characteristic of American democracy, or those Habermas argues were constitutive of the bourgeois public sphere, was that the civility, sociability, and subjectivity produced in the black public sphere could not be exercised in the hegemonic white political public. Blacks' position is characterized here by their exclusion from both state and civil society, their status as "public and private *enemies* . . . or *aliens* to the country." For Delany, perhaps surprisingly, this was not primarily a moral or political difficulty. It was, rather, a statistical problem: blacks would always be a minority in the United States. Unless blacks could become a majority—or at least that "necessary *constituent* in the *ruling element* of the country"— neither civil nor political rights would be within reach.[31] The task at hand, then, was in an important sense not political but demographic. Thus much of the speech is devoted to a statistical analysis of why such a majority could never come into being in the United States, but how, through emigration, it was a possibility in Central America. As the convention's "Declaration of Sentiments" states, "[T]he elective franchise necessarily implies *eligibility to every position* attainable; the indisputable right of being chosen and elected as the representative of another."[32] Since Delany assumed on the basis of racial history that no white man would ever agree to let a black represent him, even if that possibility were legally granted blacks could never attain full rights where they were in a minority. In short, Delany insisted, the right to vote was a necessary but not sufficient criterion for citizenship and civil rights; it had to be supplemented by a statistical possibility that blacks could take political power.

Citizenship, by this logic, could be determined demographically as at least the potential to be part of a majority. Gregg Crane has argued that this aspect of Delany's political thought inverts without overthrowing part of the logic of Justice Taney's decision in the Dred Scott case, which affirmed the tyranny of a numerical racial majority. With this in mind, Crane is implicitly critical of Delany's decision to displace the political action of his novel, *Blake,* from the slave states to Cuba, where blacks and mulattoes were a majority of the population. By doing so, Crane argues, "Delany's narrative leaves the jurisprudential question of minority rights unanswered. The move to Cuba constitutes a geographical symbol for the boundary of Delany's natural rights jurisprudence, which does not fully escape Taney's logic of power."[33]

Crane is right, I think, to say that Delany nowhere thinks through the question of civil rights for a minority; his was a plan for political hegemony for blacks (or rather, for what he calls "colored people," which ultimately seems to include all nonwhites, if we take seriously his statistical analysis of the population of the Americas). In other words, here "the people" is a term designating a *population,* rather than a social group characterized by specific attributes, manners, or behaviors. As in the case of the vigilante group in Pittsburgh, Delany did not simply reverse the hegemonic "logic of power." The three-part homology Delany makes among "a whole people," a family, and an individual should indicate that "the sovereign principle" of citizenship must be measured by other than statistical means. After all, a family does not work by majority rule. Rather, in his thought, the family figures as a site of political subjectivity organized not by power but by the bonds of sentiment.

The "Declaration of Sentiments" of Delany's emigration convention is strategically ambivalent in its deployment of these rhetorics of power and sentiment. It opens with a set of resolutions that deploy a demographic and statistically political definition of his people, using natural rights rhetoric and Delany's own argument that blacks must become "a necessary *constituent* in the *ruling element* of the country" in order to attain even basic civil rights.[34] But by the end of the list of resolutions, the declaration imbricates in this political discourse an affective, even sentimentally racialized notion of black political subjectivity, affirming an explicitly emotional attachment to racial identity through a resolution that "we shall ever cherish our ident[it]y of origin and race, as preferable, in our estimation, to any other people."[35] Here as throughout his career, Delany's political thought brings together rationalist scientific notions of race, population, and political citizenship with a more affectively based notion of racialized subjectivity. "We shall ever cherish" our racial identity, he emphasizes, but in his opening speech the identity "desired and even cherished by us" was that of citizen. As he puts it most disarmingly in *Condition,* the tone of which is mostly rational, statistical, or historical: "We love our country, dearly love her, but she don't love us—she despises us, and bids us begone, driving us from her embraces; but we shall not go where she desires us; but when we do go, whatever love we have for her, we shall love the country none the less that receives us as her adopted children."[36] Here, overlaid on the rationalist rhetoric of the nationalist treatise, is a maternal sentimental discourse: "Nationality," as Ernest Renan has remarked, "has a sentimental side to it."[37] At the same time, Delany strategically rearticulates the language of maternal love. If the United States has been a bad mother, he asserts, her children's love can be displaced onto one who loves them better. To adapt Claudia Tate's formulation, Delany here presents a "political allegory of maternal desire," an allegory in which maternal love is a matter of political choice, and in which the sentimental and the political converge.[38]

Civility and Representation

These two modes of thought, sentimental and political, converged in many of Delany's emigrationist writings and activities and intersected in explosive ways in an international incident he precipitated in 1860. He had in that year just completed a tour of the Niger Valley in West Africa, where he had successfully negotiated a treaty with the Alake of Abeokuta for land he hoped would serve as the base for a nation ruled by free blacks emigrating from the United States and Canada. The first written formulation of his plan, "A Project for an Expedition of Adventure to the Eastern Coast of Africa," deploys virtually *volkisch* nationalist rhetoric, asserting in its opening paragraphs that "[w]e have native hearts and virtues, just as other nations" and that "[w]e are a nation within a nation; — as the Poles in Russia, the Hungarians in Austria, the Welsh, Irish, and Scotch in the British dominions." "The claims of no people," it concludes, "are respected by any nation, until they are presented in a national capacity."[39]

Although "A Project" is surely one of the major documents of early black nationalism, it is both more and less than a nationalist manifesto. For Delany it represented a further break with the national public imagined by the national Negro Convention movement, and thus a further development in his conception of a black public sphere. "To accomplish so great and desirable an end" as a distinct nation, "A Project" asserts, "there should be held, a great representative gathering of the colored people of the United States; not what is termed a National Convention, represented en masse, such as have been, for the last few years, held at various times and places; but a true representation of the intelligence and wisdom of the colored freemen. . . . To effect this, and prevent intrusion and improper representation, there should be a CONFIDENTIAL COUNCIL held; and circulars issued, only to such persons as shall be *known* to the projectors to be equal to the desired object."[40] A shift in Delany's strategy of publicity is illustrated in this document. It not only narrows the previously fairly open notion of the public to which his writings and ideas are expressed, it also alters the definition of political representation, pulling back from the claim to represent the black population "en masse" and warding off "improper representation" by calling for a "confidential council" of "a limited number of known, worthy gentlemen" who possess "the highest grade of intelligence."[41]

Evident in "A Project" is the tendency toward the conspiratorial that many have noticed in Delany's thought, as well as the elitism that has led him to be described in later historiography as an "elite black nationalist."[42] Delany's elitism is undeniable, but those aspects of his political and rhetorical strategy that cut across territorial and racial boundaries complicate his designation as a black nationalist. After the exploration and acquisition of land in Africa, the next step in Delany's plan was to make an alliance between British capital and black labor and intellect that not only would constitute the economic basis for his new nation, but also, by growing cotton at lower cost, would undermine the slave system in the U.S. South. With that in mind he traveled from West Africa to Britain, where over the course of several months he lectured and raised money for his scheme in London, Glasgow, and other cities. Well received by many industrialists and abolitionists in Britain, Delany took an opportunity on this trip to gratify the long-standing interest in the emerging social sciences, specifically statistics, that he had demonstrated in the speech at the emigration convention.[43] At the invitation of the elderly abolitionist and scientist Lord Brougham, he attended the opening of the International Statistical Congress in London.

The Statistical Congress was organized according to governmentally appointed delegations representing countries in Europe as well as North and South America. As Victor Ullman points out, as a noncitizen Delany could not represent the United States, but neither had he yet satisfied the citizenship requirements of Canada, his country of residence before the African voyage.[44] He thus attended by virtue of a special royal commission granted by Prince Albert, a fact that so pleased Delany that nineteen years later he included it as a credential on the title page of his *Principia of Ethnology*. In short, while other participants were "public men" in the sense of being national representatives, Delany's status was based in norms of publicity and civility that could be termed "transnational."[45]

The tension between these norms erupted early in the meeting, as Delany became both subject and object of an international controversy over the boundaries of citizenship and civility. During the introductions, Lord Brougham chose to direct the attention of the U.S. delegates to

Delany's presence at the meeting. Addressing the U.S. ambassador, former vice president George Mifflin Dallas, Brougham proclaimed, "I beg my friend Mr. Dallas to observe that there is in the assemblage before us a Negro, and hope that fact will not offend his scruples." [46] Rather than waiting to see if the American's "scruples" were offended, Delany instead rose as if the remarks had been addressed to him. If his presence violated American national notions of civility, his retort deftly shifted the discourse to a more transnational norm. As Delany later described the incident, "I rose in my place, and said, —'I rise, your Royal Highness, to thank his lordship, the unflinching friend of the negro, for the remarks he has made in reference to myself, and to assure your royal highness and his lordship that *I am a man.*' I then resumed my seat." [47]

This event and those ensuing were covered in newspapers on both sides of the Atlantic, and all accounts make clear that a whole set of tensions— racial, national, social, and political—was played out here in a discourse of manners and civility. In a column in *Douglass' Monthly,* Frederick Douglass described the incident in just such terms, noting that "Mr. Dallas felt [the offense] at once. The hit was palpable. It was like calling the attention of a man vain of his personal beauty to his ugly nose, or to any other deformity. . . . Never was there a more telling rebuke administered to the pride, prejudice, and hypocrisy of the nation." [48] What was uncivil about the incident, then, was its insertion of a discourse of embodiment into the public sphere: not only Delany's body, described by Douglass as rising "with all his blackness, as quick and graceful as an African lion," but the white American national body, revealed as ugly, deformed, and wounded.

The American delegation took this revelation and transformed it into the kind of "narrative of traumatized identity" that, according to Lauren Berlant, is characteristic of modern U.S. citizenship. [49] Dallas himself apparently sat in stony silence, even as the delegates from other countries loudly applauded the exchange between Delany and Lord Brougham. But Augustus Longstreet, head of the U.S. delegation, stormed out of the room and refused to return to the congress. "Had the delegates received his lordship's remarks with a silent smile," he wrote in a letter to the *London Morning Chronicle,* "and Dr. Delany's response in the same way, I never should have left the Congress. But the plaudits came like a tempest of hail upon my spirit. The signs were infallible that I could not be received as an equal while the Negro was received with open arms." Dallas described Brougham's words as "a premeditated contrivance to insult the country which I represented and to provoke an unseemly discussion between the American Minister and the Negro" and referred to "the extremely unpleasant position in which this matter places me socially here."[50]

The public articulation of Delany's position as "a man" and "a Negro," however civil in its expression, violated American norms of national civility and citizenship, especially insofar as it threatened to put a representative of white America in an "unseemly discussion" with a black man. Put another way, the entire exchange—including Brougham's comment, Delany's reply, and the larger public response—located American "scruples" about race outside the norms of civility, redefined as transnational. Indeed, after President James Buchanan's cabinet met in Washington to discuss the incident, Secretary of State Lewis Cass reprimanded Dallas for failing to affirm his national identity. "Your true proceeding," he wrote, "would have been immediately to address to him and to announce to him that finding your Country through you exposed to insult . . . you would quit the meeting."[51] To be offended by such incivility—to find that your country can be insulted "through you"—is to be a national citizen.

When pressed to apologize, Lord Brougham slyly deployed the scientific discourse of "population" alongside the rhetorics of national citizenship that were really at stake and couched both discourses in quite civil language. Expressing his regret that he had insulted "our kinsmen in the United States for whom I have the greatest respect," he insisted that "I merely mentioned it as a statistical fact, which it was, and a fact, I might be permitted to add, of no small importance." Brougham surely knew that to make such an ostensibly "statistical" comment was to underscore the gap in America between political citizenship and population that had been the object of his critique. Dallas clearly recognized the sharp edge of this ostensible apology as well, for he refused to accept it.[52]

By responding as he did to Lord Brougham's complex act of interpellation Delany became—despite his protestations to the contrary in *Condition*—a "public man" of a particular sort. The story illustrates that the public for which he performed was not simply a national public; indeed, the entire complex history of Delany's shifting emigrationist thought could be cited as evidence for this point. At various times he located his projected black nation in Canada, Kansas, Central America, the Caribbean, and Africa, and he was also remarkably flexible as to what racial groups he considered potential citizens of this nation. In the very act of publicizing his black nationalism and constructing his public manhood, Delany invoked transnational norms of civility and concomitantly imagined a black public sphere that could not be contained within national borders.

Delany's most elaborate fiction of a transnational black public sphere, as well as his most fully realized representation of civility, is not one of his emigrationist manifestos but his novel, *Blake; or, The Huts of America*.[53] The early chapters of the narrative may have been begun as early as 1852, but the main body of the text was most likely written between 1856 and 1859. Robert S. Levine, who provides textual evidence for this dating, argues persuasively that the novel should be interpreted "in relation to Delany's anger and despair at the Dred Scott decision of 1857," an event that could only have underscored for Delany blacks' status as "aliened Americans." Levine notes as well that Delany's other immediate response to the decision was once again to chair a convention—this time held outside the borders of the United States in Chatham, Canada West—that "enthusiastically supported John Brown's mission to organize the slaves' resistance." Providing another detail essential for contextualizing the novel, Levine quotes a letter Delany wrote to William Lloyd Garrison in 1859, as parts of the novel were being serialized in Thomas Hamilton's *Anglo-African Magazine,* in which the author asks Garrison to help him find a publisher. His purpose in writing the novel, he tells Garrison, is to "make a pretty penny by it," to raise money to support the African exploration he was to begin the next year.[54] The novel is thus transnational in even more ways than those noted by Paul Gilroy in his discussion of both Delany's life and his protagonist's geographical wanderings as prototypical of "black Atlantic" cultural politics; its inception and circulation were intended to further, ideologically and materially, Delany's vision of a transnational black public sphere.[55]

Textually as well, *Blake*'s relation to American national civility is as complex as was Delany's at the Statistical Congress. The novel begins with a brief chapter, "The Project," the import of which will not become apparent for another thirty-three chapters. Four American men and two Cubans are gathered in Baltimore to plan the refitting of "the old ship 'Merchantman.'" The meeting takes place, Delany informs us, "during a contest for the presidency of the United States." It seems odd at first that the first sentence of the novel mentions this political matter, for it is of no apparent import to the men in the room, who "appeared little concerned with the affairs of the general government." "Though men of intelligence," Delany continues, "their time and attention appeared to be entirely absorbed in an adventure of self-interest." The only way politics seems likely to impinge upon this business matter is implied when the Cubans argue that the ship should be refitted in Cuba because of "the continual increase of liberal principles in the various political parties" in the United States. The Americans argue that Baltimore is better equipped in shipbuilding technology and that that city has "done more for the encouragement and protection of the trade than any other known place." These somewhat vague comments hint that the ship is being refitted as a slaver, but this fact is not made explicit until much later. The meeting adjourns when "for some cause, the preference for Baltimore prevailed" (3).

Delany thus opens *Blake* by setting up an apparent opposition between the individual "self-interest" of the economic market and the public sphere of national politics. Developing the political theme a bit further, the narration follows one of the participants in the mysterious meeting to his home in Mississippi, where he engages in a surprising political discussion with a woman visiting from the North, Mrs. Ballard. Questioned as to how the North will "go in the present issue"—Delany continues to avoid mentioning slavery by name—she asserts that "you will find the North true to the country." Her interlocutor, Colonel Stephen Franks, politely questions her representation of national unity by replying, "What you consider true, may be false—that is, it might be true to you, and false to us." Mrs. Ballard's rejoinder is especially telling: "You do not understand me, Colonel. . . . [W]e can have no interests separate from yours. . . . You, I'm sure, Colonel, know very well that in our country commercial interests have taken precedence of all others, which is a sufficient guarantee of our fidelity to the South" (4). The coincidence of political and commercial interests is underscored when Mrs. Ballard reveals that her husband is the judge who first ruled in favor of the Fugitive Slave Law; she also refers to the judge's "interests in another direction" as "an individual," hinting that he is implicated in the slave trade himself.

The discussion resolves potential personal and national conflict through reference to the economic "self-interest" that at first seemed to be in tension with national politics. Mrs. Ballard and Colonel Franks also deploy a gendered rhetoric of civility to help smooth over such conflicts, as she mentions that her participation in a discussion of either politics or business could be considered "unwomanly," and his reply is to "arrest the conversation . . . with true Southern courtesy." Delany thus opens his novel by representing an American national norm of civility, a norm that sutures political and behavioral meanings of civility by linking market capitalism's norms of individual self-interest to the norms of politeness characteristic of both "Southern courtesy" and notions of "womanliness." Blake's quest, and the project of the novel itself, becomes the disruption of this hegemonic civility.

The opening chapters set up a conflict between market forces and national identity that Delany quickly demonstrates to be a false opposition. This narrative and ideological false start for the novel is mirrored and doubled in the ensuing chapters, in which Colonel Franks secretly sells Maggie, the wife of the novel's eponymous protagonist, Henry Blake, who is absent on the colonel's business. This separation-of-family plot evokes emotional expectations and genre conventions established in the captivity narrative and developed in the slave narrative and sentimental fiction, especially *Uncle Tom's Cabin*. But the novel will disappoint these expectations in a most uncivil manner. For although Maggie's sale motivates Blake's escape from Franks's household, and some of his peregrinations in the rest of the story are in search of his wife, the novel is not centrally organized, either affectively or narratively, around this family breakup. As Eric Sundquist puts it in his analysis of the novel, "The surreptitious sale of Maggie, which sets in motion Blake's life as a rebel conspirator, recapitulates the by then archetypal scene of slave narratives and antislavery fiction, the separation of slave family members, but it also acts as the linchpin for Delany's critique of the far-flung, politically and economically complex regime of New World slavery."[56]

That *Blake* is not to be primarily a sentimental novel but rather a political picaresque is signaled immediately upon Blake's return to the Franks plantation. His initial reactions to his loss are couched in the language of civility and incivility, not sentimental expressions of pain and loss. His first response to the news conveyed by his pious compatriots Mammy Judy and Daddy Joe yokes liberal rights rhetoric to a renunciation of religion that his older black friends see as scandalously uncivil: "I and my wife have been both robbed of our liberty," he exclaims, "and you want me to be satisfied with a hope of heaven. I won't do any such thing; I have waited long enough on heavenly promises; I'll wait no longer. I——." Mammy Judy is scandalized by his blasphemy: "I neveh heah yeh talk so fo'—yeh sin in de sight ub God; yeh gone clean back, I reckon." Blake is unmoved by religious appeals: "What's religion to me? My wife is sold away from me by a man who is one of the leading members of the very church to which both she and I belong! Put my trust in the Lord! I have done so all my life nearly, and of what use is it to me?" (16).

In his conversation with his white mistress he seems at first to take a different, more sentimental approach: "Wiping away the emblems of grief which stole down his face, with a deep-toned voice upgushing from the recesses of a more than iron-pierced soul" (21). But most of his responses seem to both her and her husband to be characterized by their incivility, not the emotionality they expect of him. Colonel Franks berates him as an "ungrateful black dog," and the more sympathetic Mrs. Franks is barely able to restrain him from—of all things—swearing (19, 22). The ground of Blake's incivility quickly shifts from the interpersonal to the political, for it is in response to his wife's sale that he first formulates his plan to incite a black revolution throughout the hemisphere, the quest that is the main narrative thread of the novel.

The contents of this plan are, as we will see, quite mysterious. What is clear is that it requires black slaves to reinterpret their own situation and experience; as Blake remarks, "A slave has no just conception of his own wrongs" (128). Delany implicitly argues, though, that they already possess the skills necessary for such a reinterpretation. Before Blake is even introduced into the novel, the narrator remarks that "[n]ot unfrequently the mere countenance, a look, a word, or laugh of the master, is an unerring foreboding of misfortune to the slave. Ever on the watch for these things, they learn to read them with astonishing precision" (11). And the first description of the protagonist himself emphasizes that he is simultaneously "a pure Negro—handsome, manly and intelligent" and a "man of good literary attainments—unknown to Colonel Franks, though he was aware he could read and write—having been educated in the West Indies and decoyed away when young." Having juxtaposed Blake's black manhood with his literary and interpretive skills, Delany goes on in the next sentence to place in apposition Blake's private sentiments and his civility: "His affection for wife and child was not excelled by Colonel Franks's for his. He was bold, determined and courageous, but always mild, gentle and courteous, though impulsive when an occasion demanded his opposition" (16–17).

Throughout the novel, black interpretive abilities are highlighted by their juxtaposition with white ignorance and persistent incomprehension. The first example of white misinterpretation is very early in the novel, with Blake's assertion to Colonel Franks that "I'm not your slave, nor never was and you know it!" Blake means this as a statement of legal fact; he was decoyed into slavery and only stayed on Franks's plantation because he "became entangled in such domestic relations as to induce me to remain with you; but now the tie is broken!" due to Franks's sale of Maggie. But when, moments later, Mrs. Franks exclaims, "Colonel! what does all this mean?" her husband replies, "Mean, my dear? It's rebellion! A plot—this is but the shadow of a cloud that's fast gathering around us!" (19–20). In fact, Blake's act is not yet a plot. Rather, it is the beginning of his practice of reinterpreting dominant ideologies and rearticulating hegemonic institutions and practices. When he returns to the slave quarters following his altercation with Colonel Franks, he reassures Mammy Judy that despite his apparent renunciation of religion, "I do trust the Lord as much as ever, but I now understand him better than I use to, that's all." In response to Blake's claim of interpretive authority, Daddy Joe counsels patience and passivity, quoting scripture to the effect that Blake should "'stan' still an' see de salbation.'" The younger man replies that he has every intention of obeying God's word, but he adds his own interpretive twist: "[T]hat part was intended for the Jews, a people long since dead. I'll obey that intended for me . . . 'Now is the accepted time, today is the day of salvation'" (21).

By the end of the novel what looked like a renunciation of religion has been transformed into a more nuanced relation to it, as Blake announces to the revolutionary council that "[n]o religion but that which brings us liberty will we know; no God but He who owns us as his children will we serve" (258). Blake's use of the syncretic and appropriative strategies characteristic of African American Christianity is not limited to religion; his most important skill throughout the novel is his ability to come up with persuasive alternative interpretations of others' experiences. For instance, a "somewhat confused [white] ferryman" who is reluctant to transport Henry and his obviously runaway friends across the Ohio River cites as his justification the "Nebrasky Complimize Fugitive Slave Act, made down at Californy, last year" (140). This line leads to a demonstration of Blake's interpretive abilities, as he asks the ferryman, "[A]re you willing to make yourself a watch dog for slaveholders, and do for them that which they would not do for themselves, catch runaway slaves? Don't you know that this is the work which they boast on having the poor white man at the North do for them? Have you not yet learned to attend to your own interests instead of theirs? Here are our free papers,' holding out his open hand, in which lay five half eagle pieces" (140). Blake reinterprets the ferryman's situation and experience by placing the decision whether to obey the law first in a context of class conflict and then in a regional—northern as opposed to southern—rather than national framework, a task made easier by the man's already muddled understanding of the nation, in which laws are made in California. He then goes one step further by rearticulating the other man's sense of self-interest in dizzying fashion, first by offering him money, then by telling him, "[Y]our cause is a just one, and your reward is sure." Unwilling to trust the ferryman's belief in this "cause" in the face of a possibly higher bribe from the slave-catchers on their trail, Blake buys the horses that have pulled the ferry across the river and promptly shoots them.

In the following chapter, black counterinterpretation almost goes tragically awry. In high spirits because of their success in crossing the Ohio and the Wabash, and "[s]upposing their proximity to the British Provinces made them safe, with an imprudence not before committed by the discreet runaways," Blake's friend Andy leads the group in a song praising Canada and Britain for their status as havens for fugitive slaves. This time white ignorance converges with American nationalism to trap the blacks, as a white blacksmith and his wife overhear them and recognize them as runaways. "[T]hey might have passed," says the man, Dave Starkweather, "but for their singin' praise to that darned Queen! I can't stan' that no how!" His wife replies, "I'm sure I don't see what they sing to her for; she's no 'Merican. We ain't under her now, as we Dave?" And his response reveals him to be as politically ignorant as the ferryman: "No, we ain't, Ad'line, not sence the battle o'Waterloo, an' I golly, we wouldn't be if we was. The 'Mericans could whip her a darned sight easier now than what they done when they fit her at Waterloo" (143).[57] After an amusing discussion about whether Dave could beat the queen in a fistfight, the white couple tricks the runaways into waiting at their shop, and they are ultimately captured by a white mob. In contrast with Delany's experience at the Statistical Congress, Blake and his friends are not protected from American nationalism while in the United States, and they are duly punished for their violation of the norms of national civility. Fortunately for them—and thematically consistent with Delany's temperance commitments—the whites' drunkenness allows the runaways to escape that evening, and they progress without further incident into Canada.[58]

Aside from providing a combination of humor and narrative suspense in the novel, this experience demonstrates for blacks the inadvisability of expecting that they can compensate for their "aliened" status in the United States by an identification with another white national identity. Delany emphasizes this point in the next chapter, where despite the relative freedom the blacks enjoy in Canada, Andy quickly learns of "the unnatural feelings and course pursued toward his race by many Canadians." Delany provides his characters and readers with a lesson in political geography and racial history, explaining that the only right blacks have in Canada West (Ontario) is "mere suffrage-voting," that they are deprived of all the other attributes of citizenship, including jury and military duties and—apparently most galling to Delany—"the right of going into the gallery of a public building" (152–53). Full black citizenship, for him, would mean full access to the public sphere.

"Thank God for This Interchange of Sentiments!"

The escape to Canada fictionalizes both personal and political shifts in Delany's own life. Like Blake, Delany had moved to Chatham, Canada West, and had recommended that the Negro Convention movement put its energy toward the purchase of land for fugitive slaves and emigrated free blacks to farm. Also like Blake, Delany was quickly disenchanted with the Canadian option and shifted his emigrationist focus to the south—to the Caribbean, Central America, and ultimately Africa. And in another parallel, Delany used his geographical location to challenge U.S. civil and national norms, not only by exploring Africa and attending the Statistical Congress, but also by chairing a Negro Convention in Chatham that offered its support to John Brown.

Blake, however, is no autobiographical bildungsroman; it does not represent its protagonist's personal or political evolution from fugitive to emigrationist. Blake is always already ideologically coherent, and his plan is fully formed from the moment it comes to him after his wife is sold. So before and after his journey to Canada, Blake travels through the slave states and eventually to Cuba, repeatedly performing an act remarkably similar to the "confidential councils" Delany calls for in the African exploration document, the gatherings that were to lead to a "true representation of the intelligence and wisdom of the colored freemen." He holds what he calls "seclusions" with those he feels he can trust on each plantation and reveals to each "a plan for a general insurrection of the slaves in every state, and the successful overthrow of slavery" (39). One such seclusion takes place in a chapter called "Advent among the Indians," a chapter that takes place not on a plantation but in a nation: "the United Nation of Chickasaw and Choctaw Indians." The chapter opens with an incidence of incivility, as Henry comes into a room to converse with two native chiefs and finds a white doctor there as well. Henry immediately questions the chiefs as to how it is that they can reconcile themselves to holding slaves, provoking the white man to shout: "We have had enough of that" in "a tone of threatening authority." The doctor's words enrage the younger chief, who replies, "Hold your breath, sir, else I'll stop it!" In an attempt to assuage the chief's anger, the doctor responds, "I was not speaking to you, but only speaking to that Negro!" The effort at conciliation fails, however, and the doctor, "pale and trembling," leaves the room "muttering 'nigger!'"

The incident becomes for Blake a lesson in civility that is, like the exchange at the Statistical Congress, preliminary to a critique of white American notions of citizenship. Blake listens surprisingly politely to the chief's account of "the difference between a white man and Indian holding slaves. Indian work side by side with black man, eat with him, drink with him, rest with him and both lay down in shade together; white man even won't let you talk! In our nation Indian and black all marry together" (86).[59] Rather than criticizing his hosts for holding black slaves, Blake engages them in a comparison of Native American and African forms of resistance to European imperialism. The discussion culminates in Blake's decision to reveal his secret plan to the chiefs, resulting in, as the narrator puts it, "the only instance in which his seclusions were held with the master instead of the slave" (87).

Immediately following this chapter is one oddly titled "What Not," which opens with a description of the state of Arkansas beyond the boundaries of the Indian nation. Delany writes: "The most fearful incivility and absence of refinement was apparent throughout this region. . . . Law is but a fable, its ministration a farce, and the pillars of justice but as stubble" (88). He is referring to the prevalence of lynch mobs and other instruments of white mob rule in the state, one of which uses dogs to hunt him down later in the chapter. Delany goes on to juxtapose the white incivility of the region to a more highly developed black civility and civilization. As one poor white man admits later in the chapter, after his militia group has rudely burst in upon a black family and stolen their dinner, "The Negroes live a great deal better than we do." Delany here makes reference to what might be called "white trash *ressentiment*" reminiscent of Pap's diatribe against a well-dressed black man in *The Adventures of Huckleberry Finn,* but his characterization of whites as uncivilized is quite systematic, applying even where it might seem to disadvantage blacks. Even in the concluding section of the novel in Cuba, in a conversation among several whites about the complex politics of race and colonialism on the island, a man asserts that "the Negroes are more docile, contented, religious, and happy. They are civil, and more easily governed as a race than the Anglo-American; hence they make better subjects, being more submissive than they" (186).

While the speaker's claims of black docility and contentment are belied by the preparations for violent revolution that are secretly taking place all around him, throughout the novel the barbarousness of American whites is underscored. One anecdote interpolated into the Arkansas chapter emphasizes the political implications of white incivility: "[I]n the senate a misunderstanding on the rules of order and parliamentary usage occurred, when the speaker, conceiving of himself insulted by the senator who had the floor, deliberately arose from his chair . . . [and] drove a bowie knife through his body from the chest, which laid him a corpse upon the senate floor" (90).

Such "Anglo-American" incivility can refer us back once again to the uncivil exchange at the Statistical Congress. U.S. Ambassador Dallas was quite correct when he noted that Brougham's comment and Delany's reply were designed to "provoke an unseemly discussion between the American Minister and the Negro." The dialogical structure of the incident made Delany a public man in part by locating him as an interlocutor in a public act of communication, while forcing Dallas to withdraw from the public space rather than participate in such an "unseemly discussion." To the extent that the public sphere is a rhetorical construction instantiated in particular institutions, for a brief moment Delany had more public access than an official representative of the U.S. government. He had that access because he was invited to engage in the ritualized exchange of sentiments that opened the meeting, accepting the welcome offered him by Lord Brougham. What Dallas experienced—to quote *Cool Hand Luke* entirely out of context—was a failure to communicate; he could neither respond to Brougham's address from the podium nor accept the lord's apology without violating American national norms of civility.

Throughout Delany's writings, uncivil exchanges like this one, or like the one in the Arkansas legislature, are contrasted with elaborate and effective black communication networks that range in scope from massive international conspiracies to brief but meaningful exchanges such as the one between Blake and the recently captured African slave Abyssa on the deck of a slave ship, when in a glance "[s]he saw that he was a civilized man," and "the look was reciprocated" (224). Such virtually transparent communicative acts are central to Delany's notions of civility and citizenship as well as to the plot of *Blake*. The concept of communication, for Delany, incorporates symbolic, economic, and affective exchange. In his plan for an African nation in the Niger Valley, British capital and African labor were meant to produce a cotton power that would underprice and thereby bring down the southern slave system. *Blake* parallels similarly massive economic plots with a political conspiracy that often seems to consist of nothing but serialized acts of communication. The plan, Blake tells his confidants, is "so simple . . . that the trees of the forest or an orchard illustrate it; flocks of birds or domestic cattle, fields of corn, hemp, or sugar cane; tobacco, rice, or cotton, the whistling of the wind, rustling of the leaves, flashing of lightning, roaring of thunder, and running of streams all keep it constantly before their eyes and in their memory, so that they can't forget it if they would" (39).[60]

Not only does nature communicate and reinforce this plan, but "punishment and misery are made the instruments for its propagation. . . . Every blow you receive from the oppressor impresses the organization upon your mind" (40). Delany refigures virtually everything in the slaves' experience as a medium of communication. Again, what is curious is that as far as we can tell the revolution consists of nothing but this naturalized and generalized circuit of communicative exchange. In chapter after chapter, once Blake has waxed poetic about it in this way, the narrator flatly reveals nothing but the fact that he "imparted to them the secrets of his organization" (40). The incomplete status of the novel makes it impossible to know whether Delany intended to impart these secrets to his readers or not. Either way, the repetition of this epistemologically empty gesture throughout the body of the existing text makes clear that for him the act of communication is at least as important as its content. Communication serves to link the macropolitical and the economic to the micropolitical practices of social exchange. In other words, it links the political institutions of civil society to the practices of civility.

Black civility is figured in this chapter and throughout the novel not only in the politeness and hospitality with which Blake is received, but also as a well-organized communication network that will be the basis for the insurrection. Blake is surprised to find that the blacks he falls in with in Arkansas have already heard of his coming and asks, "Can you get word from each other so far apart, that easy?" His host, Aunt Rachel, replies that they have ways of communicating and that "wite folks know nothin' 'bout it." Blake replies, "[Y]ou're ahead of all the other states. You folks in Arkansas must be pretty well organized already," with "a good general secret understanding among yourselves" (89). In this chapter and in many others, Delany juxtaposes white incivility with a highly elaborated black civil society, the cohesion of which depends upon what Eric Sundquist describes as "effective networks of communication hidden from the masters . . . remarkable, in this case, for their seeming extent and complexity."[61]

Blake's plan for black rebellion is of course the key bit of knowledge communicated through these networks, but throughout the novel Delany stages scenes that demonstrate the fluidity and widespread diffusion of what we might call "counterpublic knowledge" in the black communities Blake visits in his travels. One key archive of that knowledge is the maroon community Blake stays with in North Carolina's Dismal Swamp. His sojourn with the old conjurors demonstrates his ability to appropriate all discourses for his nationalist revolution, for despite his skepticism about their superstitions, he allows himself to be named "a priest of the order of High Conjurors." At the same time, his quest is consecrated by the old men's association of him with revolutionary historical figures: "[T]he names of Nat Turner, Denmark Veezie, and General Gabriel were held by them in sacred reverence," and Blake is hailed by one old man as "a nudder Denmark" (113, 112). That these names are mentioned in the same breath as heroes of the Revolutionary War accentuates Blake's historical import; it also underscores how systematically Delany places his black nationalism in dialectical tension—but not simple antagonism—with American nationalism. Perhaps the most striking counterinterpretation of an icon of American nationality appears a few pages later, when Blake hurries by a slave prison in Washington, D.C. There he glances up to see "the National Colors," which he interprets as follows: "[S]tars as the pride of the white man, and stripes as the emblem of power over the blacks" (117).

Such counterinterpretations are both cause and symptom of the national disidentification Delany's novel is meant to produce. The structure of identification designed to be the basis of Blake's black counterpublic is harder to describe, not least because of the fact that Delany never gives us details of the plan for the rebellion. But like Whitman's *Franklin Evans*, the novel includes near its conclusion a scene of mass publicity from which it is possible to read the lineaments of that public sphere. A chapter titled "Gala Day" begins an account of the annual "National Fete" in Cuba.[62] After a description of the decorations, which centers on the presence of the "national pendants" of Spain, Britain, and the United States, the chapter turns to an account of the brutal "sport of the chase," in which bloodhounds are trained to hunt blacks. "This sport is such," Delany says flatly, "that in the training the slave is sometimes caught and badly lacerated, which produces terror in the black spectators, the object designed by the custom" (244–45).

This year, however, with the revolutionary conspiracy percolating among the populace, the response to this spectacle is different. "Never before had the African race been so united as on that occasion, the free Negroes and mixed free people being in unison and sympathy with each other. During the sport of the chase, it was generally observed by the whites that in the event of a slave being caught, instead of—as formerly— indifference on the part of the blacks, or a shout from a portion of the free colored people present, there were gloomy countenances, sour angry expressions and looks of revenge, with general murmuring, which plainly indicated if not a preconcerted action, at least a general understanding pertaining to that particular amusement" (245). Through the agency of the conspiracy, the "spectators" have been transformed into a racialized audience, a counterpublic with an alternative interpretation of what it sees. If that interpretation is manifested affectively—as "gloomy countenances" and "sour angry expressions"—it nonetheless rearticulates the identity of the spectators along politicized, racial lines. Delany represents each race as constituting its own public sphere under the broad umbrella of the National Fete, each group engaged in its own public conversation: "There was a greater tendency to segregation instead of a seeming desire to mingle as formerly among the whites, as masses of the Negroes, mulattoes and quadroons, Indians and even Chinamen, could be seen together, to all appearance absorbed in conversation on matters disconnected entirely from the occasion of the day" (245).

When the sporting event is succeeded by the "National Parade" of military might, it is "the only exhibition in which the African race took pleasure, they being desirous of witnessing the display of the troops to learn something of the character of the soldiers that might be brought against them." Even as "the crushed and oppressed people on the island" are presented with a spectacle of white power, Blake's conspiracy articulates a multiracial alliance, headed by free blacks, that systematically reinterprets the sight. This articulation is powerful enough to create a black hegemony in Delany's own terms, a demographic majority that constitutes—if only clandestinely—"a necessary *constituent* in the *ruling element* of the country." This point is underscored by the fact that in the parade itself are "several fine looking mulatto officers" who are ostensibly "the confidants of the Captain General," as well as "others of the fairest complexion among the quadroons, who were classed as white." These people, who earlier might have identified with the Spanish position in the upcoming conflict, "faithfully adhered to the interests of the African race, and . . . were ready at any moment to join them" (247).

The construction of a black counterpublic polarizes the population along lines that Delany describes as black and white, even though the former category includes all the races listed as spectators of the sporting event while the latter includes the Spanish colonizers and the even more virulently racist Americans, who are in constant conflict with one another. The moment Blake recognizes the success of his racialized rearticulation of the Cuban population is also the moment he opens up his conspiratorial counterpublic. "During the evening a general privilege was extended to any of their race in the confidence of a seclusion," creating for a moment a gathering simultaneously completely public to one race and secret from the other (249). The diverse company is witness to its own alternative national spectacle, as Blake and his mentor, the poet Placido, enter to a standing ovation and are acclaimed as the leaders of the revolution. An orchestra plays an ode to Cinque, the leader of the *Amistad* revolt, once again placing Blake in the history of black rebellion.[63]

The gathering is characterized above all by its communicative transparency; everyone seems to understand why they are there and what the plan is. "There was no empty parade and imitative aping," Delany writes, "nor unmeaning pretentions observed in their doings, but all seeming fully to comprehend the importance of the ensemble. They were earnest, firm, and determined; discarding everything, permitting nothing to interfere" (252). One practical accomplishment emerges from this meeting: the chef Gofer Gondolier demonstrates his plan to reproduce the cooking knives that will be the instruments of the whites' destruction. Otherwise what occurs is a decision to call the "Grand Official Council of the seclusion," a closed though representative body that is to choose "officers both civil and military for their future government."

Even though we do not get a representation of either the rebellion itself or the future black government, *Blake* does not go as far as the Washingtonian temperance narratives discussed in Chapter 1 in withholding direct representation of the counterpublic institutions that its creator wishes it to instantiate and help produce. But Delany does continue to emphasize the act of counterpublic communication over its content, constantly emphasizing conversation and symbolic exchange in his description of the Grand Council. Even after the National Fete the point of the group seems to consist mainly in a communicative exchange that constitutes and reproduces both a political counterpublic and a racialized revolutionary identity, rather than any particular political action. In the most concise statement of this emphasis, Blake exclaims at the climactic moment of the meeting, " 'Thank God for this interchange of sentiments!' " (258).

As this phrase indicates, it is affective expression—an "interchange of sentiments"—that both constitutes and results from the formation of the bonds of civility. The counterpublic acts of communication that the novel represents may be epistemologically empty, but they are affectively full. When Blake reveals his secret in a seclusion, his auditors consistently understand it intellectually and simultaneously feel it emotionally. For instance, one of his compatriots has two responses when he hears the plan: he remarks on its simplicity and transmissibility, exclaiming that he could explain it even to a simpleton, but he also exclaims, " 'Ah feels it! It's right heah!' " and places "his hand upon his chest, the tears trickling down his cheeks" (91). Such an emotional outburst is here figured as constitutive of Blake's alternative civil society or counterpublic, rather than as an instance of excessively emotional incivility, for it is a moment in Blake's structural transformation of the national public sphere, his conspiracy.

Blake's counterpublic communication is just as affectively based whether the seclusion in which it takes place is a clandestine conspiracy or a public meeting. "The general interest and anxiety manifested throughout the evening in the multitude of sentiments and opinions interchanged was beyond description. The greatest emotions were frequently demonstrated, with weeping and other evidences of deep impressions made" (259). Almost as important, though, the conspiracy's effects are evinced in the irrational response it evokes from whites, who throughout the novel catch exaggerated rumors of impending revolt and respond in a paranoid and repressive fashion. These circuits of almost intentional miscommunication are important not so much for their terroristic logic—as Blake explains, the more repressive the oppressors, the more blacks will remember their revolutionary role—as for their illustration of a logic of publicity. Delany sees even a secretive conspiracy as having a communicative orientation toward the hegemonic public as well as toward its more obvious counterpublic. Put more simply, even a secret separatist plot is partially a public act. In saying this I am not arguing that Delany's nationalism ultimately has as its audience a white public, nor that it is indistinguishable from forms of abolitionism aimed more directly at white public sentiments, such as moral suasionism or political coercion as Garrison or Douglass would define them. Rather, I am echoing an argument that Nancy Fraser makes in her essay "Rethinking the Public Sphere," that it is necessary to take into account the multiple forms of address in any political movement or action as interpellations of different *publics*, as opposed to, say, enclosable *communities*.[64] The conspiratorial counterpublic formed by the interchange of sentiments in the Grand Council is only one part of the revolutionary plan; the other is the stirring up of white public sentiment in disquieting ways, what one white character describes as "keeping the public mind in a continual state of uneasiness and excitement" (296).

Delany makes clear that this character mistakes the uneasy white public for the public as a whole and therefore is all the more oblivious to the actual revolution occurring around him. If whites are not oblivious, they become so paranoid as to be paralyzed by fear, seeing conspiracies everywhere: not only black conspiracy against whites, but American and British against Spanish. Indeed, the political chaos on the island intensifies to the point that the Spanish colonial government "caused the arrest and imprisonment of every white in the least suspected of seditious designs," and racial and national hostilities expand from the political sphere to civil society as "[e]very place of public entertainment, saloon, hotel, coach, cabin passage or what not—the greater part of which being controlled by Americans—were closed against Negroes and mulattoes" (304, 306–7).

Once the island is thus polarized, the revolutionary council knows that the time is right to put its conspiracy into practice. The novel ends—or rather, breaks off—with a gesture that crucially conflates the act of communication with an act of revolutionary violence. Gofer Gondolier has become a central figure in the conspiracy because, as a chef much in demand among the Spanish aristocracy, he can enter almost at will into their homes. At the same time, his profession gives him an excuse to order the manufacture of large cooking knives that he then distributes for use as weapons. At the end of the scene, Gondolier departs for one more act of counterpublic communication, "rejoicing as he left the room to spread among the blacks an authentic statement of the outrage: 'Woe be unto those devils of whites, I say!'" (313).

Gondolier's threat is the last surviving line of the novel; no further chapters have been discovered. Even if is not the ending Delany intended, the image of a black male domestic servant, armed with a knife, leaving to spread a plan of violent resistance among slaves and free blacks alike, is a potent condensation of Delany's political philosophy. From the perspective of Spanish and American whites, it is a threatening image of incivility. From the black perspective—and again, it is important to remember that Delany wants to articulate all nonwhite racial and political perspectives under a "black" rubric[65]—it is one of the acts of civil but counterpublic communication that make up both the plot of the novel and the plan for rebellion. Attention to Delany's deployment of the categories of civility and incivility, and to the relationship between affect and politics in his novel and his political writings, provides a different lens through which to view the black nationalism that historians and critics see as his most prominent characteristic. Delany's nationalism was part of his lifelong effort to give public and institutional form to the racialized sentiments at the affective core of his political thought. Sometimes those sentiments were the identificatory desires that made the members of one's own race "preferable . . . to any other people," and sometimes they were organized around that other identity he "desired" and "cherished," that of citizen. But the most consistent pattern in his writings and activism is his tendency to push at the limits of the actually existing American public sphere, to transgress and rearticulate hegemonic norms of civility in order to reveal them as merely national norms.

Early in Horatio Alger's *Ragged Dick; or, Street Life in New York,* a wealthy man hires the title character to take his young son Frank Whitney on a tour of New York City. On the trip, which takes up most of the first third of the novel, Dick displays his familiarity with the city, outwits a swindler, and tells a humorous and not entirely accurate version of his life story. He shows Frank the Bowery Theater and P. T. Barnum's American Museum, both of which the street boy has often visited. He points out the newest department stores, the New York Hospital, the Mercantile Library, and the Cooper Institute. They pass by "important public buildings" such as the City Hall, the Hall of Records, and the Rotunda. Indeed, Dick claims a personal relation to each public institution they encounter, asserting that he and the mayor "are very good friends," that Peter Cooper is "a particular friend of mine" from school, and that he and newspaperman Horace Greeley shop together for ready-made clothing.[1]

The boys then take public transportation uptown to see Central Park. When, six chapters into their tour, they finally arrive at their destination, Frank is disappointed to find that the park is still under construction. "It had not been long since work had been commenced upon it," Alger writes, "and it was still very rough and unfinished." Upon Frank's dismissive remark that his father owns "a large pasture that is much nicer," the boys decide not to enter the park. What had been the goal of the tour turns out to be only a detour. After gazing briefly at the unattractive, broken landscape, they return downtown to see Wall Street, the Custom House, and other sights in the financial district (48).

In this section of the novel, two boys from opposite ends of the economic spectrum encounter many of the institutions of the public sphere that existed in New York City in 1868, when the novel was written. In most of their tour, they see the establishments with which Dick has been familiar in his life on the street as a bootblack and newsboy: theaters, the facades of government buildings, the press, and the like; they also encounter public places devoted to economic exchange, from department stores and shop windows to a bank and a cheap clothing bazaar. For my purposes, the most significant place the boys encounter is the one they decide not to enter. Central Park—neither a seat of government nor a place of trade—was a new kind of institution of the public sphere, one that was both literally and figuratively under construction in 1868. Designed to be simultaneously didactic and pleasurable, Frederick Law Olmsted's Central Park was one of many midcentury attempts to construct a cultural public sphere for the masses, instilling in "the dangerous classes" norms of gentility and civility and allowing the "middling classes" to display their own adherence to such norms.[2] Contemporaneous descriptions of Central Park often compared its functions to those of other relatively new institutions like public libraries and public schools, calling it "a great free school for the people . . . a magnetic charm of decent behavior, giving salutary lessons in order, discipline, comeliness, culminating in mutual good will."[3]

Such public institutions were to be neither domestic nor commercial; rather, they were differentiated from the parlor and especially the marketplace. Olmsted declared that Central Park should display "the greatest possible contrast with the streets and the shops."[4] Official regulations prohibited the "display [of] any sign, placard, flag, banner, target transparency, advertisement or device of business . . . nor shall any hawking or peddling be allowed on the Central Park."[5] Olmsted's ideal was continually threatened by plans to add to the park such structures as "auditoriums, restaurants, burial grounds, trotting tracks, playgrounds, athletic fields, zoos, statues, even museums."[6] His intransigent opposition to the park's commercialization was one of the factors that in 1878 led to his dismissal from his position as Central Park's landscape architect. Constructing a public institution distinguishable from the market was apparently not a simple or uncontroversial project.[7]

Literature, especially fiction, was at the time of Alger's writing a locus for playing out similar conflicts over the distinction between the public sphere and the market. While the antebellum novels and institutions discussed in Chapters 1 and 2 did their cultural work primarily on the bodies of grown men, later in the nineteenth century there was increasing focus on the character of younger men and boys. Organizations like the Boy Scouts and the Young Men's Christian Association (YMCA) grew exponentially during the period, aiming, like Olmsted's Central Park, to reinforce genteel values in the middle-class boys and men who flocked to their meetings and activities.[8] At the same time—and, some feared, in competition with the institutions explicitly designed for such social control—writers and publishers targeted adolescent males as a distinct and identifiable reading public, beginning dozens of series of genre fiction as well as nonfiction historical adventures and boys' biographies.[9] Story papers, dime novels, and police gazettes all aroused the concern of moral arbiters; indeed, any narrative read predominantly by young men and boys drew such attention. While boys' literature certainly predated the Civil War—the Ned Buntline novels that Tom Sawyer reads in Twain's fiction were popular in the 1840s, for instance—it was in the 1860s and 1870s that popular books for boys came into their own both as reading material and as profitable commodities.

The seemingly self-evident fact that these books were simultaneously works of literature and commodities, that they interpellated boys both as a reading public and as a mass audience, made them sites on which authors and cultural arbiters vied to define the roles men and boys were to play in the economic market and in the developing mass-cultural public.[10] In this chapter, I read Horatio Alger's novels and the responses they provoked as moments in the struggle to control the transformation of the cultural public sphere in the second half of the nineteenth century. Alger's narrative formula was designed to enlist his readers in the construction of a literary counterpart to the ideal realm of leisure, discipline, and genteel performance Olmsted envisioned. His stories were reformulations of the traditional association of masculinity with publicity. In other words, Alger's fiction interpellated boys as virtuous, "manly" individuals destined to play a role in a version of the public sphere that his novels were helping to construct.

Like Olmsted, Alger tried to imagine a public realm distinct from overtly commercial values and linked to an older model of republican virtue. And like Olmsted's plans for Central Park, Alger's novels provoked controversy. His fiction intervened in at least two kinds of public space, two institutions of the public sphere that existed in some tension with one another. One, the public library, is an institution that seems public in a paradigmatic sense. Though most readers today associate Alger's name with didactic and moralistic writing, in the 1870s his novels were at the center of a conflict over the kinds of books that should be bought by public libraries, a controversy that I will examine in some detail in the next section of this chapter. The main reason Alger's novels created a controversy in this institution of the public sphere is that they so clearly placed themselves and their boy protagonists in a second, more problematic space that could only be considered "public" from a particular angle: the economic market. This chapter thus engages implicitly in an argument mentioned in the Introduction, a debate with theories and histories of domesticity that describe the domestic as "private" and place the domestic sphere in binary opposition to an economic realm defined as "public." The efforts of Olmsted and Alger to define their public spheres as distinct from the economic market point to the problem with this conceptualization, which is quite simply that under capitalism the economic realm is in important ways private, not public.[11]

Despite his best efforts, then, Alger's novels provoked controversies about the possibility of distinguishing between the public sphere and the realm of economic exchange, controversies that were articulated as anxieties about masculinity and the market. What young males bought, what they read, and what they became were all intimately intertwined with contemporary notions of the public sphere. To some of his adult readers, Alger's form of address to a reading public made up of boys and young men was a morally dubious means of "pandering" to his audience's basest desires and pleasures, a further step in the regrettable and ongoing commodification of the reading public. Because, to use Linda Kerber's words, masculinity and the public sphere were "reciprocal social constructions," anything that seemed to debase the contemporary public sphere put the meaning and stability of masculinity into question, and vice versa.[12] That is not to say that the public sphere was simply masculine. Indeed, the fact that Alger's fiction was at the center of controversies in which definitions of both masculinity and publicity were at stake is evidence that neither these terms nor the relations between them were stable in this period.

The Public and the Market

The 1879 conference of the Library Associations of America, held in Boston, inspired unusually widespread interest for a gathering of librarians. Because of the large crowd drawn by the special focus of the meeting, "Fiction in Libraries and the Reading of Children," sessions had to be moved from the original site to "the spacious hall of the Young Men's Christian Association," which was filled to capacity. The editors of the special double issue of the *Library Journal* in which the conference papers and proceedings were printed attributed the unexpected turnout to the fact that the topic was not only of special concern to librarians, but of political and social interest to the public at large: "[T]he close and eager attention given by this large auditory, lasting persistently long beyond the dinner hour, emphasized the fact that this discussion was one the public wanted to hear—a demand further responded to by the general press, which carried the word of the Conference far beyond its immediate hearers. Surely no question can be more vital to far-sighted men, since it touches at the roots of public education. It has to do with an education including but wider than that of the schools; and public education is at the root of our system of government." [13]

The librarians here made a strong claim for their institution's place at the core of the national public sphere, pointing as evidence to the library's links with the schools, the press, and the democratic state. Many of the papers reprinted from the conference took up this issue by asking, implicitly or explicitly, what the word "public" meant in the phrase "public library." The lead article in the journal, for instance, was titled "The School and the Library: Their Mutual Relation," and the question was addressed by the professional librarians who addressed the conference as well as by professors like William T. Atkinson and luminaries like Reverend James Freeman Clarke and Reverend Thomas W. Higginson.[14] The speakers had no trouble asserting the "mutual relation" between the public library and institutions like schools and churches whose public status seemed morally unambiguous. What sparked the most debate was the public library's relationship to the economic market, a relation that was unavoidable because it was increasingly evident that books were commodities. Unlike a church or a school, the market had no moral screens, no way of distinguishing between good and bad books. If the library was to make a claim to promote public virtue, it had to distinguish itself from the market on some such grounds.

Every speaker agreed that there were some books none of them would consider including in their libraries: S. S. Green, a librarian from Worcester, Massachusetts, placed the works of "Ouida" and "translations of many French novels" in this category. Green succinctly delineated the main terrain of contention at the conference when he asserted that while "no librarian would think of putting an immoral book into a library," a more difficult problem is raised by those books whose morality is ambiguous, "written by men who mean well." "The question to which good men who have studied library economy give different answers is, whether such books as those of which the writings of William T. Adams ('Oliver Optic'), and Horatio Alger, Jr., are examples among books provided for the young, and of Mrs. Southworth and Mrs. Hentz, among works wished for by older persons, ought to find a place in public libraries."[15]

The debate revolved around two related issues. One was essentially a theoretical or psychological question about reader response: What effect did morally ambiguous fiction like that written by Alger and Optic have on its audience? This question provoked strongly gendered rhetoric. Those who, like T. W. Higginson, defended such fiction's place in the public library affirmed its readers' manliness and the importance of that manliness for national and racial hegemony:

> It is not a bad impulse but a good one which makes the child seek the reading you call sensational. The motive that sends him to Oliver Optic is just that love of adventure which has made the Anglo-American race spread itself across a continent, taking possession of it in spite of forests, rivers, deserts, wild Indians and grizzly bears. The impulse which leads him to Jules Verne is the same yearning of scientific imagination that has made the American the foremost inventor of the world. How much of the great daring of our American civil war was nurtured by tales of adventure, reaching lives that had until that war *no* outlet! You cannot repress these yearnings—you fortunately cannot. They are the effort of the young mind to get outside its early limitations. You cannot check them by prohibition. That is apt to defeat itself.[16]

In rebuttal, Professor Atkinson proclaimed: "I cannot quite agree with my friend, Mr. Higginson's rather rose-colored view of the influence of the Oliver Optics of this day. I don't think it is the really clever boys who are much addicted to Oliver Opticism, and on the limp mind of the ordinary boy I think it has a mischievous influence. He settles down into it and does not rise above it: it is well if he does not sink below it."[17]

A compromise position that developed in the course of the conference deployed a form of developmental psychology and the newly invented category of adolescence to argue that even if such fiction is not good in itself, boys inevitably outgrow it. James Freeman Clarke argued that one should "let boys revel in Oliver Optic and Horatio Alger. This literature is false to life, tawdry in sentiment, full of impossible incidents. But let them have it, go through it, and outgrow it. It will lead to something better in many cases." [18] Green provided a fuller account of this developmental theory of reading, justifying such "impossible" literature in the boy's early years on the ground that it at least instills the habit of reading in youth, a habit with a value in itself:

> It is becoming fashionable to sneer when the librarian says that the boy who begins with reading exciting books comes afterwards to enjoy a better class of literature. There is truth in the statement, nevertheless. A boy begins by reading Alger's books. He goes to school. His mind matures. He outgrows the books that pleased him as a boy. If boys and girls grow up with a dislike of reading, or without feeling attracted toward this occupation, they will not read anything. But if a love of reading has been cultivated by giving them when young such books as they enjoy reading, then they will turn naturally to reading as an employment of their leisure, and will read such books as correspond to the grade of culture and the stage of intellectual development reached by them. They will thus be saved from idleness and vice. [19]

Not every participant in the conference was convinced by this logic. Charles Francis Adams Jr., for instance, replied, "Now, that insipid or sensational fiction amuses I freely admit, but that it educates or leads to anything beyond itself, either in this world or the next, I utterly deny. On the contrary, it simply and certainly emasculates and destroys the intelligent reading power." [20] At stake in this discussion was the boy reader's frankly phallic white masculinity: does the reading of books like Alger's inspire the impulse to spread "Anglo-American" manliness across a continent, or does it reinforce the limpness of the ordinary mind? Is the goal of reading to motivate or to contain a boy's aggressive masculinity? That the speakers had different attitudes toward a boy's masculinity becomes clear if one compares Higginson's vision of imperialist manliness with the views of Green, who also supported libraries' purchase of Alger novels, if less enthusiastically. Green concluded his half-hearted apologia for Alger by asserting, "Perhaps there is no book that the average Irish boy likes better than one of Mr. Alger's stories. Now such a boy is likely to learn that his powers are subject to limitations, and not be led by these books to feel an overweening self-reliance." [21] For Higginson, the virtue of Alger's novels was that they inspired precisely such self-reliance, while Green argued that this effect would be contained by their reader's encounter with ethnically inflected real-world constraints on the very "yearnings" Higginson valorized.

Juxtaposed with the debate over books' effects on the masculinity of boy readers was the linked but more broadly political question of the meaning of the word "public." On this question the participants were almost as starkly divided as they were on the first issue. Most agreed that libraries, like Olmsted's parks, should carve out a space between "instruction" and "rational entertainment." What was more problematic, though, was the relation between the public library and the market. Again discussing Alger and Optic, James Freeman Clarke asserted that "the Public library is for the same purpose as the Public Garden, Public Baths, music on the Common provided by the city, or fireworks on the Fourth of July. Why do we provide these things at the public expense? Because they tend to refine and elevate the people, because they tend to make them contented, cheerful and happy, because they tend to prevent crime by giving a taste for something better than the drinking saloon. Thus they make the whole community more safe and peaceful—they take the place of a police—they supplement the Public Schools."[22] How, then, were libraries to respond to the popularity of Alger and Optic—writers who, all agreed, neither refined nor elevated their readers? How could libraries fulfill their "police" function of maintaining public order through private reading?

Charles Francis Adams Jr., who insisted that sensational fiction "emasculated" its readers, felt that using "public money" for the "wholesale purchase of trashy and ephemeral literature" was unjustified not so much because such literature should not be read, but because "those who wish to do so should be willing to pay for them, as they do for their theatres."[23] The public library is differentiated from the theater precisely by its public status, which is again defined as its separation from the market. Books that are "made to sell," Adams argued, belong in the market—subscription libraries and bookstores—and not in the public realm.

The basis of Adams's distinction between market and public links this debate back to the one about the moral and psychological effects of reading. Adams interpreted the market as an immoral reversal of the ideal scene of reading. Rather than serving as the transparent medium of communication between boy and man, reader and author characteristic of virtuous publicity, the literary mass market is governed by a reading practice that is dangerously unidirectional: the reader is read by the market and thereby turned into a consumer. "The publisher of today," Adams argued, "understands the popular appetite almost perfectly well. . . . He studies the market, and not his own inner consciousness; the result is that he publishes what the market will take."[24]

Adams insisted that there is nothing essentially immoral about this procedure, for it is the economic logic of capitalism and the basis of some of America's highest literary accomplishments (his example is *Harper's Monthly*). However, he argued, it is essential that one literary relation be kept apart from this dynamic: the public library's relation to children, especially boys. The books of Alger, Optic, and others should be relegated to the logic of the market and not allowed in the public library. Reading boys in public—the construction of a reading public that is essential to the targeting and creation of a male mass audience—is precisely the problem that the public library is designed to contain, because targeting boys erodes the distinction between the public and the market. Using Alger as his main example, Adams proclaimed: "I fear the public libraries are, by degrees, approaching somewhat near to what it is not using too strong a term to call *pandering*."[25]

When Adams and others figure the relation between morally questionable books and their readers as a kind of "pandering"—whether defined as "minister[ing] to the gratification of another's lust" or as catering to "the baser passions" in general[26]—and raise the specter of the public library operating on the model of "bread-and-circuses," their rhetoric condenses sexual and economic anxieties into a single worry about the meaning of male reading in the public sphere. In Habermas's comments on the part played by the rise of the novel in the development of the bourgeois public sphere, discussed in the Introduction, the economic market plays a role as circumscribed as the one prescribed by cultural arbiters like the librarians at the Boston conference. The book itself is made widely available in the form of a commodity, but it is important to Habermas that the logic of commodification does not penetrate either the content of the book itself or the "psychological" relationship between reader, text, and author. Once such penetration occurs, with the dominance of "manufactured publicity and nonpublic opinion," the audience itself becomes a commodity to be bought and sold by television networks and advertisers, a development Habermas says signals the end of authentic publicity. The accusation of "pandering" leveled at Alger demonstrates that late-nineteenth-century cultural analysts were anxious about tendencies similar to those that Habermas decries, such as the tendency to put forms of subjectivity—in this case, again, boys' masculinity—on the market to be "read" and targeted by authors and publishers.

Adams's fear was that an uncontrolled distribution of popular books like Alger's would collapse the public sphere into the mass market, thus making readers and citizens into consumers. Alger's books were at the center of this controversy, and yet they are not obviously any more mass-cultural or sensationalistic than many others. The questions they aroused among nineteenth-century guardians of morality may have been due to the way his characters court the very relations Adams fears. Pandering is not a threat to the Alger boy. Indeed, as several critics have noted, the paradigmatic encounter between the boy and his older mentor is depicted as a kind of virtuous seduction, in which the boy's rewards are what Alger, characteristically conflating the economic and the affective, calls in *Ragged Dick* "the pleasures of property" (105). The encounter is equally and simultaneously an act of reading, of transparent communicability, in which each participant—usually in a public space like a street or a train car—interprets the other's performance of virtuous masculinity. The model of transparent communicability such encounters offer to the reader entails the very pandering Adams decries. In Alger's novels, masculinity is on the market at every moment.

Reading Well and Looking Good

In Alger's own view, as represented in his fiction, the relationship between the market and the public parallels the relationship between the book and the reader. Alger typically foregrounds his protagonist's illiterate status early in his stories. At one point in *Julius; or, The Street Boy Out West,* the title character says of another, "I know him like a brick." "The common expression," Alger informs us, "is 'like a book'; but that would hardly have implied any close knowledge on the part of Julius, for he knew next to nothing of books."[27] "I ain't much on readin'," says the hero early in *Ragged Dick,* "It makes my head ache" (28). Along with the acquisition of property—a bank account, a gold watch, and a new suit of clothes— the Alger boy's success is marked by his learning to read.[28] But literacy is not just the means to an economic end that one might expect it to be in an Alger novel, even though it is usually accompanied by the hero's upward mobility. More important, the boys develop a relation to books that makes reading a significantly public act, and the path to economic success in the Alger novel runs parallel with a path toward a closer connection to the public sphere.

To be sure, few of Alger's characters enter public life in any conventional sense of the term; they neither participate in social movements like temperance nor found counterpublic political institutions like Negro Conventions. Publicity in its most positive form is never conceived of as a theatrical or artistic performance; in fact, *Phil, the Fiddler* describes Phil's escape from having to play his violin on the street for money as a welcome relief from being "at the service of the public."[29] Nor do the characters enter into a direct relationship to the state; the hero never really comes to be or even know the president or the mayor, although he jokingly claims both. When asked "What's the use of studying so much," Dick responds, "If my feller-citizens should want me to go to Congress some time, I shouldn't want to disapp'int 'em; and then readin' and writin' might come handy" (107). In only one Alger novel does the hero's transformation from rags to respectability have an overtly social component: the author claimed that *Phil, the Fiddler* exposed and thereby ended the exploitation of Italian street musicians by their *padrones*. Critics have generally seen this novel as anomalous; Gary Scharnhorst and Jack Bales claim that "in Phil more than in any other novel Alger wrote, his altruistic impulses were at war with his formula," because "his angry story had to end happily."[30] *Phil, the Fiddler* only seems to violate the norm if we see Alger's formula as a set of narrative conventions rather than as a mechanism for character formation that works through publicity. Alger makes explicit in Phil his notion of literature as serving a socially ameliorative function, asserting that it fulfills that function precisely by publicizing the problem it is meant to address. This logic of publicity applies whether the dilemma to be addressed is framed as one of personal finance or of social exploitation. Indeed, in this fictional context there seems to be no difference between the two problems. Even the musicians' abuse is framed as linguistic and psychological rather than political or economic. Few of the boys "acquire even a passable knowledge of the English language," and their inability to communicate about their own situation is clearly the source of their oppression. Until he masters English, Phil cannot even "analyze his own emotions."[31] Alger's books themselves are meant to perform this communication or translation. Literature's function is to produce a public sphere in which the economic manipulation represented in *Phil, the Fiddler* by the boys' *padrones* will be immediately visible.

While publicity implies visibility and openness in Alger's novels, the publicity to which the Alger hero aspires is not primarily a social space. In fact, the stories typically narrate the boy's trajectory out of public spaces like the street and toward both the economically private world of business and the socially private domestic sphere. Publicity is instead an aspect of an individual's character. All of the positive adjectives Alger repeatedly uses to introduce his protagonists—"frank," "honest," "bold," "attractive," and "manly"—refer to some degree to an ideal of transparent legibility. Making this link concisely, the protagonist of *Struggling Upward*, when asked by a confidence man, "And whom do you represent?," replies, "Myself for the most part."[32] The prerequisite of virtuous publicity is simply that the boy's interiority and surface appearance are identical, that individuals represent themselves.

In the ideal version of Alger's public sphere, the moral character of things and especially people is immediately legible to anyone trained in sympathetic observation.[33] One can recognize an honest boy, whether by means of his outward actions or his physiognomy, and he will recognize you in turn. Some such scene occurs in virtually every novel; the Alger hero meets a businessman in some public place, and each judges the other in an instant. Dick's "open face," along with his claim to "know all about the public buildings," convinces Mr. Whitney that the boy is a suitable tour guide for his son in *Ragged Dick*. "I may be rash in trusting a boy of whom I know nothing" the man says, "but I like your looks" (107). Even when one Alger character, tricked into assisting in a robbery, is caught in the act, the victim can immediately sense the boy's integrity: " 'You have an innocent face,' responded the young man kindly. 'I am sure you are a good boy.' "[34] This ability to be read as attractively virtuous is at the core of the Alger hero's success. As another boy's benefactor puts it with disarming ambiguity: "He is a very good looking boy, and he looks *good*, which is still better."[35]

That such self-evident self-identity is a fantasy—albeit a fantasy at the core of Alger's world—is made clear in a paradigmatic scene from *The Store Boy* in which a businessman and the young protagonist meet on a train. Each immediately evaluates the other as honest, and they discover that they are both on their way to unmask the same swindler. The man proposes that they unite, since the impostor "wants to swindle both of us—that is, those whom we represent."[36] His hesitation is symptomatic: the "us" and "those whom we represent" are in theory inseparable, a point already underscored by the judgments each has made based on appearance.

Alger's novels are just as committed to an ideal of transparent communicability as are Delany's writings. The scenes in which older men recognize the virtue of the Alger hero serve narrative functions not unlike those in which black slaves recognize Delany's hero Henry Blake as their political leader and instantaneously join his cause. Unlike Delany, however, Alger valorizes legibility and transparency as primarily individual characteristics, not as prerequisites for the formation of a political counterpublic. It would be misleading to refer to them as purely personal traits, though, for literacy and legibility mark the Alger hero's ability to participate honestly and profitably in the economic market. It is this association that allows the boy of the street to move so seamlessly into the world of business, for "Street boys . . . are by their circumstances made preternaturally sharp" and "Wall Street men are good judges of human nature."[37]

Along with the hero's ability to read human nature comes another form of literacy: an often playful mastery of language. Alger is enamored of puns and plays on language, as when, on the tour of New York, Frank Whitney is mystified by a man who "came out of a side street, uttering at intervals a monotonous cry which sounded like 'glass puddin'.'" "'Glass pudding!' repeated Frank. . . . 'What does he mean?'" Dick is amused by Frank's misunderstanding of the glazier's cry, "Glass put in" (41). The boy's "sharpness" and his "active sympathy," which allow him to interpret these linguistic ambiguities as well as the more dangerous ambiguities of the confidence man, are signs of and means toward his moral and financial rise. They link Alger's moral cause—the construction of a public sphere of linguistic and economic exchange based in confidence, active sympathy, and transparency of communication—with his hero's personal quest for success. Alger's analogy between individual and social publicity relies for its legitimacy on a corresponding connection between literacy and legibility, between reading well and looking good.

The Alger boy's virtuousness, an older male observer remarks in *The Store Boy*, "is of the old-fashioned kind. It is not the kind now in vogue."[38] His combination of literacy and legibility is not "in vogue" because, as John Cawelti has persuasively argued, Alger's ethos derives from an older republican model of public masculinity. The representation of literature as public disclosure of hidden wrongs—whether personal or social—and the association of literacy with public virtue were characteristic of the republican rhetoric that Alger appropriated.[39] As historians have pointed out, early American writers and politicians alike represented the political public and the reading public as analogous, even identical. The act of reading was, David Paul Nord argues, "a form of participation in the new social order of postrevolutionary America."[40] When Dick describes himself as having "diffused intelligence among the masses"—meaning that he has sold newspapers—his phrasing is classical republican rhetoric, a phrase used since the eighteenth century to describe the public function of print (38). As Michael Warner points out, George Washington affirmed in his farewell address that "a general diffusion of knowledge" was one of the prerequisites for the continued survival of the republic.[41] Dick's claim that his ragged coat had been owned by Washington, who "wore it all through the Revolution" and then "told his widder to give it to some smart young feller" (5), shows that Alger was intent on making his hero's ideological ancestry clear.

As if to underscore the association between print culture and Alger's publicity, the hero's apparent virtue often becomes public reality when he is put into print himself. When Frank Courtney in *The World Before Him* hears a group of people reading a story of a boy who has prevented a theft, he modestly remains silent. But when asked, "Don't you wish it had been you, Courtney?" he replies, "It was," causing "a great sensation . . . all eyes were turned upon our hero."[42] Exposure to such an admiring public gaze quite properly embarrasses the hero, but it simultaneously confirms that he is on a moral trajectory toward success. The boy thus both needs and desires such print publicity, because it guarantees the transparency of representation that makes his virtue visible—or, in other words, confirms that he in fact represents himself.

When Dick is told that a newspaper is advertising an unaddressed letter under the name of RAGGED DICK, his pride in having received a letter—in itself an act that signifies access to a proto-public sphere of literate exchange—is doubled by his excitement over seeing his name in print.[43] This is the first moment in the book in which Dick's openness to being read is equaled by his ability to read. Dick's reading of his own name also marks a turning point in the narrative, a confirmation that the boy is on the road from rags to respectability. Upward economic mobility and the moral development of character are figured in Alger novels as a kind of publication, a chain of publicity that begins within the novel, where an experience like seeing his name in the newspaper is enough to motivate a boy to further good deeds, and moves through each series of novels, where the spectacle of the hero's actions influences his "ward" for the better, to the boy reader himself, who is subject to a discourse of moral suasion that assumes he will be improved by his identification with the character in print.[44] The communicative act, here metaphorized as print literacy, possesses a reciprocal structure that almost seems designed to ward off the charge of a critic like Charles Francis Adams, who argued that writers and publishers of popular boys' fiction read their audience all too well, that the mass literary market amounted to an amoral "pandering." Reading Alger's books, like entering Olmsted's parks, put one in a public place safe from such pandering, providing some degree of immunity to the potential deceptiveness of the market.

Although the Alger boy's combination of literacy and publicity establishes an apparently stable, proper, and legible character that both he and the reader can build upon, it can also produce in the protagonist a crisis of identity, evidence of one contradiction in the novels' construction of masculine publicity. For there is a disjunction between print and persons, between publicity and subjectivity, that makes the boy uncomfortable, threatening to reveal his "manliness" as a masquerade. The "incredulity" of Frank Courtney's audience when he announces that he is the hero of the newspaper story they have been reading is appreciated by the boy himself, who "was glad that his name was not mentioned in the account, as he didn't care for such publicity."[45] To "care for such publicity," to enjoy his notoriety, would be to represent oneself in an improperly theatrical manner. In short, the Alger hero's ability to "look *good*" is a potentially dangerous quality because it risks making his performance of virtue look like a confidence game.[46] Frank's embarrassment at being in the public eye, like Phil the Fiddler's aversion to being "at the service of the public," indicates that the Alger boy fears the publicity he courts. Publicity, Alger warns his readers, may undermine the very virtue it is meant to guarantee.

Even Dick, among the most self-assured of Alger's heroes, is unnerved by having to match his identity to his printed name when he goes to pick up the advertised letter. He fears that the postal officials will not give him the letter, because he no longer fits the advertised description of Ragged Dick, but at his friend Fosdick's suggestion he dons his old clothes, disapprovingly surveys himself in a mirror, and sneaks out (118). The discomfort Dick shows when forced to assume his former identity threatens to reveal both roles—the street urchin and the respectable working boy—as fictions. Early in the novel, when Mr. Whitney buys him a new suit, Dick is "so transformed in dress that it was difficult to be sure of his identity." "That isn't me, is it?" he exclaims, leaping away from his own image in a mirror and comparing himself to Cinderella (18–19). Now, though, he better understands the relationship between dress and identity: "I believe in dressin' up to your name," he says to the postal clerk who questions his right to the letter, and that assertion and the boy's raggedness are enough to convince the clerk that the letter is indeed for him (119). The boy's statement is humorous in part because it goes against the grain of the narrative as a whole, in which Ragged Dick changes his name to Dick and then to Richard Hunter. It would be more accurate to say that Dick believes in changing his name to match his dress.

The changes in identity that are so central to the Alger narrative come to seem like a kind of theatrical performance, a willed assumption of a role. This tendency is taken still further in *Adrift in New York; or, Tom and Florence Braving the World,* where names and identities are even more flexible. When the novel's protagonist, known as Tom Dodger, wakes up after being kidnapped, drugged, and put on a slow boat to California, he is mistakenly addressed by the captain as Arthur Grant. Dodger's renaming makes him strangely happy: "He had recently felt the need of a name," he says to himself, "and didn't see why this wouldn't answer his purpose as well as any other." And, like Ragged Dick's recognition of himself in the newspaper, the writing of this new name stabilizes his identity: " 'I must write it down so as not to forget it,' he resolved. 'It would seem queer if I forgot my own name.' " Grant/Dodger's later transformation into the heir to a fortune is paralleled by his assumption of yet another name, Harvey Linden.[47]

The fact that boys can take on and dispose of names and identities at will is a source of hope that their lives and fortunes may be concomitantly changed. The replacement of an epithet like "Ragged Dick" with a "proper name" like Richard Hunter does more than make the boy respectable and employable; it is a manipulation of signs that both marks and causes a shift in his identity and social position. It is thus an essential part of the fantasy of upward mobility and personal mutability that made Alger's novels so popular and pleasurable. Karen Halttunen has argued that the Alger hero's manipulation of appearance marks a decisive shift in the moral connotations of theatricality in middle-class culture. Whereas earlier in the nineteenth century the figure of the confidence man was a threat to the bourgeois system of economic and symbolic exchange, in Alger's novels and in the advice books published for young men in the latter decades of the century, the confidence man becomes a figure to emulate. "[T]he manipulation of others through artifice was coming to be accepted as a necessary executive skill," Halttunen writes, citing as evidence an advice book writer who extolled "the arts by which we read the hearts of men, and artifices by which we mould them to our purposes . . . it is not enough for us to *do*, we must also *seem*."[48]

This positive valuation of conscious manipulation had been latent in American narratives of success since Benjamin Franklin's *Autobiography*, and it is an important element in Alger's formula. Figured most often as a kind of theatricality, such manipulation is an essential part of the Alger hero's character, an available figure for his emergent publicity. However, it is also in tension with the model of virtue, legibility, and literacy that just as certainly structures Alger's narratives. The very idea of the confidence man militates against the fantasy of a transparent publicity, undermining both its individual and its social manifestations. Thus the books are filled with performances that are clearly misrepresentations, signs of insincerity, based in deceptive appearances or imposed on the boy hero by villainous confidence men and stepmothers. The most threatening form of theatricality is enacted when characters do consciously what Alger's heroes do inadvertently: manipulate others' sympathy. For instance, Luke Gerrish, the villain in *Silas Snobden's Office Boy,* is seen on the deck of a boat "posing for sympathy"—misrepresenting himself as "an honest, hard working man, with a crazy child to support," in the hopes that "he might draw a few dollars from the sympathetic, but indiscriminating crowd of passengers whom he had imposed upon by his sham tears."[49]

Among the most ruthless criminals in Alger's fiction, Gerrish is guilty of worse than self-misrepresentation: he forces the young boy he has kidnapped to participate in his performance by dressing as a girl. To be taken in by such a confidence game is humiliating; to be forced to participate in one is still worse. Thus a boy like the title character of *Mark, the Match Boy* is unwilling, despite his poverty, to stoop to begging because it necessitates a manipulation of sympathy. On the surface Mark's refusal to beg seems to be rooted in simple honesty and pride in his independence. The way Alger presents these qualities, however, reveals that they are meant to be read as correlative to a fundamentally masculine aversion to theatricality. In the same scene in which Mark refuses to borrow a shawl because he "had a boy's natural dislike to being dressed as a girl," he is told to his dismay that he is "just the chap to make a good beggar," that his appearance would make it possible for him to perform for sympathy and money. As if Alger were anxious to differentiate between the boy's appearance and a morally ambiguous theatricality, in the next breath Mark declines an invitation to the Old Bowery Theater.[50]

Even though Mark and other Alger characters express a gendered antipathy to theatricality, they also display a seemingly natural theatrical propensity. Many of Alger's heroes appreciate the theater: on the first page of *Ragged Dick,* for example, Dick announces that he has spent the previous evening at the Old Bowery, and *Julius; or the Street Boy Out West* opens with a detailed and humorously affectionate description of an evening at "The Grand Duke's *Oprea* [*sic*] *House,*" a "theayter" where the hero's friend Pat Riley performs as "Miles O'Reilly, the Great Minstrel Komedian and Jig Dancer."[51] Another Alger boy, who escapes from the orphanage by joining an acting troupe, is told by the stage manager that he has "the dramatic instinct."[52] Indeed, a supposedly instinctive or inadvertent performance is virtually the only form of agency allowed to a boy in his trek to publicity. The Alger boy must constantly be waiting for an opportunity to attract the attention of an audience, ideally a wealthy male observer whose daughter must coincidentally fall off the ferryboat when the hero is the only person watching. However, Alger insists that his hero does not "calculate" on such opportunities for success. Even the detailed charts of living expenses Alger likes to reproduce in his novels cannot be signs of the boy's own Franklinian frugality; they are most often direct communications from author to reader that the character neither produces nor reads. And when an Alger hero outwits confidence men by use of their own tricks, as occurs twice in the opening chapters of *Ragged Dick,* it is always to help others who have been swindled, never on his own behalf.

Alger's insistence that his heroes do not "calculate" often leads them to deny their own agency in their success. When in *The Store Boy* Ben Barclay is accused of having "played [his] cards well" by getting on his mentor's "blind side" and knowing "how to feather [his] own nest," his only response is to insist that all the blindness is on his own side, and that his ignorance is a sign of his own virtue. "I don't understand you," he says. "I can't accept the compliment, if you mean it as such. I don't think Mrs. Hamilton has any blind side, and the only way in which I intend to commend myself to her favor is to be faithful to her interests."[53] The often-noted passivity of the Alger hero is fundamental to his virtuousness; although his preferred path to success is recognition from an affluent observer, anything consciously designed to attract such notice would be a morally ambiguous theatrical manipulation of an audience, a performance of masculinity. Virtuous publicity and active agency—both of which are seen as constitutive of masculinity—are thus placed in tension with one another.

Alger's public sphere is, again, an attempt to mediate these contradictions. Even though the books' narrative trajectories typically take the hero away from socially and politically public spaces, his actions always take place on a public stage, whether he means for them to or not. Male actions in Alger novels are inherently public, performed for an audience larger than the boy's intimate circle of friends. The books lead us to expect that, no matter where the boy is, someone he does not know is watching and waiting to reward virtue or the appearance of virtue. A contrast with two of the very few cases in which Alger created female protagonists illustrates his interdependent definitions of masculinity and the public sphere. Although Alger rarely gave girls or women prominent roles in his boy books, his only books for adults were efforts at fairly conventional sentimental women's novels. In one, *A Fancy of Hers,* a young, rich, attractive heroine leaves her active urban social life to become a schoolteacher in a small New Hampshire town. Mabel keeps her identity a secret and spends a summer making anonymous charitable contributions, never publicizing her virtuous acts. When a talented artist who knows her from her previous life arrives, quickly becoming an appreciative one-man audience for her performance, she allows him to think—without ever actively deceiving him— that she is teaching because she has lost her social position, and his opinion of her increases with her perception that she is *not* acting to win anyone's sympathy or money.

Their marriage and departure from the town coincide with the end of the novel, and so we never see any public response to the heroine's virtuous performance. Like the Alger boy who performs virtue while disavowing his performance, Mabel avoids having consciously to play the part attributed to her, but nonetheless she causes the artist to sympathize with and even fall in love with her. The virtuousness of the performance is marked by the fact that, as Mabel says, "I can't say I calculate" on getting married, just as the Alger boy does not "calculate" on getting rich.[54] Unlike Alger's boys, however, Mabel ends up in the domestic rather than the public sphere, and the fact that she is already rich guarantees that her theatricality is not a means of entering the realm of economic exchange. She retreats happily into domesticity, never revealing the fact that she has been performing for a virtuous purpose to anyone but the man she marries. In contrast, the Alger boy never escapes the notice of benefactors, even if his virtue is hidden beneath a veneer of filth, because the publicity in which he exists makes him immediately legible. And in Alger's only attempt to place a girl at the center of his standard formula, *Tattered Tom,* he starts the novel with his heroine seemingly on the standard path to the public sphere—she is dressed as a newsboy—but by the end she is firmly ensconced in respectable domesticity.[55] Both Mabel and Tom are reinscribed in a feminine privacy, whereas the telos of the male protagonist's performance of virtue is publicity.

The Pleasures of Property

Alger's ambivalent representation of public masculinity lies at the center of his formula's appeal, marking for readers both the pleasures and the dangers of his fiction. Toward the end of *Ragged Dick,* Alger describes the change that the title character has undergone in the following terms: "He was beginning to feel the advantages of his steady self-denial, and to experience the pleasures of property" (105). This sentence in part supports the most standard interpretation of Alger's moral stance: Work hard and save and you will become rich. But the phrase "the pleasures of property" sweetens its offer of financial success with a promise of something more seductive, a reward more affective than economic. Given that Dick's "steady self-denial" has included giving up the activities he found enjoyable in his former life—the Old Bowery Theater and Barnum's museum—what new pleasures accrue to a boy who still owns little more than a single suit of clothing and a small bank account?

In place of the artifice and theatricality available at Barnum's and the Old Bowery, *Ragged Dick* offers its protagonist and audience the more authentic pleasures of reading. Of course, reading is presented not as a pleasure but as a virtue. Yet it quite literally replaces the theater in Dick's schedule as well as in his affections; at Frank Whitney's behest, he stops spending his nights at plays and instead gives his friend Fosdick a space in his bed in exchange for reading lessons. Reading, then, carries with it the virtues and pleasures of homosocial male companionship. But reading is not only a practice; it is also represented as a property relation. Frank's father—who tells Dick that he got his own start as an apprentice in a printing office, where he developed "a taste for reading and study"—advises the boy to " 'Save your money, my lad, buy books, and determine to be somebody, and you may yet fill an honorable position' " (55–56). Reading is essential to the virtuous respectability toward which the Alger hero aspires, and buying books is a form of consumerism in which it is virtuous to take pleasure, even the intimately homosocial pleasure of reading in bed with a friend. Alger thus offers his readers an affective lure—rather than a narrowly political or economic one—to accept their interpellation into the public sphere.

Alger was not the only writer of his time to represent reading as a virtuous property relation that comes with an affective bonus. Essays and books aimed at young men and boys who were aspiring to middle-class respectability counseled their readers not only to read more, but to purchase and collect books. It is perhaps unsurprising that a volume commissioned by Appleton's Home Books, purveyors of atlases and moral guidebooks, argued that "[a] book that is really worth reading is worth owning," especially since this advice is closely followed by a sales pitch for "Appleton's American Cyclopaedia" and several of the company's other publications.[56] But similar advice came from less overtly interested sources as well. For instance, Noah Porter, then president of Yale University, argued in *Books and Reading* that "[r]eaders of books desire to become the owners of books. . . . Hence, books like everything else which is desirable come to be sought for and valued as property."[57] Another educator, Charles F. Thwing, without qualms compared a home library to furniture: "A library, of at least some sort, is as essential to a home as are tables, chairs, and beds. . . . [Books] are in a sense the 'fixtures' of a home."[58]

For these writers, books were commodities that it is virtuous not only to possess but also to enjoy. As Thwing—whose title, *The Reading of Books: Its Pleasures, Profits, and Perils* makes this very point—went on to say: "A peculiar pleasure, moreover, belongs to the possession of a library, be it large or small, and to the reading of one's own books. In his own collection one takes a personal interest."[59] But there are limits to this "peculiar pleasure," limits that were regularly marked by a rhetoric of theatricality and display. In *The Choice of Books*, Charles F. Richardson, like Thwing, compared books with furniture, arguing that "the plainest row of books that cloth or paper ever covered is more significant of refinement than the most elaborately carved étagère or sideboard."[60] Similarly, Thwing proclaimed that "[o]rnamental volumes, designed to adorn the centre-table, teeming with coarse engravings, and vapid in their thought, are not to be tolerated."[61] And Porter condemned those who "buy books for *show*," who "like the sight of elegant books in substantial and costly bindings."[62]

The wish to own books "for show" was not suspect just because it was a waste of money, or because of a simple puritanical distaste for decoration. These writers denounced "showy" books for the same reason they regularly condemned "the trashy literature in which [young men] delight"—books whose covers were surely not guilty of being too decorative, even if they may have been "showy" in a different way.[63] Both sorts of books raised anxieties about the commodification of culture the advice writers were trying simultaneously to ward off and to control for their own purposes, about the way popular literature blurred the boundary between the market and the public sphere. This is the same reason that popular theater and theatrical display served as markers of inappropriate behavior in both Alger's fiction and Olmsted's Central Park. As with many of Alger's boys, the fact that Dick spends his leisure time at places like the Old Bowery Theater is a sign that he has not yet adopted the values and habits that will eventually lead to his success. Similarly, visitors to Central Park were meant to forgo their own theatrical practices and pleasures. "No shows of any kind are allowed on the Park's grounds," Olmsted declared, listing specific types of popular entertainment he wished to see banned: "[J]ugglers, gamblers—except those disguised as gentlemen—puppet shows, peddlers of flowers," and several others.[64]

Writers like Porter praised young men's "desire to become the owners of books," and yet they condemned works of "cheap literature" as "simply a reflex of the commonplace aims and the vulgar feelings of the mass of readers for whom they are written. They are made to *take* and made to *sell*, and they both *take* and *sell*, because they humor what their readers like."[65] Similarly, one of the librarians at the Boston conference capped a lengthy tirade against boys' "sensational, detrimental, immoral . . . flat, weak trashy" reading by setting out its worst characteristic: it is "all meant to sell."[66] This anxiety about commodification was present even in those who represented books as commodities like furniture, and who, like Porter, praised the economic democratization of reading, the fact that "[b]ooks of all sorts are now brought within the reach of most persons who desire to read them."[67] Even the most overtly commercial of these texts, Appleton's *Home Library,* warned its readers to "[b]eware of the itinerant book-peddler," because "most of his books are made to sell, and are not worth reading."[68]

These authors' aversion to "selling" was not rooted in any antipathy toward market capitalism; many of the literary advice books were bound with advertisements not only for other books but also for other commodities. The copy of Appleton's *Home Library* I examined includes promotions for stained glass and gas fixtures as well as for *Webster's Unabridged Dictionary* and a book of reminiscences of great authors. Moreover, many writers included a list of books deemed necessary to comprise a respectable library, thus blurring the distinction between moral advice and advertisement.[69] On the one hand, reading was not supposed to be a display of conspicuous consumption, but at the same time, it was undoubtedly imbricated in consumerist ideology. The counsel offered was thus somewhat contradictory: the most virtuous "pleasures of property" derived from buying things that are not "made to sell." Once again, the logic of the market came into conflict with an ideal of public virtue.

Here, though, the conflict between the market and the public was staged at the level of individual psychology rather than in the formation and legitimation of a public institution like the library. All of these advice books and articles demanded that young men and boys ask themselves the questions in Porter's subtitle: *What Books Shall I Read and How Shall I Read Them?* The two questions were linked quite deliberately; what matters most is how a book asks to be read, the kind of response that it provokes in its audience. The literary advice writers developed what can without exaggeration be described as a theory of interpellation and identification. They argued that the subject-position produced by the books they decried was not a member of a reading public; it was instead a consumer. Of "the ready-made literature turned out by the fiction-mills," Arthur Penn says: "[I]t is not right to call the consumers of stuff like this readers. Charles Lamb speaks of books which are not books, so these are readers who are not readers. They read with the eye alone, while the brain is inert."[70] Penn and others claimed that boy books produced, in place of a virtuous reading public, a mass audience, and they depicted that audience in the language of passivity, vulgarity, feminization, narcissism, commercialism, and consumerism that has characterized much of the discourse on mass culture ever since.[71]

Porter's deployment of this rhetoric is revealingly contradictory. On the one hand, he argues in answer to the questions in his title, one should only read what is made to be read in the proper way. He approvingly cites Robert Southey's rules for distinguishing "whether the tendency of a book is good or evil," which advise readers to "examine in what state of mind you lay it down." If the book has made you "dissatisfied and impatient under the control of others" or weakened your "self-government, without which both the laws of God and man tell us there can be no virtue and consequently no happiness," then you have been reading an immoral book. "If so — if you are conscious of all or of any of these effects — or if, having escaped from all, you have felt that such were the effects it was intended to produce, throw the book into the fire, young man, though it should have been the gift of a friend!"[72] According to Porter, one can immediately apprehend the intention and effect of a book and can judge it accordingly. In other words, the book itself predetermines its reader's responses, and books exist in the same sphere of transparent legibility that Alger creates for his boys. Yet elsewhere in *Books and Reading,* the Yale president argues that *how* one reads is at least as important as the content or intention of the book itself, that the same book might be read in different ways.[73] "*Passive* reading is the evil habit against which most readers need to be guarded, and to overcome which, when formed, requires the most manful and persevering efforts."[74] Novels — Porter's examples, like those in the librarians' debate, are women's sentimental novels and boy books — are the kinds of literature that are most likely to elicit this seductively passive response, for the novel reader "often becomes for the time an unconscious imitator or a passive reflex of his author." "So complete a subjection" to an author is dangerous, having "a tendency to make us one-sided and unnatural."[75]

Porter distinguishes between two kinds of reading: one "manful" and virtuous, the other passive, feminizing, and "dangerous." The reader of mass-cultural trash, especially boy books and sentimental novels, risks becoming "almost an intellectual idiot or an effeminate weakling by living exclusively upon the enfeebling swash or the poisoned stimulants that are sold so readily under the title of tales and novels." In contrast, the virtuous reader "will find in himself . . . the manhood that he has and which he is bound to think of and care for."[76] Protecting and cultivating this apparently quite fragile manhood is, finally, the purpose of reading.[77]

Even virtuous reading, however, requires a degree of readerly passivity, or at least a tentative acquiescence to the author's power. At times this passivity is figured as an intersubjective relation of sympathy between author and reader. The reader "sympathize[s] with the feelings which [the author] experienced," Porter writes, and throughout his text he reiterates that when we read we must "widen and make yielding our sympathies," to the point where we "yield our feelings to [the author's] control by that pliant sympathy which is requisite for our enjoyment of his enthusiasm."[78] Sympathy in this context designates a communication of affect that in Porter's language verges on the erotic. Alger conceived of his fiction as evoking a similar communication of affect between reader, character, and author: "A writer for boys should have an abundant sympathy with them," he asserts. "He should be able to enter into their plans, hopes, and aspirations. He should learn to look upon life as they do. . . . A boy's heart opens to the man or writer who understands him."[79] But while Porter and Alger share the notion of sympathy, their conceptions differ in their intended result. Alger seeks not the critical reflection that Porter advocates, but imitation. "Perhaps" he says, "although [Dick] was only a bootblack, [readers] may find something in him to imitate" (44). As didactic fiction, Alger's novels depend on the reader's acceptance of precisely the role that Porter warns against—becoming "an unconscious imitator or passive reflex of his author"—just as his model of success necessitates a degree of patience and passivity, at least until the opportunity arises to save a rich man's daughter from drowning or to unmask a pickpocket.

In its motivations and mechanisms, this description of sympathy recalls the sympathetic identification valorized above all in the women's sentimental novel, which entails a potentially self-negating surrender to the emotions of a suffering heroine. I will both spell out and problematize this representation of sympathy as feminine and self-negating in Chapter 4. But it is important to resist the temptation to see the deployment of sympathy in Alger's fiction as a straightforward feminization of the male reader. Such an interpretation is certainly invited by Porter's image of the novel reader as an "effeminate weakling" and by the statement by Charles Francis Adams Jr., quoted earlier, that such fiction "simply and certainly emasculates and destroys the intelligent reading power."[80] Porter, however, insists that this passivity can be a form of masculinity, for male sympathy allows the reader to find "the manhood that he has."[81] Alger argues as well that his "abundant sympathy" is most evident in the fact that his heroes are "manly boys," which he contrasts to the "goody-goody boys" with whom his readers are unwilling to identify.[82]

What guarantees that male sympathy is not feminizing is, simply if tautologically put, that it is a relation between males. Porter advises that "when a man reads he should put himself in the most intimate intercourse with his author, so that all his energies of apprehension, judgment and feeling may be occupied with and aroused by what his author furnishes."[83] Perhaps to contain the feminizing potential of sympathetic male reading, the writers of literary advice books consistently represent the relation between readers and authors and between readers and books as an affectively charged form of homosocial companionship. As Charles Thwing writes, "The book is a friend who never fails to respond to every emotion."[84]

The metaphor of books as companions is not peculiar to the second half of the nineteenth century, but in that period the image acquired new connotations. Thwing writes that "the reader buys books gradually. He gains them, as he gains friends, one by one."[85] Here Thwing, like Alger, blurs the distinction between an affective relation and a economic one; three pages earlier he has described books as a kind of decorative furniture—"the 'fixtures' of a home"—while here they are figured as friends.[86] While the advice books claim to differentiate the public virtue enacted in male reading from the commercialism of the market, ultimately the public and the economic come to be instances of the same "pleasures of property." In other words, these books stage some of the same tensions between the public and the market, the affective and the economic, as does Alger's fiction.

Some of Alger's critics and biographers have read his homosocial conflation of the economic and the erotic as related to the event that occasioned his decision to become a full-time boy book writer: his dismissal in 1866 from the ministry in Brewster, Massachusetts, for what the Unitarian Church report called "the abominable and revolting crime of unnatural familiarity with *boys.*"[87] In fact, one of the few nineteenth-century readers familiar with Alger's pederastic sexual history, a Brewster deacon named Solomon Freeman, articulated his antipathy to Alger by linking the scandal to his writing. In a letter to the general secretary of the church, Freeman expressed the fear that Alger's pernicious influence carried through his fiction and voiced indignation that "he was still permitted to contribute to the respectable periodicals, particularly those intended for boys to read." The danger lay not in the content of the stories, which the letter does not mention, but in Alger's inexcusable desire to place his stories and himself in the public eye after the scandal. Above all, Freeman declared,

Alger should not have the pleasure of seeing his name in print: "[H]is name should never have appeared in any production before the public." The church secretary agreed, replying that he was "sorry ... at the readiness to come forward into public so soon, on the part of Mr. Alger."[88] Alger's indiscreet desire to publicize his "familiarity with boys" apparently persisted for several years, for in 1870 Henry James Sr. expressed surprise and annoyance that "Alger talks freely about his own late insanity—which he in fact appears to enjoy as a subject of conversation."[89]

The indignation of Freeman and James was echoed more than two decades later in an 1893 issue of *The Literary World* by an anonymous reviewer who presumably knew nothing of the Brewster scandal. This writer proclaimed himself or herself "indignant not only with the writer, who might do something better than pour forth this unceasing stream of sensational, impossible literature, but with the boys who persistently read, enjoy, and talk them over." For that writer, Alger is clearly guilty of a scandalously successful pandering, one that produces enjoyment in its objects. However, the reviewer acknowledges that "it is only fair to say that the writer intends always to lay stress on the qualities of energy, truth, and manliness," implicitly granting not only that Alger and his boys "mean well," as the Worcester librarian had asserted, but also that they possess a marginal, though recognizable, masculinity.[90] The review simultaneously demonstrates the instability of masculinity's meaning. I have been arguing here that late-nineteenth-century shifts in the semantic and ideological connotations of the concepts of masculinity and publicity put the meaning and stability of both terms into question. For many readers, Alger's fantasies of masculine publicity came to epitomize the very transformations they seem designed to contain: the theatricalization and putative "emasculation" of masculine character, the shift in the cultural meaning of writing for a male readership from an act of virtuous and transparent communication to a species of pandering, and the commodification of the reading public into a mass audience.

In whatever sense they "pander" to their readers, as commodities and as stories about financial success Alger's novels inevitably engage with the market as a social structure. I began this chapter by looking at the way his writings were inadvertently implicated in a controversy over their position in a paradigmatically public institution, the library. Despite their ideological and material engagement with such institutions of the public sphere, unlike the temperance fiction discussed in Chapter 1 or Delany's black nationalist writing analyzed in Chapter 2, Alger's novels tend to abjure the representation of publicity in the form of such institutions. Instead, publicity is an aspect of what he and his contemporaries would have called "character." By that I do not mean that publicity becomes purely a matter of individual psychology. Quite the contrary; it is consistently figured as at the very least a reciprocal, intersubjective communication, whether in the form of the mutual personal legibility that enables the affective and economic exchange between the wealthy mentor and the attractively virtuous boy or in the form of the exchange of literacy and intimacy between boys. But perhaps the most important of the figurations of publicity in the Alger novel are the forms of interpellation and identification his formula establishes between author, character, and reader. The next three chapters will analyze such forms of interpellation and identification in novels ranging from the 1850s to the 1890s in order to trace the history of their development. Though the following chapters may seem to represent a shift in focus from the state to the individual, from the political to the psychological, virtually all of the terms that serve as building blocks for my analysis have already come up in this first section: sympathy, theatricality, interpellation, identification, and affect.

II

Performing Publicity

CHAPTER 4

**AN UNEQUALED SYSTEM OF
PUBLICITY** THE LOGIC OF SYMPATHY IN
WOMEN'S SENTIMENTAL FICTION

Henry James proclaimed in 1906 that for decades "the American woman
. . . has had at her service an unequalled system of publicity."[1] Such publicity, James argued, mostly manifests itself in the newspapers' constant
attention to women's clothing, appearance, and social and matrimonial
engagements. Most disturbing to him was women's unrivaled ability to
take "possession of the public scene," by which he meant that women easily
dominate a social space like a train car or a park.[2] In James's view, the feminization of American culture did not take the privatizing and domesticating form described in most accounts of nineteenth-century gender relations. On the contrary, women "are encamped on every inch of the social
area that the stock-exchange and the football field leave free; the whole
of the social initiative is in other words theirs, having been abandoned to
them without a struggle."[3]

James's essays on *The Speech and Manners of American Women* seem to
anticipate and even exceed current revisionist critiques of the notion that
strictly gendered separate spheres structured American culture and society
in the nineteenth century.[4] In James's topsy-turvy depiction of gender and
the public sphere, the masculine realm is surprisingly constricted, while
women control everything that falls under the sign of the "social," the
"cultural," and the "public." Throughout the essays he intricately conflates
these three terms, remarking, for instance, that "the ladies' culture-club is
the most publicly taken engagement, surely, that ever was."[5] James depicts
as feminine all the acts of open, communicative exchange that writers like
Alger and Delany had in previous decades placed at the core of their public spheres and claims that most of the nation's institutions of the public
sphere have been hegemonized by women. In a manner that would, several decades later, become a convention of antifeminist backlash discourse
and so-called "postfeminism," he ascribes a great deal of power—virtually
"the whole of the social initiative"—to the aggressive public women he
caricatures.

James's essays include numerous narrative illustrations of his point, many of which involve women engaged in a practice most commonly represented as individualizing and privatizing: reading. By his account, women's reading is both cause and symptom of femininity's scandalous publicity. Like the librarians and cultural arbiters who debated the value of purchasing Horatio Alger's fiction for public libraries, James describes the kinds of reading he disparages as a form of consumption. He is horrified to see one woman on a train, "sated with her strange commixtures" of food she has been "engulfing," proceed to "seek to combat digestive drowsiness with one of the horrific printed and figured sheets that succeed in darkening, to the traveller's eye, so much of the large American air."[6] James fears that such consumption of popular magazines filled with "literature . . . almost solely from the hands of women" has created a "female society," a "great feminine collectivity asserting itself as against all interference and so quite effectually balancing against any discipline of friction within the herd."[7] In his view, if anything has changed since the 1850s—the years of his youth, and another period in which culture seemed in danger of feminization—it is that Hawthorne's infamous "mob of scribbling women" has been supplanted, or at least supplemented, by this "herd" of uncritical readers trampling across formerly masculine public spaces.

James was not alone in figuring the reading public in such ominous and gendered terms, nor was he the first to do so. What is, for my purposes, important about these essays is that they represent the relation between gender and reading as a "struggle" for control of the cultural public sphere. There were, however, other ways of imagining this struggle, other ways of representing the relation between reading and publicity, that James fails to acknowledge. The next three chapters explore several such possibilities. The present chapter discusses Louisa May Alcott's attempt to address and construct a feminist reading public through the conventions of women's sentimental fiction in her 1873 novel *Work: A Story of Experience*.[8] Chapter 5 returns our focus to the representation of masculinity in analyses of works by Fanny Fern, Nathaniel Parker Willis, and James himself. The masculine figure under discussion there, the dandy, is a significantly different sort of "public man" than those represented by Whitman, Delany, or Alger, one whose publicity and masculinity are manifested less as "representative identities" than as theatricalized performance.[9] Chapter 6 emphasizes another genre of masculine public performance popular in the nineteenth century: the "bad-boy book" written by successful middle-class men such as William Dean Howells, Mark Twain, and Charles Dudley Warner.

What these fictional forms have in common is that they link the constitution of gender identity to their fictions of the public sphere by both representing and eliciting particular forms of identification. Like other recent literary historians engaged in rewriting the history of the American novel, I deploy the term eighteenth- and nineteenth-century critics and writers would have used to designate this complex of identificatory structures: "sympathy." Sympathy has recently become the subject of extensive analysis in critical and historical studies on American literature and culture, especially in works about the antebellum period. Earlier, in the Introduction, I quoted Theodore Parker, an American theorist and advocate of sympathy, who defines it as a recursive emotional exchange: "Feeling, he must make others feel."[10] Unlike most analysts of sympathetic identification, who see sympathy as a primarily privatizing emotional exchange between reader, text, and author, I read this affective form, which lies at the core of the sentimental structure of feeling, as a paradigmatically public sentiment. This claim can be supported by the fact that Parker sees this "great power of feeling" as best exemplified by oratory, perhaps the quintessentially public genre. It also follows and expands upon Habermas's brief yet pivotal discussion of literature in *The Structural Transformation of the Public Sphere*. Habermas claims that "the psychological novel" of the late eighteenth and early nineteenth centuries produced and pioneered the forms of identification characteristic of liberal citizenship and subjectivity.[11] The novel, Habermas argues, mediates between private personality and public sociality because it enacts the division of public and private in each reader. The novel can do so merely by evoking the reader's sympathetic identification. "The relations between author, work, and public," Habermas writes, "became intimate mutual relationships between privatized individuals who were psychologically interested in what was 'human,' in self-knowledge, and in empathy." Such "empathy," when experienced in fiction, constitutes an identificatory subjectivity, allowing "anyone to enter into the literary action as a substitute for his own, to use the relationships between the figures, between the author, the characters, and the reader as substitute relationships for reality."[12] While these identifications are importantly "intimate," the subjectivity they constitute is neither purely private nor purely individual. Habermas goes on to say that "the empathetic reader [of the novel] . . . recreated within himself the private relationships displayed before him in literature; from his experience of real familiarity (*Intimität*), he gave life to the fictional one, and in the latter he prepared himself for the former," and, in turn, for participation in the political public.[13] Like James, Habermas argues that the shape, boundaries, and makeup of the public sphere are at stake in the way people read, that James's "struggle" for the "social initiative" takes place in part in the forms of identification evoked in works of fiction.

My contention in these three chapters is that writers as diverse as Alcott, Fern, Willis, Howells, and Twain might well agree with James and Habermas in their descriptions of the reading public. However, instead of merely mourning the disappearance of the public sphere by lamenting women's appropriation of "the social initiative . . . without a struggle," these authors stage that struggle, strategically representing and eliciting sympathetic identifications as forms of public sentiment. At the very least, by positing alternative identifications, they expose what Habermas calls "the fiction of the *one* public," the universalizing ideology proclaiming that what defines the "individuals who came together to form a public" is a common "humanity" evinced by their ability to participate in the affective communicative exchange exemplified and performed in the novel.[14] My readings of these novels build on Habermas's claim that novelistic identifications imply and produce particular forms of publicity and argue that implicit in the novels' production of public sentiment are alternative, sometimes critical, fictions of the public sphere. At the same time, the affective basis of identification's public orientation problematizes any reading of nineteenth-century American novels as foundational of a range of subaltern counterpublics. I will argue toward the end of this chapter, and at greater length in the last two, that the sentimental politics of affect produces an affective and identificatory category that theories of the public sphere have trouble accounting for. Alcott and Willis, among others, refer to this category as the "personal," and as we will see, it irrupts into sentimental discourse at just the moments when it threatens to become most political. As if to invert the later feminist slogan that "the personal is political," at crucial moments sentimentality seems to insist that the political is personal.

Emotion and Equivalence

To understand the production of the personal out of the political in literary texts, we must turn again, briefly, to an exploration of the relationship between the political public sphere and the literary public. Habermas—again like James—underscores the gendered disparity between the political public and the reading public. He points out that "[t]he circles of persons who made up the two forms of public were not even completely congruent. Women and dependents were factually and legally excluded from the political public sphere, whereas female readers as well as apprentices and servants often took a more active part in the literary public sphere than the owners of private property and family heads themselves."[15] In other words, the two publics have never coincided demographically, diverging most obviously along the lines of gender. Women, as James notes anxiously, seem to dominate the reading public, thereby threatening to expand their "social sphere" and thus, potentially, to challenge men's hegemony in the political public.[16]

This lack of congruence between political public and reading public is one of the anomalies that analyses of nineteenth-century sentimentalism have to address. It is not a newly recognized problem. In her novel *Work: A Story of Experience,* Louisa May Alcott foregrounds the question always latent in popular women's fiction: If women possessed in abundance the affective and psychological capacity to enter the literary public as readers, what was to prevent them from participating in the political public as citizens? Sentimental fiction is a crucial site for such an interrogation because its ostensibly exclusive address to women brings out the conflict between the evidently public task of appealing to a mass readership and the ideological status of this particular readership as the guardian of the private sphere. This conflict is most evident in the genre's relation to its implied audience and in its central demand that its readers identify emotionally with its characters. To constitute a female mass audience for their products, the writers drew on the normative assumption that it was women— genteel, white, literate women in particular—who were characterized by their willingness and ability to extend this emotional identification to characters who are represented as being like them. It thereby produced a differently gendered fiction of the public sphere.

Even the most conservative prescriptive texts of domestic ideology asserted that women possessed the emotional capacities requisite to membership in this affectively demarcated reading public, representing the ability to sympathize as the primary trait defining feminine character. Margaret Coxe's 1839 conduct manual, *The Young Lady's Companion,* written in the form of letters to the author's orphaned niece, affirms this notion of femininity in the very arrangement of its contents. Opening with one brief letter on the "importance of forming just views of life," the book continues with five chapters on "female influence." According to Coxe, the "just character" a woman should work to form through her influence is not her own. Judging by the number of pages devoted to it, her addressee's own moral salvation is relatively unimportant compared to that of the children she raises, the company she keeps, and the husband she chooses, each of which is allocated at least one chapter. The woman's own moral salvation is almost entirely reducible to that of the people around her.[17]

Many of the most popular sentimental novels overtly reinforce this description of femininity as selflessness. For instance, Maria Susanna Cummins's 1854 best-seller, *The Lamplighter,* repeatedly insists that a woman's moral rightness and personal satisfaction rest entirely upon her ability to make others happy, that is, upon "that kind of regard which causes one to find gratification in whatever tends to the present or future welfare of another."[18] Similarly, Christie Devon, the protagonist of Alcott's *Work,* is described as "doing good, as women best love to do it, by bestowing sympathy and care with generous devotion" (83). Even when a censorious contemporary reviewer of *Work* characterized Christie as "a female who was not a woman . . . [who] never so much as dreamed of womanly selflessness," the anonymous writer affirmed the norm: a woman is ideally self-negating and other-oriented.[19]

Sentimental novels deploy this definition of femininity in part as a means of addressing and constituting their readership. In the circular logic characteristic of all acts of interpellation, female readers are asked to identify themselves as women on the basis of the assumption that they are emotionally equivalent to the novel's female protagonists, that they too are both capable and worthy of sympathy. Sympathetic identification thus works through a logic of equivalence based on affect. Any being capable of feeling, ostensibly regardless of social differences such as race and age, can evoke sympathy, especially from a female character or reader who has had comparable feelings herself. This seemingly unrestricted logic of sympathy has often been taken to be the egalitarian core of the sentimental politics of affect. As Philip Fisher has influentially argued: "The political content of sentimentality is democratic in that it experiments with the extension of full and complete humanity to classes of figures from whom it has been socially withheld[:] . . . the madman, the child, the very old, the animal, and the slave. Each achieves, or rather earns, the right to human regard by means of the reality of their suffering."[20]

Fisher's use of the word "experiment" is especially suggestive for an analysis of *Work,* the original subtitle of which was *Or Christie's Experiment.*[21] As Alcott makes clear in her use of the word at various points in the novel, the subject of Christie's "experiment" is her own sentimental subjectivity. And her experiment's results are, by the end of the novel, as politically democratic as Fisher could wish: Christie is affiliated with a group advocating the rights of working women and is at the center of "a loving league of sisters, old and young, black and white, rich and poor" (343). Along the way, Alcott explores some of the contradictions within the concept of sympathy, and her protagonist discovers both the pleasures and the dangers of sympathy's unrestricted logic.

Throughout *Work,* as in most sentimental fiction, the motivating force behind the character's actions is the subordination of the protagonist's self in a sympathetic identification with an other. Correspondingly, the heroine's willingness to subordinate herself to others is the sign that she is worth the reader's sympathy. But in the process of modeling forms of identification, sentimental fiction also figures alternative social identities for its readers, identities that may conflict with normative femininity. Readers are then placed in a problematic position. Interpellated through codes of traditional femininity, in the course of the narrative they are asked to identify with and take up subject-positions that repeatedly violate these codes. At times, *Work*'s generalization of sympathy causes feminine selflessness to be seen in a different, more unsettling light than in the novel's happy ending. Christie spends the first half of the book moving from job to job in an unnamed city. Her last urban occupation is as a seamstress. When she loses this job—and along with it her only friend, Rachel—she falls deeper and deeper into both poverty and depression. Wandering to the edge of a wharf, Christie considers suicide. At first she seems to feel simple loneliness, a lack of sympathetic ties: "[N]o one waited for her, no one would care if she staid for ever." But then she falls into a hallucinatory trance and experiences a series of nearly psychotic identifications: "Something white swept by below,—only a broken oar—but she began to wonder how a human body would look floating through the night. It was an awesome fancy, but it took possession of her, and, as it grew, her eyes dilated, her breath came fast, and her lips fell apart, for she seemed to see the phantom she had conjured up, and it wore the likeness of herself" (124).

Christie's identity, the boundaries of her ego, are clearly in crisis in this scene. Later in the novel, when she addresses a working women's organization, she is applauded for her "self-possession" (428), but in this earlier scene her identifications take "possession of her," and she momentarily loses the ability to distinguish between self and other. This confusion does not result from an inability to sympathize; on the contrary, Christie's identification with her own image projected onto the oar *is* a sympathetic identification. The psychotic aspect of her fantasy—the hallucinatory equivalence between her self and the floating object—derives from her willingness to extend the category of subjectivity to an inanimate object, briefly to equate the oar with "a human body" and thence to equate herself with a corpse. Domestic ideology's image of femininity is transformed into a nightmarish parody of self-effacement, a fantasy of death.

Perhaps worst of all, Christie's sympathy gets turned back upon her own image; she is paralyzed, even fascinated, by the image of *herself* floating by. Her fascinated gaze downward into a body of water that reflects back an image of herself, and her inability to decisively identify the reflection as her own, evoke a narcissistic scenario: "So plainly did she see it, so peaceful was the white face, so full of rest the folded hands, so strangely like, and yet unlike, herself, that she seemed to lose her identity, and wondered which was the real and which the imaginary Christie" (124). What attracts her to the water is the image of her own death, the "peaceful . . . white face" and "folded hands" of a "phantom." It is no wonder that she would "lose her identity" in a sympathetic identification with her own corpse. This identification results in a self-loss that takes the form of a temporary splitting of her identity between "the real" and "the imaginary Christie." " 'Was I going to drown myself?' " she asks when Rachel unexpectedly appears to rescue her. Her friend's curious reply is " 'No, dear; it was not you that meant to do it, but the weakness and the trouble that bewildered you' " (125). To restore Christie's sense of self, Rachel rhetorically divides it.

In its manifest content this scene is unusual for the sentimental genre, in which heroines do not typically contemplate suicide. But Christie's identification with a hallucinated corpse is continuous with the extension of the logic of sympathy at the affective and political core of the sentimental structure of feeling, as is Rachel's pedagogy of self-division and self-negation. The selflessness implicit in the norm of sympathy leads sentimental characters to extend it indiscriminately and essentially involuntarily. Recall the scene from *The Lamplighter* cited in the Introduction, in which the protagonist's stepmother throws the girl's kitten into boiling water. Cummins leaves open the question of which is to make the reader more angry, the murder of the cat or the danger in which the girl is subsequently placed by being thrown out into the snow with no shoes. Gerty's identification with the cat marks her as a character to be sympathized with, but it also demonstrates that sympathy could indiscriminately extend beyond or even supersede identifications with human beings.

As I argued in the Introduction, in the sentimental structure of feeling sympathy conflates two aspects of identification. A reader is asked to feel *like* a fictional character, but also to feel *with* the fictional figure. In the process of asserting an affective connection between subjects, sympathy can negate their subjectivity by conflating the *analogy* it posits between them with an illusory and risky *coincidence* between them.[22] The idea that one can analogically feel *like* another person feels can be overshadowed by the paradoxically narcissistic and self-negating desire to feel *with* that other person, to imagine that the experiences of two subjects entirely coincide. Christie's crisis on the pier is an extension and exaggeration of this risk: feeling both *with* and *like* a dead body, she nearly becomes a corpse herself. The imaginative equivalence at the basis of sympathy thus doubles back on itself.

Nowhere is this balancing act between analogy and coincidence more precarious and visible than in the sentimental novel's paradigmatic scenario: the death of an innocent child and the transformations resulting from mourning. Most often, as when Eva dies in *Uncle Tom's Cabin*, a sentimental death induces its survivors to redouble their efforts in whatever spiritual or social cause the novel is championing, inspired by the example of the virtually angelic deceased. As such, it is a straightforward example of the way sympathetic identification transforms the most intimate experiences into public acts. The death of Christie's husband, David, is also a perfect illustration of this dynamic. He has volunteered to fight in the Civil War and is shot trying to rescue an escaping slave woman and help her bury her dead child. Christie arrives to find him barely alive, and since she has been working as a nurse, she is allowed to stay with him in the hospital until his death. In a moment of anguish, she asks, "Why did you pay such a price for that girl's liberty?" David's reply limns the identificatory logic of such death scenes in fragmented phrases: "Because I owed it; — she suffered more than this seeing her baby die; — I thought of *you* in her place, and I could not help doing it" (315).

David juxtaposes an affective comparison ("she suffered more than this") with an identificatory analogy ("I thought of *you* in her place"), and this combination produces an involuntary emotional response ("I could not help doing it"). Here, in condensed form, is the logic of sympathy, complete with the multiply mediated identification with suffering posited by Adam Smith and Jean-Jacques Rousseau in their early theorizations of sentiment ("she suffered . . . seeing her baby die").[23] Also typical of sympathetic identification are the disciplinary tone and "reproachful look" with which David admonishes Christie, to use Stowe's phrase, to "feel right," to direct her sympathies properly. David's next affective instructions reorient those emotions toward public action, revealing the title of the novel itself to be an imperative toward such a politics of affect. "Such a beautiful world!" he says, "and so much good work to do in it. . . . Don't mourn, dear heart, but work; and by and by you will be comforted." To enact such a transformation, however, there has to be an unsettling amount of identification involved in mourning. "I will try," Christie replies, "but I think I shall soon follow you, and need no comfort here" (315). Though she is ultimately inspired to social action by David's death, she initially responds by identifying completely with the lost object and incorporating its characteristics, appearing "as tranquil, colorless, and mute, as if her soul had followed David, leaving the shadow of her former self behind" (317). She becomes, like him and with him, a corpse, experiencing a self-loss that seems symbolically and physically to destroy her. For someone with Christie's "sympathetic nature," loss of the other is equivalent to loss of the self, even death.

Like Gerty's concern for her boiled kitten, Christie's identification with a corpse is marked as conventional, even positive. Although her neighbors comment on the excessiveness of her grief, they also make it clear that the sentimental cult of mourning provides a framework within which they can understand it: "[T]hose who loved her said despairingly to one another: 'Her heart is broken: she will not linger long'" (317). Only the birth of her daughter and the opportunity it provides to shift her sympathies from a morbid to a maternal direction can cure her of her desire to join David in the grave. Whereas in the months after her husband's death " 'He will not come to me, but I shall go to him,' seemed to be the thought that sustained her," Christie's first words when her child is placed in her arms are " 'Don't let me die: I must live for baby now' " (316, 321).[24] This is the kind of displacement toward the domestic typically attributed to the sentimental novel. But the baby, Pansy, is described in the last sentence of this novel as "a hopeful omen, seeming to promise that the coming generation of women will not only receive but deserve their liberty," thus once again linking Christie's domestic sentiments and the more public sentiments the novel aims to produce and provoke (344).

Both the identifications entailed in the sentimental death scene and Christie's crises of identity reveal the experience of sympathy to be a potential threat to the sympathizer's identity. Sentimental sympathy, even in its most conventional manifestations, is predicated on a loss of self; it is in some sense depersonalizing. Nonetheless, as female bildungsromans, sentimental novels set up their characters' quests for sympathy as searches for identity.[25] Their heroines are often willing to violate what appears to be the primary norm of domestic ideology in order to fulfill the sentimental ideal of sympathy. For example, Alcott's *Work* begins with its orphaned heroine's departure from her guardians' household. Christie wishes for an autonomy not available in her home—"I must go where I can take care of myself"—and hopes that her "experiment" will lead to some public accomplishment, that "you'll soon hear good news of me" (7). From the opening pages Christie articulates her desires in explicitly political terms, proclaiming that "there's going to be a new Declaration of Independence" (5). Alcott comically juxtaposes Christie's political discourse with that of her domestically content Aunt Betsey, who "curiously interlarded her speech with audible directions to herself" from the recipe she is completing (6). This opening passage underscores the complete domestication of Aunt Betsey's character, not only through the integration of her activity and her speech, but also through the integration of culinary discourse into the narration itself ("interlarded").

Despite its expression in political rhetoric, Christie's dissatisfaction with her surrogate family is emotional at its core, arising from the fact that the household is not organized around a properly affective axis. The lack she feels is a lack of sympathy, of a basis for the family's existence that would transcend both her uncle's obsession with money and her aunt's wish for peace and quiet. Her response to this lack is to go to the city and take up various occupations. From the outset, *Work* complicates the conventional opposition between the masculine public sphere of work and money and the emotional realm of family ties—what Nancy Armstrong aptly calls the "economy that is not money"—by having Christie leave the domestic sphere in search of precisely those values it is supposed to uphold and reproduce.[26] The opposition the novel posits and attempts to resolve, then, is not simply that between the domestic sphere and the market, between home and work.[27] Instead, Christie's republican rhetoric points to a distinction between feminine domesticity and political publicity, a conflict that it is ultimately her mission to mediate.

That Christie begins her search for sympathy by entering the marketplace is unusual for the sentimental genre, but the fact that she breaks up a family and a home is not. Indeed, sentimental narratives have a surprising tendency to disarticulate domestic spaces. Rather than insistently fixing heroines in their proper places, many novels begin with young girls leaving their homes, either by being orphaned or by their own choice. And instead of concluding with happy marriages or otherwise restoring their heroines to normatively defined families—in which case the initial departure from the family could be read as ultimately supportive of domestic values—the novels often place their heroines in situations that are notable for their deviations from that norm. While the new stasis that resolves the novels' narrative tensions is still described, at least metaphorically, as a "family," it always represents a transformation of the group initially designated by the term. Sentimental plots repeatedly transgress both the internal and the external limits of the family structure that domestic ideology held up as its overt ideal.

Even though it is consistently depicted in familial rhetoric, sympathy often turns out to conflict with ties of kinship. The orphaned Ellen Montgomery in Susan Warner's *The Wide Wide World* rejects both her aunt's household and, later, an offer of adoption from the rich relatives who take her to Scotland. In both cases, she prefers sympathetic ties with the Humphreyses, neighbors whose now dead daughter had been her dearest friend and mentor. Ellen upsets her relatives by calling John Humphreys her "brother," explaining that "[h]is sister called me her sister—and that makes me his" (509). This especially disturbs her relatives because Ellen refuses to call her uncle "father" even after he has legally adopted her. Other popular sentimental novels such as Catharine Maria Sedgwick's *Hope Leslie* and Cummins's *The Lamplighter* also stage the dissolution of their heroines' families in their opening pages or have recently orphaned girls as their main characters, or both. Throughout the genre, the voluntary affinities of sympathy prove stronger than the ties of kinship.

The representation of sympathy serves at least two related functions within sentimental narratives. As we have seen, it establishes the character of the sentimental heroine as other-oriented, selfless, and emotionally tied to those who have helped her or who need help themselves: in a word, "feminine." Even as it establishes individual character, sympathy provides a normative standard by which heroines—and, by extension, readers as well—can judge a group, community, or situation. The confluence of this norm with the heroine's own identity permits her to reject even her own family without seeming to violate the standards of femininity. The dissolution of family structures that occasions so many sentimental narratives is seen as a natural outgrowth of supposedly selfless female character, an appropriate attempt to transgress the boundaries of the domestic in order to expand the boundaries of domestic values.

Carrying the "experiment" of sympathy into the family itself can lead to unexpected consequences. Instead of proposing that one should love one's family, it asserts, in effect, that one's family will be whatever one loves. Sympathy brings the values of contract and consent into the heart of the domestic sphere, imagining that the term "family" can designate something chosen, rather than a given set of biological or legal relations. Like romantic love in the marriage plot, sympathy in the sentimental plot is the affective core of an individualistic ideology, what Gillian Brown identifies as "domestic individualism."[28] But the novels set limits to sympathy's logic, often by raising the specter of incest as the ultimate, excessive domestication and privatization of affect. At the end of *The Wide Wide World* Ellen ultimately marries John Humphreys—the man she has insisted on calling her brother—in a match that can only be described as quasi-incestuous, as they have lived together like siblings since Ellen was quite young. *The Lamplighter* concludes with not one, but two quasi-incestuous marriages. First Gerty's adoptive sister, Emily, marries the mysterious Phillip Amory, who has revealed himself to be not only Emily's lost step-brother but also—in one of the most bizarre series of coincidences in American literature—Gerty's father. As if to complete the totalization of the family metaphor, Gerty marries Willie Sullivan, the boy she has grown up with as a brother. Thus a novel whose main character initially lacked even a last name ends with a situation in which virtually all the surviving characters are related to one another, some in multiple ways.

Perhaps the most startling example of a work of sentimental women's fiction that depicts incest as the telos of sympathetic identification is Elizabeth Stuart Phelps's *The Gates Ajar,* which consists entirely of conversations between a bereaved sister and her Aunt Winifred. The younger woman is comforted by her aunt's assurances that in the afterlife she will be able to resume the extremely close emotional and even physical relationship she once had with her brother. Contemporary reviewers, especially when they were opposed to the unorthodox theological principles Phelps espoused, did not hesitate to point out that the sister's love seemed to go beyond the bounds of filial affection.[29] However, this potentially scandalous implication did not prevent the novel from becoming one of the best-sellers of the 1860s.[30]

The novels often try to explain away the incestuous implications of such conclusions by remarking on the "natural" tendency of two people who have been raised in close proximity to form sympathetic and romantic ties. But such comments really only beg the question; after all, that logic could legitimate an incestuous romance between any members of a household. Foucault's argument in *The History of Sexuality* is more to the point here: the valorization of sympathy was a part of "the affective intensification of the family space" that characterizes bourgeois society's regime of sexuality, and incest marks that regime's internal limit. Incest, Foucault says, "is an object of obsession and attraction, a dreadful secret and an indispensable pivot. It is manifested as a thing that is strictly forbidden in the family insofar as the latter functions as a deployment of alliance, but it is also a thing that is continually demanded in order for the family to be a hotbed of sexual incitement."[31]

In *Work,* too, the license sympathy grants to transgress the boundaries of the family leads to a virtually incestuous violation of a family's internal limits.[32] In the chapter titled "Companion," Christie is hired as a companion for a sick young woman in a pleasant but eccentric and secretive family. It turns out that there is hereditary madness in the father's line, and that his four Carrol children must not marry if they wish to avoid having children who will perpetuate the illness. The sick girl and the oldest brother have already fallen into the melancholia that precedes the madness, and in fact the girl commits suicide by the end of the chapter. But Christie advises the two younger siblings to live for each other, to let their mutual sympathy sustain them and ward off the madness.

Bella and Harry seem to interpret Christie's suggestion to mean that they should act as if they were married. When the young woman returns at the end of the novel to update Christie on their activities, she reports that she has been keeping house while Harry has been training to become a doctor, and the two are virtually inseparable. Even their assertion that they will never marry anyone else now sounds like a declaration of romantic love: " 'We shall always be together,' " Bella says, " 'and all in all to one another, for we can never marry and have homes apart you know' " (335). Bella and Harry are faced with a double prohibition against marriage; the incest taboo prevents them from marrying each other, and the genetic heritage of their family prevents them from marrying anyone else. Nonetheless, the narrative conflicts of their plotline are resolved, like most sentimental narratives, by the formation of a tie that both is and is not familial.[33]

The telos of sentimental narratives is often just such a simultaneous extension and containment of the power of sympathy. But in validating such conclusions by metaphorically equating these sympathetic groups with families and traditional notions of domesticity, the novels do not innocently draw upon "the affective intensification of the family space." Collapsing the voluntary affinities of sympathy with the compulsory ties of kinship, the recombinant families that resolve the narratives carry within them the internal limit of incest.[34] When Christie tells Bella to "make Harry's home as beautiful and attractive as you can," she is ostensibly helping them to form a pleasant little household and a circle of friends, but the phrase is uncomfortably close to advice an older woman might give to a new bride. Even when it deploys thoroughly domestic rhetoric—or perhaps especially when it does so—the sentimental novel raises the threat of incest.[35]

Performing Sympathy

We have explored two sets of tensions within the logic of sympathetic identification that intensify sentimental fiction's affective charge. First, we saw how the equivalential logic of sympathy places its notion of individual subjectivity in conflict with conventional concepts of femininity. This conflict is evinced in the crises of self and selflessness that pervade both sentimental narratives and the cultural conventions that inform them, such as the practice of mourning. Second, we saw how sentimental novels' use of familial rhetoric risks incestuous implications by implying that family ties can be based on affective and consensual cathexes as well as on biological or conventional bonds. At this point such ties cease to be bonds of kinship, and the family as a normative category becomes incoherent.

In pointing out the ways sentimental fiction explores the limits and logical contradictions of sympathetic identification, I am not saying that the genre is simply ideologically incoherent. Sentimental novels have ways of working through their contradictions. After all, mourning does not lead to a complete dissolution of the female protagonist's identity, nor does the fear of incest prevent her from forming social ties or entering into a marriage. Granting that sympathy threatens either to violate the integrity of the individual or to enclose one incestuously within a constricted family circle, sentimental novels sometimes imagine that instead of isolating the heroine these threats open her up to a different set of identifications, sympathies that promise her a newly intersubjective, social identity. This new identity is figured in the groups that resolve the novels' conflicts, groups that range in character from the quasi-incestuous family alliances at the conclusion of *The Lamplighter* to the "loving league of sisters" gathered in the kitchen at the end of *Work*. In each case, the group becomes a site from which the protagonist can work to extend the value of sympathy to all those around her.

For sympathy to be extended socially, however, it has to be *performed*. As we saw in Freud's story of boarding school girls imitating their friend's "fit of hysterics," cited in the Introduction, sympathy in sentimental fiction is essentially mimetic. Protagonists—and, in turn, the readers who identify with them—are repeatedly presented with displays of suffering, scenes that are inevitably followed by demonstrations of the power of sympathy to ease pain. The presumption is that readers will imitate what they have witnessed, extending the narrative series of sympathetic identifications into the real world. As in the conduct manual described above, the value of an act of sympathy can only be measured by its "influence," by its effect on others. Thus the literary representation of sentimental sympathy is always a public sentiment, oriented as it is toward implied and actual audiences.

In *An Old-Fashioned Girl,* published two years before *Work,* Alcott depicts a scene perfectly exemplary of the mimetic and performative logic of sympathy. The protagonist referred to in the title, Polly, describes the death of her brother Jimmie to her mischievous young cousin Tom and his sister Fanny. Her emotional narration of a quite conventional sentimental death scene leaves Tom "full of sympathy, but he didn't know how to show it." When Polly mentions a slight resemblance between Jimmie and Tom, he is "seized with a sudden desire to imitate this boy." [36] He and his sister, who have done nothing but bicker up to this point in the novel, say a few affectionate words to each other, and their relationship becomes far closer than it has been. This scene is a perfect allegory of sentimental performance. Readers are meant to be "seized with a sudden desire to imitate" — not the main character's actions so much as her identifications — and thereby to make attachments analogous to the newly strengthened familial bond between this young brother and sister.

While sentimental novels are rarely subtle about their desire to perform and produce such identificatory imitation, they are extremely ambivalent about any implication that their performance of sympathy might be visible as a form of theatricality. Like the Alger heroes discussed in Chapter 3, sentimental heroines must perform virtue instinctively, inadvertently. Polly notices Tom's change in behavior, but Alcott emphasizes that "she didn't know that she had made the sunshine." [37] And in *Work*, Christie herself usually wields her "influence" — to use the novel's own terms — "unconsciously." For instance, she reveals her ability as an actress when she "loses herself" in her role and thereby moves her audience, and the effect she has on her first suitor, Philip Fletcher, is directly proportionate to her lack of awareness of it. Just as the sympathetic sentimental subject risks sliding into selflessness, so too the theatrical performance of sympathy is premised on a lack (or disavowal) of any consciousness or selfhood.

In her analysis of theatricality and sincerity in middle-class culture, Karen Halttunen argues that by the 1850s participants in the parlor theatricals that became popular in the period were willing to admit that "middle-class social life was itself a charade." [38] But sentimental novelists in that decade and later were reluctant to give up theatricality as an unambiguous marker of insincerity. While they depend for their emotional force on the performative character of sympathy, these writers almost always portray overt theatricality as inauthentic. *An Old-Fashioned Girl* contains a scene in which Polly attends an actual theater with her cousin Fanny. Polly tries to "feel with" the scantily clad young girls on the stage, "dazzling, exciting, and demoralizing the spectator," but the only feeling she gets from thus extending her emotions is "shame." [39] The danger of theatricality is that, like sympathy in general, it encourages identification without limits. Polly's sympathizing with the "spectacle" makes her "want to go under the seat," she says afterward, but not because she cannot identify with the actors. On the contrary, that night she dreams "dreadfully of dancing in jockey costume, on a great stage; . . . the audience all wore the faces of her father and mother, looking sorrowfully at her, with eyes like saucers, and faces as red as Fanny's sash."[40] Polly's identity is at risk in a theatrical situation because she is all too apt to identify sympathetically with—and even, in fantasy, to merge with—wholly unappealing characters. Both the real incident and the dream focus on a theatrical spectacle's effect on its audience. Theatricality seems to be dangerous both because spectators might identify with what they see and, at the same time, because they might not. When Polly identifies with the spectacle she feels shame, but when she does not identify she is divided from society by her desire to crawl under the seat. "People seemed to like it," she says, "but *I* don't think it was proper."[41] Her dream marks this impropriety with multiplied images of parental disapproval.

Although sentimental fiction asserts that theatricality is dangerous because it can evoke an "improper," inauthentic form of sympathy, its representations of even the most authentic sympathy are often indistinguishable from theatricality. Polly's description of her brother's death is itself a bravura performance, one that has precisely its intended effect on its audience. The entire story of *An Old-Fashioned Girl,* like most novels centered on a virtuous heroine, consists of incidents in which the mere sight of Polly's virtuousness makes others feel compelled to be virtuous. Even if Alcott insists that Polly's moralizing power is exerted unconsciously, it is an example of the power of performed sympathy. What distinguishes one scene from another is ultimately not the presence or lack of theatricality; it is the heroines' effectiveness in performing sympathy on and for their figured or actual audience.

Theatricality, however strongly disavowed, is thus essential to sentimental literary conventions. It is also, like sympathy, integral to normative femininity. In *Work,* when Christie becomes an actress she is described as having "no talent except that which may be developed in any girl possessing the lively fancy, sympathetic nature, and ambitious spirit which make such girls naturally dramatic" (44). While the novel struggles to dissociate theatricality and authenticity, here its description of a "sympathetic nature" includes being "naturally dramatic." Christie's talent consists in her ability to bring out a sympathetic response in an audience through her own self-effacement: "When her parts suit," remarks the elder member of the acting company, "she forgets herself entirely and does admirably well. . . . She's got that one gift, and it's a good one" (47).

Despite its association with normative femininity, theatricality undermines such norms because acting leads a woman both to "lose herself" in a role and to have, in a sense, too much self. In a scene that anticipates the dangerously depersonalizing narcissism of her later contemplation of suicide, Christie pleasurably examines herself in the mirror before she goes on stage as "Queen of the Amazons" in a mythical military drama. Here an identification with her own image is temporarily inspiring: "[E]ven this poor counterfeit pleased her eye and filled her fancy with martial memories of Joan of Arc, Zenobia, and Britomarte" (41). Her close friend and fellow actress Lucy warns her, "Don't admire yourself any longer," and Christie leaves the mirror to present her image to a larger audience. But as her fame grows so does her interest in the opinion of her audience, and a woman's conscious concern for others' opinions threatens her "sympathetic nature." "She had no thought now beyond her art, no desire beyond the commendation of those whose opinion was serviceable, no care for any one but herself" (49). The move from the mirror, in which she is her own spectator, to the stage, where she presents herself to the view of an audience, like the apposition of others' "commendation" and her exclusive self-regard, indicates that the poles of theatricality are isolated individuality and the anonymous masses. At no point is the audience an intimately sympathetic society.

At first the actress fails to see the dangers of her new occupation. Then, at the height of her career, Christie suddenly realizes that her friend Lucy has stopped loving her because of a mistaken belief that they are competing for a man's affection. In the middle of a performance Christie's "genuine pity" comes to the fore once again, and "Lucy felt comforted without knowing why" (54). Sympathy emerges, surprisingly, on the stage itself, and both the actresses and their characters benefit, for the women's real emotions allow them to project and display their feigned emotions more effectively. From this moment on, Christie and the rest of the cast give the best performance of their careers. But just as it seems that this episode has made sympathetic friendship and theatrical performance wholly commensurable, a piece of scenery falls from above, seriously injuring Christie as she dives to keep it from hitting Lucy. Alcott's legitimation of her heroine's acting collapses as the dangers of sympathy and theatricality converge; the opposition between them becomes too problematic to sustain. At one point Christie's talent is evidence of her sympathetic nature, and a moment later it is the cause of her lack of sympathy. Her success causes her to forget the feeling of authentic sympathy, but then her "genuine pity" brings her to new heights of success.

Christie's subsequent decision to quit the stage shows that she has learned there are potentially fatal risks involved in producing what Alcott disparages as "mimic scenes" of sympathy.[42] These risks make acting difficult to reconcile with the form of female character Christie is coming to represent, and she decides not to resume her career when she recovers from her injuries, thinking to herself that "[o]thers might lead that life of alternate excitement and hard work unharmed, but she could not. The very ardor and insight which gave power to the actress made that mimic life unsatisfactory to the woman" (57). The problem with acting is more than the "alternate excitement and hard work" it entails. What Christie really learns from her experience is that the community formed by the theatrical display of sympathy is not the intimate community that is the sentimental novel's utopia. She is performing sympathy, but for the wrong audience. Proper sympathetic identification integrates a female protagonist into a sympathetic community, as in the "homes" Christie enters and the rhetorically familial groups that conclude other sentimental novels. All other acts of sympathy are mere "mimic scenes," too privatizing and individualizing to be compatible with normative femininity.

The theater is not the "home" Christie finds with the Wilkinses and later with the Sterlings because it is both too public and too individual: it produces a relation between a depersonalized, potentially "demoralized" audience and a performer so narcissistically caught up in herself that she has lost the other-orientation that defines femininity. Later in the novel Christie is surprised when the play-acting she does to entertain the Wilkins children meets with no disapproval from the morally upright Sterlings and the minister, Mr. Power; this is because it takes place not in the morally suspect sphere of the theater, but within the confines of an undeniably domestic and intimate space. Domesticity's mediation is the only thing that can limit and thus redeem her theatricality. Even so, domesticity does not fully privatize theatricality. Mr. Power may relegate Christie to a private home at first, but as Elizabeth Keyser points out, he serves as "both model and mentor" for Christie, preparing her for what Alcott calls playing "a nobler part . . . on a wider stage."[43] That "stage" is, eventually, activism and public speaking.

The sentimental novel, as a cultural origin of what Lauren Berlant has called "the intimate public sphere," was designed to produce a literary version of the intimate space of performance figured in a scene like the one with the Wilkins children.[44] The genre disavowed overt theatricality long after parlor theatricals became an acceptable form of genteel entertainment, but its model of sympathetic identification was implicitly theatrical. Moreover, its notion of female character can be aptly described as, to use Habermas's words, a "subjectivity . . . always already oriented to an audience."[45] Habermas uses this phrase to describe the link forged in the eighteenth century between the domestic, the literary, and the public spheres. "In the intimate sphere of the conjugal family," he argues, "privatized individuals viewed themselves as independent even from the private sphere of their domestic activity—as persons capable of entering into 'purely human' relations with one another. The literary form of these at the time was the letter . . . through letter writing the individual unfolded himself in his subjectivity."[46] Letters, diaries, and ultimately the novel were "experiments with the subjectivity discovered in the close relationships of the conjugal family. . . . Subjectivity, as the innermost core of the private, was always already oriented to an audience (*Publikum*)."[47]

Alcott herself grew up in an environment devoted to experimenting with similar performative principles. Many of the childrearing experiments of her father, Bronson Alcott, seem to have been intended to make his children constantly feel as if they were performing for others, for an audience that ranged from their own consciences to the intellectuals and tourists who came to visit their home and Fruitlands, the utopian community he founded in 1843.[48] Alcott's childhood diaries from that year reveal that she expected her supposedly intimate writings to be read by others, including her father, his philosophical partner, Charles Lane, and especially her mother, Abigail May Alcott. On November 29, Louisa's eleventh birthday, she invited her mother to write in her diary. The older woman's intervention shows that it was not only Bronson who saw their daughter's character as ideally oriented to an audience. In a striking example of what Richard Brodhead calls "disciplinary intimacy," Abigail Alcott simultaneously inscribed her own status as the audience for her daughter's diary and redirected the young girl's disciplinary gaze at her own development, figured as self-expression and self-understanding: "DEAR LOUY,— Your handwriting improves very fast. Take pains and do not be in a hurry. I like to have you make observations about our conversations and your own thoughts. It helps you to express them and to understand your little self. Remember, dear girl, that a diary should be an epitome of your life.

May it be a record of pure thought and good actions, then you will indeed be the precious child of your loving mother."[49]

Brodhead comments in a discussion of another such diaristic dialogue that "Alcott stands as a striking model of an historical individual constructed on a culturally organized plan for identity formation disseminated in the antebellum decades."[50] As in most of the Alcott family's pedagogical practices, including Louisa's own writings, at stake in this communicative exchange is the reader's character itself. She is being trained to think of herself even in her supposedly most intimate moments as performing for an audience. And the audience here, like Polly's in her theatrical nightmare in *An Old-Fashioned Girl,* conjoins the gentle disciplinary gaze of the mother with the girl's own gaze inward. Even the diary is not simply, in Habermas's phrase, "a letter addressed to its sender"; it is written with other readers in mind. Intimacy and interiority, for Alcott, were oriented toward a public.

Sentimental Publicity, Sentimental Personality

Christie's near-suicide midway through *Work* marks a transition between two different ways of imagining a "subjectivity oriented to an audience." In the first half of the narrative all her "experiments" are privatizing and individualistic, and each fails for precisely that reason. Her jobs as governess, actress, and seamstress, among others, are temporary because they do not result in the sympathetic community she desires. The inadequacy of these individualist solutions is in each case marked by incidents almost as forceful as the blow to the head she receives on the stage. In another chapter, for instance, she takes to reading in bed at night because she cannot find real friendship in the home where she works as a servant. Her reading seems at first to fulfill her emotional needs, for it "peopled the silent house with troops of friends." But one night she falls asleep, tips over the candle, and, when the house nearly catches fire, is ignominiously dismissed (28–29). Like most accidents in sentimental novels, these recurrent mishaps teach Christie and the reader a lesson: none of these paths will lead to her goal, sympathetic community.

When Rachel arrives at the wharf to rescue Christie from narcissistic suicide, she leads the bewildered woman to a kind of place she has never seen before. To Rachel's reassuring voice saying, "Now, dear, come home," Christie can only reply "Home! ah, Rachel, I've got no home, and for want of one I shall be lost!" (127). Literally this is true, as Christie has just left her boardinghouse, unable to pay the rent. The word "home" here, as throughout the genre, designates something more than where one lives. It is an almost utopian space of sympathy and community, the lack of which indeed results in one's identity being "lost." The home to which Rachel sends Christie is not her apartment; it is the warm though chaotic abode of Cynthy Wilkins, a laundress and mother of too many children to count. Within seconds of her arrival, Christie is welcomed into the family, and "[a]s Rachel predicted, she found herself at home at once" (130). Just as Christie is on the verge of being "lost," the discovery of a new home opens up the possibility of the construction of a new self.

The erasure of identity that sympathetic identification can enact, at first linked to a threatening dissolution of individuality, is then even more emphatically tied to sympathy's potential to form groups and reconstitute social identities around them. When Christie is brought to this safe haven, her lack of a positive identity troubles her; she protests the warm welcome she receives by saying, "But you don't know any thing about me, and I may be the worst woman in the world" (168). What she does not yet understand—and what Mrs. Wilkins explains to her—is that the other woman's sympathy is predicated precisely on Christie's abjection, on the possibility that she "may be the worst woman in the world." Her self-effacement is both a limit and a necessary moment of sympathetic identification.

Sentimental sympathy, at least in its feminine manifestations, is thus characterized by those elements that form its limits: a contradictory ideology of femininity as selfless, the incitation and repression of incest, the deployment and disavowal of theatricality. The convention of sentimentality is to suture these tensions through the closure of a quasi-familial collective. The virtually incestuous pseudo-familial communities that form around Gerty in *The Lamplighter* or Ellen Montgomery in *The Wide Wide World* function as acceptable happy endings in part because they reject their theatricality. They are closed groups; unlike most representations of sympathy in the novels, they do not seem to be performed for an audience, and their "influence" is not figured in the text. They are meant to be at least as affecting to their extradiegetic audience, but by this point a long succession of allegories of interpretation have instructed the novels' readers in the proper emotional response to such scenes, and that response does not need to be reiterated.

Christie's arrival at the Wilkins residence, her move into the Sterling household, and her marriage to David Sterling all seem to place her back on a path parallel to that of other sentimental heroines. Her quest for sympathetic community leads her toward a "home" that can serve as the novel's happy ending. The limits of sympathy—which have threatened her character, her livelihood, and even her life—can be contained or at least forgotten in such a home. But Alcott's project in the second half of *Work* diverges from the narrative and affective conventions of the genre. In the final chapters, she experiments with the logic of sympathy by taking it public.

One of the reasons *Work* so clearly articulates and extends the logic of sympathy has to do with its extended period of composition. Alcott wrote the novel over the course of twelve years, from 1861 until its publication in serial form in 1872. Begun when the sentimental novel was still dominating the literary marketplace, *Work* was not completed or published until the genre was, by most accounts, past its peak. Although many sentimental writers—Harriet Beecher Stowe and Elizabeth Stuart Phelps, for instance—were still producing popular novels in 1872, such writers felt as if their time had past. Early that year Stowe wrote a letter to Alcott noting these changes, expressing her trepidations about the tastes of the mass audience, and congratulating the younger woman for her popularity: "In my many fears for my country and in these days when so much seductive and dangerous literature is pushed forward, the success of your domestic works has been to me most comforting. It shows that after all our people are *all right* and that they love the right kind of thing."[51] In Stowe's view, Alcott's writings were virtuous because they retained the values of domesticity, and the national public was "all right" because it retained a taste for sentimental novels. She clearly read Alcott's fiction as continuous with her own and that of her contemporaries who first cultivated the nation's taste for "the right kind of thing."[52]

The occasion for this letter was Alcott's agreement to write for the *Christian Union,* a monthly edited by Stowe's brother Henry Ward Beecher. First Stowe and then Beecher, appreciative both of Alcott's ability to produce "domestic works" and of her "success" with the immensely popular *Little Women* in 1868–69, *An Old-Fashioned Girl* in 1870, and *Little Men* in 1871, had solicited her contribution to the magazine. The first installment of *Work*—revisions of the novel she had begun more than a decade before under the title *Success*—appeared in Beecher's journal on December 18, 1872; it ran in twenty-seven more installments, through June 18, 1873.[53] Although Alcott had changed the title, most of what she contributed could well have been written in the 1860s or even 1850s. She stages problems of the boundaries of the domesticated family, the definition of femininity, and the dangers of theatricality in ways that allowed readers like Stowe to treat the book as if it were a classic sentimental novel. Where *Work* differs from earlier examples of the sentimental genre, however, is in its effort to reimagine sentimental literature's domestic utopias as institutions of the public sphere. The classic sentimental tale resolves the anxieties it arouses about selflessness, incest, and theatricality by presenting us with a depiction of a group that it represents as a family. In place of such domesticating closure, the last chapter of *Work* offers its readers three overlapping images of feminine—even feminist— collectivity. Alcott represents each as addressing—though perhaps not resolving—several of the contradictions within the logic of sympathy that she staged earlier in the novel.

The first of these images is a condensation and refiguration of Christie's earlier acting career. Her final public performance takes place not on a stage, but right next to one. Christie describes her attendance at a public meeting called to bridge the gap between genteel women fighting for women's rights and working women struggling for better working conditions. She goes merely to listen to the speeches by genteel women interested in helping others, but she grows frustrated as she realizes that each speaker seems to misread her audience. The reason these speakers cannot communicate with their listeners is, of course, a problem of sympathy. Though they are sympathetic in the broadest sense of the term, none of the speakers properly identify with the working women. Through the whole meeting, Christie sits in the audience, as "impressible" as anyone else. She "admired, regretted, or condemned as each spoke; and felt a steadily increasing sympathy for all" (331). In short, she is the perfect sentimental reader of the scene, responding as instructed and interpreting each of her varying responses as a form of "sympathy."

However, Christie does not stop with sympathy; rather, she transforms sympathy from a purely affective interaction into a form of political mediation. Her impressions lead to an active desire to "bring the helpers and the helped into truer relations with each other" (331). "Truer relations," of course, turn out to be more appropriate sympathetic ties. When Christie spontaneously stands up to make "her first speech in public since she left the stage," the first move she makes to bring these relations about is to break down class distinctions by refusing to get up on the platform.[54] This democratic gesture draws cheers from the crowd and ensures her an attentive audience. Alcott says here that Christie's acting experience "stood her in good stead now, giving her self-possession," precisely what was denied her on the stage. Though different in its results, the scene follows the same logic as the earlier scene in the theater. Just as Christie's acting ability and her virtue rise up along with the "genuine pity" she felt for her friend Lucy in the play, here her self-possession arises simultaneously with her sympathetic relation to the audience.

Christie's oration makes her a minor celebrity overnight. Alcott gives us only one sentence of her speech, the one in which she announces her refusal to get up on the stage. Standing on the lowest step, she proclaims "I am better here, thank you; for I have been and mean to be a working woman all my life" (332). "Working woman" is not a term she has applied to herself before this moment; in fact, Alcott remarks in the previous paragraph that many in the audience knew her in a variety of other roles, including "Mr. Power's friend, David Sterling's wife, or an army nurse who had done well." But following the logic of sympathy I have described in this chapter, identification has turned into identity, "significant analogy" into "coincidence." Instead of describing the political content of the speech, Alcott dramatizes Christie's formation as a subjectivity oriented toward her audience. The women see her not only as "a genuine woman [who] stood down there among them like a sister" but also as "one of them; for the same lines were on her face that they saw on their own" (333). Sympathy here reaches its public apotheosis: it is mutual and reciprocal, simultaneously producing identities and breaking down the distinctions between them. Again, Theodore Parker's phrase for the sympathetic orator—"Feeling, [s]he must make others feel"—describes Christie's role here perfectly.

Christie's foray into public speaking is represented as a logical culmination of the development of her character and her search for independence. If the sentimental novel were nothing but a kind of female bildungsroman, this scene would be the one in which Christie's character appeared as a fully formed, self-identical subject of possessive individualism. Anyone reading the novel in this way, however, would come to the conclusion a few pages after this scene that Christie's self-fashioning has been a failure, for her own account of her oration makes the individualistic interpretation difficult to sustain. "I don't deserve any credit for the speech," she says, "because it spoke itself, and I couldn't help it" (342). As in earlier scenes, sympathetic identification leads to a depersonalizing loss of self, albeit a morally valorized one. Just as the woman appears to become a speaking subject, she undercuts her individuality by modestly describing herself as a passive conduit for speech, lacking both agency in and knowledge of her own actions. The act of speaking is identical with the fact of being spoken, or being spoken *through*. Sentimentality's assertion of a feminine subjectivity, predicated on that subjectivity's self-negation, apparently resituates the female subject in the domestic place already carved out for her. Her self is once again defined as other-oriented, selfless.

What makes this scenario seem like a version of feminism instead of (or in addition to) being an example of conventional feminine self-abasement, is Christie's—and Alcott's—claim that her selflessness allows her to speak on behalf not only of her abnegated self, but of women in general. Again, Christie's speech is not quoted; its content is described almost exclusively by negation. "It was not a long speech, and in it there was no learning, no statistics, and no politics" (333). Indeed, its politics are as purely a politics of affect as Martin Delany's contentless "interchange of sentiments." [55] Christie performs and embodies the public sentiments, political action, and institutional alliance that the meeting is meant to effect. "Yet more impressive than anything she said," Alcott writes, "was the subtle magnetism of character, for that has a universal language that all can understand." The working women see in her a "figure with health on the cheeks, hope in the eyes, courage on the lips, and the ardor of a wide benevolence warming the whole countenance stood out full of unconscious dignity and beauty" (333). Correspondingly, she recalls later that the genteel "ladies had been as grateful as the women; had begged her to come and speak again, saying they needed just such a mediator to bridge across the space that now divided them from those they wished to serve" (333–34).

To the extent that Christie appeared on the stage as a "character" and a "figure"—an embodiment of political ideals—this scene is continuous with women's merely symbolic participation in the nineteenth-century public sphere as analyzed by Mary P. Ryan. Ryan argues that in the "ceremonial space" of antebellum holidays, festivals, and parades, women's public appearances as Columbia, the Maid of Erin, and other such figures on floats and stages served, paradoxically, to reinscribe their status as private. "Women entered upon the public ceremonial stage primarily to represent private values," she writes. "The second sex was clearly implicated in the ineluctable process that fractured public culture and spurred a retreat from public spaces on celebratory occasions." Ryan goes on to observe a subtle but significant shift in the postbellum period, when women in public ceremonies "seemed to represent, if not themselves, gender itself. . . . [T]here seemed to be something visually and culturally satisfying in the female presence itself" that could "disarm and dissolve the contentious differences in industrial America," most notably class differences.[56] Ryan summarizes her historical account: "Early in the nineteenth century, sexual difference served primarily to differentiate men from women and to mark off the public sphere as masculine territory. In the 1830s and 1840s, more refined gender distinctions buttressed the social boundaries within the public, helping to recast social identity in terms of ethnicity. During the 1870s, those ceremonies enacted in the name of charity gilded class divisions with gender symbols. Simultaneously, an increasing array of feminine symbols articulated a differentiation of social space, giving new cultural power to the private sphere and undermining the publicness of ceremony."[57] Alcott's depiction of Christie's speech stands uneasily between the two functions of women's public display that Ryan describes. On the one hand, she positions her character literally "just off the public stage," to use Ryan's phrase, thereby marking her distinct class position, while on the other hand, her plea for understanding between the classes, again in Ryan's terms, "in a single stroke divided the public between the rich and the poor and then bound them together again on hierarchical but benevolent terms."[58]

What Alcott adds to this mix is a sentimental politics of affect designed to reconcile the class and gender politics of the scene. The logic of sympathy here works to mediate the tensions between theatricality and authentic sympathy, between ideals of feminine selflessness and Christie's "new Declaration of Independence." Alcott's implicit claim is that Christie's identificatory identity makes her able to embody these mediations. In this claim she is an early example of a strain within feminism that would later become perhaps too familiar, one in which the middle-class white woman sees herself as the universal subject. As Alcott writes, Christie is "fitted to act as interpreter between the two classes" because "from the gentleman her father she had inherited the fine instincts, gracious manners, and unblemished name of an old and honorable race; from the farmer's daughter, her mother, came the equally valuable dower of practical virtues, a sturdy love of independence, and a great respect for the skill and courage that can win it" (334). Alcott here apotheosizes the virtues of the same class fraction that is at the center of her children's novels from *Little Women* on:

downwardly mobile but insistently genteel New England families whose daughters, like Christie and Alcott herself, sometimes had to work outside the home.⁵⁹

However constrained the content of Alcott's vision of class politics, the scene at the working women's meeting represents a rare and significant effort to link the genre conventions of the sentimental novel to the representation of a key institution of the public sphere, a class-based social movement. The second public sphere institution Alcott uses to provide closure to part of the novel's plot seems at first either to be puzzlingly anachronistic or to reinforce what Ryan calls "the cultural power of the private sphere." Bella Carrol returns in the last chapter to tell Christie that she and her brother have still not fallen prey to the family melancholia, which good news she attributes to Christie's advice that they simulate a life as a happily married couple. Bella is also hoping for some more inspiring words from Christie about how the couple can "settle down and be as happy and useful as we can." Both women begin with the assumption that the only thing that can keep the siblings sane is selfless, sympathetic activity. Bella's complaint is that while her brother Harry has a profession through which he can serve others, "I have nothing after my duty to him is done." She has come to Christie because she wants to get involved in charity work. Much to her surprise, however, Christie says that although her monetary donations are welcome, "pretty creatures like you" should not spend their time mingling condescendingly with the poor, as "so much pity and money are wasted in sentimental charity." Instead, she says to Bella, "[You] can find plenty of work in your own class" (338).

Bella thinks at first that Christie wants her to become a political speaker like herself, but Christie's response to that idea is curious. "Now Bella," she says, "that's personal; for I made my first speech a night or two ago" (338). Christie's claim that her publicity is "personal" reflects once again Alcott's sense that there is something particular about her character that fits her for such a role in the public sphere. She then goes on to suggest a sphere of influence for Bella: "I want you to try a little experiment for me." The Carrols are to set up a fashionable household, to invite the cream of high society to visit, and thereby to form a sympathetic group around them. In short, they are to transform and legitimate their quasi-incestuous sympathies by making them quasi-public. "I don't want you to . . . try to reform society at large," Christie says, "but I *do* want you to devote yourself and your advantages to quietly insinuating a better state of things into one little circle" (437). Christie essentially asks the Carrols to transform their union and their home into an organization identified by Habermas, and by historians of the early European and American public spheres, as a quintessential institution of the public sphere: a salon.[60] Christie explicitly evokes the history of the salon by disavowing it, saying, "I don't ask you to be a De Staël, and have a brilliant *salon*" (338), but she makes clear that that is almost precisely her intention. She asks Bella to invite people to her home "as intelligent men and women, not as pleasure-hunting beaux and belles." She is to change her wealthy friends' way of identifying themselves by giving them "conversation instead of gossip; less food for the body and more for the mind. . . . In short, show them the sort of society we need more of, and might so easily have if those who possess the means of culture cared for the best sort, and took pride in cultivating it" (339).

Embedded in this suggestion to form a salon is Alcott's implicit theory of the relationship between what she calls "culture" and "society." In the essays cited at the beginning of the chapter, Henry James consistently conflated these realms with the "public" and expressed his sense that women possessed power over nearly all spheres that could be designated by these terms. Alcott here explicitly agrees with the idea James puts forward, claiming that "[w]omen lead in society, and when men find that they cannot only dress with taste, but talk with sense, the lords of creation will be glad to drop mere twaddle and converse as with their equals" (340). Histories of the salon have identified it as the proto-public institution where this claim to conversational gender equality was most often made. In his important analysis of British American salons in the eighteenth century, David Shields cites a woman named Elizabeth Magawley who, more than a century before Alcott's novel, made almost precisely the argument Christie makes here. In Shields's words, "Magawley indicated that the conversation of mixed company was controlled in large measure by the conversation of ladies," and she set about to attract "men of sense into a space dominated by women" by asserting "that within the feminine company there existed women of sense worth communing with." Drawing on Dena Goodman's analysis of French salons, Shields concludes that salons had "given French women a hand in affairs of state by incorporating men of affairs into a conversation superintended by women." In the British American context Shields discusses, salons became the site for development of a particular politics of affect based on "the elevation of feminine sympathy into a political principle."[61]

This last phrase, though meant to describe eighteenth-century practices, applies equally well to the strain in the sentimental novel that allowed Stowe to compare Alcott's writings with her own. Implicit in the juxtaposition of a woman of 1730 with Alcott's fictional figure created 140 years later is that some continuities exist between the eighteenth-century "cult of sensibility" and the nineteenth-century "culture of sentiment." Critics and historians have recently focused on literary and philosophical connections between these structures of feeling.[62] Alcott's invocation of the salon suggests that at least one author saw potential institutional continuities as well, and that she might not have agreed with Ryan that her granting of "cultural power to the private sphere" would serve to undermine the public sphere.[63] At the very least, imagining such a public institution seemed to Alcott to provide a kind of closure for the gothic, incestuous subplot of her sentimental novel.[64]

These two institutionally public resolutions to *Work*'s plot are supplemented by a third and final ending, one that mediates between, on the one hand, the public political discourses of middle-class reform and working-class agitation and the social transformation implied in the formation of a salon and, on the other hand, the domestic ideals that provide the ideological, narrative, and characterological underpinnings for the genre. I am referring, of course, to the image of the six major female characters sitting around a table, hands joined, "a loving league of sisters, old and young, black and white, rich and poor, each ready to do her part to hasten the coming of the happy end" (343). Joined by Christie's daughter, who cries out, "Me too!," the women see themselves as a kind of sentimental vanguard of a millenialist feminism. As Christie puts it, "We all need much preparation for the good time that is coming to us, and we can get it best by trying to know and to help, love and educate one another,—as we do here" (343).

Condensed in this last chapter are not only Alcott's specific political commitments to feminism, but the even broader politics of affect she develops out of the conventions of the sentimental novel. Like the conclusions of other sentimental novels, this scene presumes that the reader has been subjected repeatedly to its sentimental allegories of interpretation and so gives the reader an opportunity to put that sympathy into practice. *Work*'s conclusion is typical in that it contains an image of a sympathetic community figured as a metaphorical family, though the constituency of this community is unusual in that it crosses rather than affirms lines of class and race. It is somewhat more explicit than most examples of the genre in its insistence that its sympathetic community has public implications; while such conclusions are always performed for an imagined audience, here the women are described as "each ready to do her part to hasten the coming of the happy end," an "end" seen as personal, social, and political.

What is also unusual about this scene is that it tries to resist sympathy's tendencies to transform its identifications into identities, to mistake its significant analogies for affective coincidences, and to construct "the fiction of the *one* public." Just as the group of women sits down at the table "like a flock of birds of various plumage and power of song, but all amicably disposed, and ready to peck socially at any topic which might turn up," Mrs. Wilkins looks up and notices a new painting on Christie's wall (341). It is a rendition of a scene from that virtually sacred urtext of sentimental Christianity, *Pilgrim's Progress,* "a quaint and lovely picture of Mr. Greatheart, leading the fugitives from the City of Destruction." The subject matter of the painting, though, is almost irrelevant, for three of the women offer their own interpretations of it, each of which is equally but differently sentimental. Mrs. Sterling "looked up with her devout eyes full of love" to see "just a hint" of her dead son David in the image of Mr. Greatheart. Rachel/Letty sees the likeness of Christie's daughter Pansy in the child he carries, and Hepsey, the former slave, "tearfully" asserts that the escaping women he leads " 'oughter bin black' . . . for she considered David worthy of a place with old John Brown and Colonel Shaw" (342).

These personal interpretations both overlap and differ, but whatever conflicts exist are elided in the scene's emotionality. Indeed, Christie herself offers no interpretation of the painting; instead she "said nothing, because she felt too much" (342). The illustrator of the first edition of *Work,* Sol Eytinge, renders this scene by reducing the interpretations put forward to a single common denominator: he places a portrait of David over the women's heads. His emphasis on the women's commonality of identification captures only one aspect of the logic of sympathy Alcott condenses in this scene, the tendency toward a coincidence of interpretation and identification. In their variety, however, these acts of interpretation assert not only the common femininity of the observers in their primarily personal and emotional responses to the image, but also their particularities of race, age, and personal history. Like the conclusions of most sentimental novels, this one offers its readers a fantasy that affective intensity—each woman's sentimental view of the painting, Christie's excessive emotion—can enable communication across these differences.

It is the fantasy of transparent communicability that cements the sentimental novel's status as what I have been calling a "fiction of the public sphere." The texts and institutions analyzed in earlier chapters also rely on such fantasies to figure their relationships to their literary and political publics. The affective exchange that interpellates the listener at a Washingtonian experience meeting and the reader of the temperance novel, the "interchange of sentiments" at the climactic meeting in Delany's *Blake,* and the legibility of the Alger boy to his mentor all depend on their publics' willingness to imagine themselves as participating in this sort of transparent communicative exchange. What we see developing in the sentimental novel, however, is a tendency that will be examined more fully in Chapters 5 and 6. Just as Christie insists that her public performance as a speaker for working women is a "personal" experience, so antebellum male writers like Nathaniel Parker Willis and postbellum authors of "bad-boy books" represent publicity as an aspect of character, a part of their protagonists' performative forms of "personality."

The tensions within the logic of sympathy signal that in the sentimental novel, perhaps more than in the other genres I have discussed, the author is aware of the difficulties entailed in transforming a fantasy of communicability into a performance of publicity. The tensions between Alcott's own authorial celebrity and her desire for political activism were even more difficult to address. Increasingly convinced that feminism was to her generation what abolition had been to that of her parents, Alcott became a regular contributor to the *Woman's Journal,* protested women's exclusion from the centennial celebrations in Concord, and attended the 1875 Women's Congress in Syracuse, New York. At an earlier public appearance at Vassar College she had agreed to stand on a platform, rotating slowly and silently so that the audience could get a good look at her, but at Syracuse she resisted such theatricalization and specularization, fleeing the stage when she found herself besieged by autograph seekers.[65] As we saw in *Work,* sympathetic identification and its subjectivity oriented toward an audience risk both self-negation and theatricalization. In her own life Alcott evidently grew wary of such theatricalized political embodiment, paralleling the trajectory described by Ryan from symbolic public spectacle to an "offstage" performance that entailed valorizing the social and cultural power of the private sphere. In *Work* she created a protagonist who, in her audience orientation, conjoined the performative and identificatory conventions of the sentimental novel with an appeal to feminist public sentiments. For Alcott, then, the transparent communicability and emotional exchange characteristic of the logic of sympathy could form the basis of a politics of affect that would interpellate her already substantial reading public as a feminist political public.

No one was more skeptical about the sentimental politics of affect than Henry James, and nowhere is his skepticism more savagely displayed than in *The Bostonians*. Written a decade after Alcott's *Work*, James's novel seems to pick up exactly where Alcott's leaves off, depicting a milieu in which feminine sympathy rules the social and political world.[1] The women in James's novel each embody different aspects of the culture of sentiment, and two of them in particular represent the unseemly results of mixing sympathy with publicity. Of Miss Birdseye, an elderly woman who has spent her life working for abolition and women's rights, James writes that "all her history had been that of her sympathies." These sympathies are to James's mind distressingly public sentiments, and their publicity has apparently prevented Miss Birdseye from acquiring either private property or, above all, personal identity: "[S]he had never possessed anything, and it was open to grave doubt that she could have entertained a sentiment so personal" as romantic love. She is described as an "essentially formless old woman" who lives in "a common residence of several persons, among whom there prevailed much vagueness of boundary." To the extent that Miss Birdseye possesses a personality at all, it is actualized in institutions of the public sphere: "[S]he belonged to any and every league that had been founded for almost any purpose whatsoever. This did not stop her being a confused, entangled, inconsequent, discursive old woman."[2] Unlike Christie Devon in *Work,* for whom public speaking is a "personal" activity, for Miss Birdseye the political conception of sympathy is antithetical to the personal.

Miss Birdseye's sympathies threaten personal identity in part because they break down the distinction between the feminine domestic and the masculine public spheres that the novel's male protagonist, Basil Ransom, forcefully asserts over the course of the novel. "Her charity," James writes, "began at home and ended nowhere." Here he may be parodically paraphrasing an 1853 sermon on "The Public Function of Woman" by Theodore Parker, Alcott's model for Mr. Power in *Work*. Parker's widely published sermon begins, "The domestic function of woman, as a housekeeper, wife, and mother, does not exhaust her powers. Woman's function, like charity, begins at home; then, like charity, goes everywhere."[3] Through his portrayal of Miss Birdseye, James asserts that such a model of "woman's function" will "consume" the woman herself: "She had been consumed by the passion of sympathy; it had crumpled her into as many creases as an old glazed, distended glove. . . . And yet people said that women were vain, that they were personal, that they were interested!" (64–65).

So much for the politically public version of feminine sympathy. My concern in this chapter is with another form of public sentiment: the expressly performative modality of sympathy that, I will argue, is at the basis of sentimentality's theory of personality. In *The Bostonians* theatrical performativity is embodied in Verena Tarrant, the novel's empty center and the site of its sexual and political conflicts. Verena is introduced as an "inspirational speaker" on the subject of women's rights. What makes her speeches moving—and what makes her appealing to Basil Ransom—is that she, even more than Christie Devon in *Work*, is spoken *through* by political discourse. "It isn't *me*," she insists, and her spectators are worried before she begins that her "performance" might be a mere "melodrama." Their fear is dispelled when "she was in possession of her part," which means, paradoxically, that she is entirely unconscious of what she is saying: "[S]he didn't mean it, she didn't know what she meant." During these performances, "it was impossible not to perceive that she was in perfect possession of her faculties, her subject, her audience" (265). But Verena's "self-possession," James says, is not a prerequisite for individual agency. It is, rather, a part of her "public character," playing out the same contradiction Alcott figures when her character's "self-possession" during her political speech is nearly negated by her own claim that it "spoke itself, and I couldn't help it."[4] Verena is thus empty of both politics and character; not only is she unaware of the meaning of her statements, she is also "neither more nor less willing to say it than to say anything else" (85).

This, at least, is Basil's interpretation of her performance, based on Verena's repeated denials of her own agency. The narrator then steps away from Basil's perspective long enough to comment, "I know not whether Ransom was aware of the bearings of this interpretation, which attributed to Miss Tarrant a singular hollowness of character" (85). Basil's interpretation is James's point: Verena's "public character" *is* hollow, and not only because Basil sees her as "meant for something divinely different—for privacy, for him, for love" (269). Her bizarre form of asubjectivity is the logical consequence, within James's view of sentimental culture, of trying to perform femininity publicly—or, as James paradoxically puts it, of giving in to "the mania for producing herself personally" (251).

Though *The Bostonians* most thoroughly mingles publicity and personality in its representation of femininity, the novel is almost as skeptical about the sustainability of masculine personality in public. Basil Ransom has the same desire we saw in the Horatio Alger hero in Chapter 3: he wishes to get his name into print. Specifically, Basil wants to publish articles in journals of conservative opinion. In this desire for print publicity, he is like all the significant male characters in the novel. His desire is perhaps less strong than that of the writer and columnist Matthias Pardon, who wishes for "a state of intimacy with the newspapers, the cultivation of the great arts of publicity," and for whom "all distinction between the person and the artist had ceased to exist; the writer was personal, the person food for newsboys. . . . All things, with him, referred themselves to print" (139). Even marriage, for Pardon, is a form of publication—"[I]f Matthias Pardon should seek Verena in marriage, it would be with a view to producing her in public"—and he sees his romantic feelings as public sentiments: he has "a remarkable disposition to share his affection with the American people" (140). Nor does Basil's desire for publicity match that of Verena's father, Selah Tarrant, whose "ideal of bliss was to be as regularly and indispensably a component part of the newspaper as the title and date, or the list of fires, or the column of Western jokes," and for whom "human existence . . . was a huge publicity" (121). While Tarrant wants "to go in [the newspaper] himself, bodily," Basil wishes to epitomize a rigorously abstracted rational publicity: "He had always had a desire for public life," which he conceives of as causing "one's ideas to be embodied in national conduct" (198). "Should he not be able to act in that way upon the public opinion of his time, to check certain tendencies, to point out certain dangers, to indulge in much salutary criticism?" (206).

Basil further describes his public aspirations to Verena as they take the elevated train to Central Park and—unlike the boys in Alger's *Ragged Dick,* who turn away at the sight of the incomplete public space—take a lengthy walking tour of the now well-landscaped park. "I have an idea," Basil explains to Verena, "that my convictions exist in a vague, unformulated state in the minds of a great many of my fellow-citizens. If I should succeed some day in giving them adequate expression I should simply put into shape the slumbering instincts of an important minority." He even takes seriously Verena's exclamation that "adequate expression" would entail his becoming president and, in his words, "breath[ing] forth my views in glowing messages to a palpitating Senate" (323). This curiously erotic fantasy of his public voice is deflated, however, when Verena reminds him that he has not yet succeeded in publishing a single article. He is cowed for a moment, but then her harping on this failure leads him to assert his aspiration all the more aggressively. His "interest," he says, "is in my own sex; yours evidently can look after itself. That's what I want to save" (327).

This is the one moment in the novel where Basil's vision of masculine publicity is put in direct dialogue with Verena's feminine publicity, so it is worth examining closely. What he wants to "save" men from is precisely what she, her mentor Olive Chancellor, and Miss Birdseye represent:

> [T]he most damnable feminization! I am so far from thinking, as you set forth the other night, that there is not enough woman in our general life, that it has long been pressed home to me that there is a great deal too much. The whole generation is womanized; the masculine tone is passing out of the world; it's a feminine, a nervous, hysterical, chattering, canting age. . . . The masculine character, the ability to dare and endure, to know and yet not fear reality, to look the world in the face and take it for what it is—a very queer and partly very base mixture—that is what I want to preserve, or rather, as I may say, to recover; and I must tell you that I don't in the least care what becomes of you ladies while I make the attempt! (327)

This outburst—rather hysterical and canting itself—produces more debate, but ultimately leads to an exchange that syntactically places Basil, like Selah Tarrant and Matthias Pardon, in print himself. Verena unexpectedly says, "I hope very much you *will* get printed." Even though Basil corrects her by saying, "Get my articles published," it is not hard to see that Verena has rhetorically effaced the difference between Basil's publishing and being published, in the same way that it is never clear whether it is her feminist ideas or her *self* that is made public in her own performances (333). Later, when he gets an article accepted by the *Rational Review,* Basil works to establish a difference between their forms of publication. "The simple fact that it is to be published makes an era in my life," he says to Verena. "This will seem pitiful to you, no doubt, who publish yourself" (360). But the fact that he has rushed to her to boast of his success, and that he immediately goes on to assume that his publication means that he will succeed in wooing her romantically, shows that for Basil no less than for Verena, publicity is personal. Indeed, as he puts it himself, before publication "I felt very blue; it didn't seem to me at all clear that there was a place for me in the world," but being published has restored him to self-confidence and self-identity (360).

Another Kind of Public Man

Basil Ransom possesses a "desire for public life," and yet he disavows any form of performance that would appeal to any but the most limited audience. At best, he thinks, "an important minority" will share his public sentiments. However, there is a type of masculine character in several of James's works who quite overtly performs for an audience. In his early novel *Roderick Hudson,* and then again in two novels of the "middle period," *The Princess Casamassima* and *The Tragic Muse,* James placed the peculiarly performative figure of a dandy at or near the center of his narratives. For the dandy, while publicity is a style of performance, it is also an aspect of his personality. As Richard Sennett puts it, the European dandy is emblematic of the way "personality entered the public realm" beginning in the 1830s and 1840s.[5] For James's dandies there is a conflict between the public and the personal, between political activity and aesthetic preoccupation.[6] At least in the dandy's American manifestations, the connection between his public performance and the political public sphere is highly mediated and tenuous. As we will see, the plot of *The Princess Casamassima* underscores this point most emphatically: when its protagonist, Hyacinth Robinson, tries to combine the aesthetic sensibility of a dandy with revolutionary political activity, it leads — inexorably, it seems — to his self-destruction.[7]

Later we will examine how James's dandies are manifestations of the same gendered tensions between personality and publicity that he approaches more explicitly in novels like *The Bostonians,* where he deals directly with the public sphere of politics and social movements, and *The Reverberator,* where he anatomizes the publicity of the mass media.[8] First, though, an exploration of the implications of the dandy figure for the key concepts indicated in the title of this chapter—the public and the personal—requires a history of the American dandy as James found and developed him. The genealogy traced here is prompted by a curious coincidence of names. Thirty years before James created Hyacinth Robinson, Fanny Fern depicted a dandy named Hyacinth, first in her popular newspaper column and then in her best-selling novel, *Ruth Hall*. Both Apollo Hyacinth in the newspaper sketch of that title and Hyacinth Ellet in *Ruth Hall* were widely known in the 1850s to be based on Fern's far more famous brother, the dandy, poet, travel writer, journalist, and editor of the *Home Journal*, Nathaniel Parker Willis. I read all these Hyacinths as critiques of—or, to use Lauren Berlant's more evocative and accurate formulation, "complaints" about—the inadequacy or impossibility of men's fulfillment of their prescribed public roles.[9] Played out in each of these representations is a tension between a masculinity fulfilled in its public performance and one that is more affective, privatized, and personal. None of them, of course, fully resolves the contradictions they stage, but their representations of a dandified masculinity point in very different directions, directions that lead to very different formulations of public masculinity.

In recent criticism, neither Fern nor James is portrayed as respecting the distinction between a domestic and privatized femininity and a public masculinity defined in terms of participation in the economic market. Biographically and fictionally, Fern transgressed the boundary between domesticity and the market through actions like negotiating a prenuptial agreement with her third husband, becoming the highest-paid newspaper columnist in America, and writing a popular autobiographical novel in which the heroine's strict adherence to domestic ideals pointedly fails to provide support for her children, leading her to enter public life as a domestic writer. James's complex relationships to both masculinity and the market are also well known to readers of recent work focused on his sexuality, his relation to British aestheticism, and the "friction with the market" that reached its apex with the commercial failure of his two novels written with the most conscious intention of reaching a large and remunerative audience, *The Bostonians* and *The Princess Casamassima*.[10]

Fern's *Ruth Hall*, published in 1855, is currently celebrated for its complexly critical reformulation of the cult of domesticity, as well as its status as the one women's novel to win exemption from Hawthorne's infamous condemnation of the "damn'd mob of scribbling women." The book's initial notoriety, however, was based less on its critique of ideologies of womanhood than on its scathing satire of masculinity. As Joyce Warren has noted, "[C]ritics castigated Fanny Fern for her negative treatment of her father, brother, and in-laws." When Fern's identity as Sara Willis Eldredge Farrington was revealed shortly after the novel's publication, its sales increased in part because of "readers particularly eager to see the author's portrait of her famous brother."[11] Nathaniel Parker Willis is satirized in the novel as Hyacinth Ellet, Ruth Hall's hypocritical, greedy, and callous brother who refuses to help her out of her economic distress. The vituperative tone of Fern's portrayal of Willis could have been no surprise to her most dedicated readers, who two years earlier had read "Apollo Hyacinth" in the *Musical World and Times,* a periodical edited by another brother, Richard Willis.[12] Fern continued using her brother as a foil for at least a decade, later mocking the reluctance of "Hyppolite Hyacinth" to alienate his magazine's southern subscribers by taking a stand on the Civil War.

In Fern's portrayal of Willis, as in her satires on men throughout her literary and journalistic career, her complaint takes a form that seems contradictory, at least within a conceptualization of nineteenth-century masculinity as occupying one of two gendered separate spheres. Fern criticizes men for being simultaneously too "effeminate" and too "public." The gendered tension in her portrayal is marked in the name she gives her brother in the earlier sketch, which conjoins in one figure the beautiful young boy, Hyacinth, with Apollo, the god who loved him.[13] On the one hand, the conflation of the two mythical characters effectively conveys the charge of self-love, self-absorption, and narcissism that Fern levies at Willis and attributes to publicly successful men in her other writings. On the other hand—though it may turn out to be the same one—the name designates a character who is scandalously feminized and illegitimately sentimental. "I am acquainted with Apollo Hyacinth," Fern writes. "I have read his prose, and I have read his poetry, and I have cried over both, till my heart was as soft as my head, and my eyes were as red as a rabbit's." This ability to provoke tears, which she says is enough to "raise the price of pocket handkerchiefs," is Apollo Hyacinth's public vocation. "I have listened to him in public," Fern continues, "when he was, by turns, witty, sparkling, satirical, pathetic, till I could have added a codicil to my will, and left him all my worldly possessions." It is precisely this capacity to make his sentiments reach into the economic realm that demonstrates, for Fern, his hypocrisy and inauthenticity. She complains of his penchant for borrowing money and never returning it, his unwillingness to extend his sympathies so far as to donate to a cause he would otherwise publicly advocate, and his tendency to ignore friends in need "until they have been extricated from all their troubles."[14]

"Apollo Hyacinth" was followed three months later by a column entitled "Have We Any Men Among Us?," which denounced "*milk-and-water husbands and relatives*" who failed adequately to police the boundaries between domestic and public spheres, allowing and even encouraging others to "invad[e] the sanctity of [a woman's] private life."[15] For Fern, even as her novel and the public example of her own career seemed to advocate women's freedom to enter into public life and the market, men were to uphold the separation between the spheres in their own economic and affective lives, confining their sentimentality to the domestic sphere and refraining from public performances of sentiment that could only, in her view, be hypocritical and feminizing.

The worst of Fern's men engage in an unending public performance that leads them to a potentially feminizing concern with aesthetic appearance and display. Fern attributes Apollo Hyacinth's faults to what she calls his "keenness of perception, and deep love, of the beautiful." "His tastes are very exquisite," she writes; he has an "exquisitely sensitive nature." It is no wonder that, shortly after *Ruth Hall* appeared, some readers of the pseudonymous novel began to suspect that the model for Hyacinth Ellet was Nathaniel Parker Willis. Willis's reports from British high society, his breezy but affected writing style, and his proclivity for fine dress had marked him as the public figure in American life most resembling a Regency dandy. At various times in the 1840s, he was referred to as "the American Pelham," "the American d'Orsay," and "the very Dr. Johnson of dandyism."[16] Oliver Wendell Holmes's 1885 reminiscence of Willis, like more contemporaneous accounts, focuses on his personal appearance and his showiness, his orientation toward an audience: "He came very near being very handsome. He was tall; his hair, of light brown color, waved in luxurious abundance, and his cheek was as rosy as if it had been painted to show behind the footlights, and he dressed with artistic elegance. He was something between a remembrance of Count d'Orsay and an anticipation of Oscar Wilde."[17]

In *Ruth Hall*, Fern attributes Hyacinth Ellet's lack of sympathy with Ruth's plight to a similarly portrayed dandyism. Hyacinth is "handsome, and gifted" and foppishly "elegant" to the point where, after Ruth's enthusiastic hug of greeting, he replies, " '[K]iss me if you insist on it, Ruth, but for heaven's sake, don't tumble my dickey.' "[18] Early in the novel he is contrasted with the "manly form" of Ruth's first husband, Harry, whose "handsomeness" even Hyacinth admires, but after Harry Hall's death "Hyacinth's regard for his sister evaporated in a lachrymose obituary notice of Hall in the Irving Magazine" (178). By the end he is described by the male magazine editor who has helped Ruth out of poverty as "a miserable time-server. . . . Fashion is his God; he recognizes only the drawing-room side of human nature. Sorrow in satin he can sympathize with, but sorrow in rags is too plebeian for his exquisite organization" (207). In short, the character has the same capacity for inauthentic public sympathy and self-absorption as Apollo Hyacinth and is condemned accordingly.

Hyacinth's affective crime, then, is the disjunction between his public performance of sympathy in such texts as the "lachrymose obituary" and his lack of authentically personal sentiments. Fern aligns this hypocrisy with a transgression of the line between public and private—or rather, with the charge that he draws such a line in the wrong place. When he appears in *Ruth Hall,* Hyacinth is presented as pure performance, sheer theatricality; Fern even describes his private thoughts as "soliloquized" (177). In one such soliloquy, Hyacinth demonstrates that his entire subjectivity is contained not within a public/domestic binarism, but in a dubious world of publication and puffery. He is musing to himself about the potential embarrassment he faces if word gets out that he refused to help Ruth in her time of need, especially since he has since been claiming, inaccurately, to have had a hand in her literary success. "If I am badgered on the subject," he soliloquizes, "I shall start a paragraph saying, that the story is only a publisher's trick to make her book sell. . . . I don't think a paper of any influence would attack me on that point; I have taken care to secure all the more prominent ones, long ago, by judicious puffs of their editors in the Irving Magazine" (177–78). Hyacinth thus brushes aside his domestic, familial obligations; for him, the public/private distinction inheres instead in a theatricalized separation between public performance and clandestine, behind-the-scenes stage managing.[19] In short, his private life—whether the term "private" designates something affective and personal, the conventionally conceived domestic realm, or the realm of economic private interest—is subordinated to, or even submerged in, his public persona. If, as Lauren Berlant has argued, Fern mocks what the author herself called the " 'female woman' . . . who trivializes herself," she equally mocks the man who, like the dandy in her representation of him, trivializes his masculinity. Her "female complaint" about men is that they are insufficiently masculine, that they fail to fulfill their performative obligations.[20]

Willis's Incivilities

The form of Fern's attack on her brother was especially apt, since Nathaniel Parker Willis had made his name by publicizing private lives. Indeed, in an illuminating recent study of Willis, Thomas N. Baker argues that he pioneered "the modern *culture of celebrity*," which Baker describes as "the personality-saturated ethos that prevailed in the United States by the time of Willis's death in 1867."[21] After Willis established a reputation in the late 1820s as an author of religious and occasional poetry, a sketch-writer, and a gift-book editor for the popular publisher Samuel Goodrich, his "gossipy travel book *Pencillings by the Way* exploded on the Anglo-American literary scene in 1835."[22] For the rest of his career, Willis capitalized on what Baker aptly calls the "enthusiasm for turning so-called private experience to public account," initiating the readers of his magazine sketches into the conversations, habits, and feelings of European and American elites.[23]

The personal life Willis most successfully publicized was his own. At about the time of his graduation from Yale, he began publishing poetry pseudonymously, and his topics gradually shifted from the pious to the profane. Under the names "Cassius" and "Roy," he began to write about the pleasures of flirtation and coquetry and to put into print as well as practice his favorite quotation from William Godwin: "A judicious and limited voluptuousness is necessary to the cultivation of the mind, to the polishing of the manners, to the refining of the sentiment, and to the development of the understanding."[24] Through Godwin, Willis drew on the vestiges of eighteenth-century sensibility's links between aesthetic sensation and moral sentiment, though he tended to skirt the earlier emphasis on the "judicious and limited" nature of the sensations and its link to the virtue of the sentiments to be cultivated.

Not for the last time, however, Willis overestimated the sanctity of pseudonymousness and the potential for print to remain impersonal, as in 1828 the *New York Enquirer* revealed his identity to its readers. A minor scandal ensued, during which Willis's apparent proclivity for publicizing his love life was publicly criticized. While the scandal was one of the events that led to his excommunication from the Congregationalist Park Street

Church, it also helped cement his reputation as someone whose private sentiments and experiences were to be circulated publicly and consumed avidly by his readers. Willis quickly learned that this form of personal publication was his calling. His very personality became capital to be invested and exchanged; as Sandra Tomc puts it, "In Willis's view, indeed, no property, however personal, however rich in sentimental value, should be exempt from circulation." As an example, Tomc cites the 1843 magazine column where Willis went so far as to provide—"purely in the way of advertisement," as he frankly admitted—a description of his country estate, which was on the market at the time. In his columns, Willis put forward a "vision of a mode of life—even his own personal life—as something now alienable and made available to all."[25]

Willis's most successful self-circulating performance was the construction of his persona as the voice of the "Editor's Table" at the *American Monthly* magazine. Beginning at the end of 1829, Willis's editorials presented both his personality and his possessions to his readers. Nearly every issue included a description of some aspect of his studio garret, including his collection of antiques, his books, his furniture, his dogs, and his other material effects, all of which produced a sense of a highly stylized and yet individualized aesthetic taste. No less prominently featured were his own more personal affectations, which included a fondness for Romantic and French literature that his clerical father would have found scandalous, his habitual sickliness, his habit of holding an ivory-handled fork to keep his palms from sweating, his foppish style of dress, his fashionable lateness to social events, and everything else that epitomized his emerging dandy persona.[26] Willis's style of "rambling, familiar gossip" was the perfect medium for this artfully casual self-presentation. As Baker says, Willis perfected the "trade in personality, a commercial enterprise dedicated to packaging inner experience and private relations for broad public consumption."[27]

Willis's persona at the *American Monthly* exhibited in print the traits that historians and analysts have attributed to the British and Continental dandy. Indeed, the famous characterizations of the "dandiacal body" in Thomas Carlyle's 1838 *Sartor Resartus* could serve as a description of Willis in the years before and after its publication. "The Dandy," Carlyle writes, "is a Clothes-wearing Man, a Man whose trade, office and existence consists in the wearing of Clothes. . . . [A]s others dress to live, he lives to dress."[28] This does not mean that the dandy was simply superficial and inauthentic; as Richard Sennett puts it, "For Carlyle clothes had become 'unspeakably significant,' because appearances made in the world are not veils but guides to the authentic self of the wearer."[29] Three decades later, a Horatio Alger protagonist could change his name to match his appearances, and Alger would see this malleability as a sign of his virtuous transformation, not of superficiality—though, as we have seen, cultural arbiters in Alger's day were not always persuaded by this display or performance of virtue.[30] In the dandy's performativity we can see an antecedent to this debate about whether or not clothes make the man. The dandy's subjectivity, Carlyle goes on, exists in its performance; he asks only "that you would recognise his existence; would admit him to be a living object; or even failing this, a visual object."[31]

In this "visual" aspect and his desire for recognition, the dandy exemplifies in extreme form Habermas's claim that "[s]ubjectivity, as the innermost core of the private, was always already oriented to an audience (*Publikum*)."[32] But Willis's dandyism also exemplified this subjectivity's apparent antithesis; in the next sentence, Habermas writes that "[t]he opposite of the intimateness whose vehicle was the written word was indiscretion and not publicity as such."[33] Willis's reputation was built on blurring the line between "indiscretion" and "publicity as such," on a series of betrayals of intimacy. While the earliest of these were the youthful indiscretions that led to his excommunication in 1829, the most famous occurred in England in 1834. Three years earlier, too deeply in debt to continue as a magazine owner and too embroiled in sexual scandals to effect a match with a wealthy woman, Willis had merged his Boston-based *American Monthly* with the *New York Mirror* and signed on as the new periodical's assistant editor under George Morris. He had spent most of the next three years perambulating the Continent, briefly considering a new career as an artist in Florence, socializing in Paris with the likes of the artists Horatio and Henry Greenough and his old acquaintance, the doctor and philanthropist Samuel Gridley Howe, and entering into a surprising range of social and cultural circles on the basis of a set of letters of introduction and a hastily provided position as an attaché to the American diplomatic mission. All the while he sent letters back to the *Mirror* describing his social success and the habits of both American expatriate circles and the increasingly elite circles in which he moved.

In June 1834 Willis found himself entering a circle he had once only been able to read about in fiction: an aristocratic salon in London. Using his considerable charm, Willis ingratiated himself with Lady Marguerite

Blessington, who had published her correspondence with Lord Byron and was then the companion of the notorious dandy, Count Alfred D'Orsay. Through her Willis gained access to the most fashionable salon in London, which she hosted in her home. Also in attendance was Edward Bulwer, the creator of the fictional dandy who had provided Willis with his nickname, "the American Pelham." All of fashionable London seemed to agree that no visiting American since Washington Irving had made so favorable an impression on high society. Willis's success was partly based on his personality, of course, and on the letters of introduction he carried. In addition, his travel writings had been widely reprinted in England, as had some of his poetry, all to great acclaim. And surely Willis's own sense of style did not hurt, as he appeared in their midst as if he were a character from one of Bulwer's novels, sporting clothing at the cutting edge of fashion, carrying an ornate cane, and wearing a coat in the style of George Stultz, the favorite tailor of the dandy set.[34]

So long as Willis used his dandy persona to gain access to the ambiguously public domestic space of a literary salon, his presence was genially accepted by all concerned.[35] However, as he did throughout his career, Willis compulsively and profitably made public what was ostensibly private. All the while he was a guest at Lady Blessington's, he was sending dispatches about the conversations he overheard at the salon back to New York for publication in the *Mirror*. When he earlier had published of his personal peccadilloes, Willis had overestimated the sanctity of pseudonymousness; in this case he overestimated the national and geographical distance between the English and American reading publics. "Our periodical literature is never even heard of" in England, Willis wrote in his first missive to his American readers, in spite of the fact that his own writings had been acclaimed there. "Of course there can be no offense to the individuals themselves in anything which a visitor could write, calculated to convey an idea of the person or manners of distinguished people to the American public. I mention it lest, at first thought, I might seem to have abused the hospitality or frankness of those whom letters of introduction have given me claims for civility."[36]

Willis's "claims for civility," along with his letters of introduction, were soon at risk of being invalidated. In part because of his own growing prominence in the English literary market, and in part because he was writing about political and cultural figures who were of great public interest, very shortly after his sketches of Lady Blessington's salon appeared in the

Mirror they began to be pirated and reprinted in the English press. First the *Liverpool Journal* and then other periodicals demonstrated that the borders between national publics were not as hermetically sealed as Willis had imagined. Although Lady Blessington herself quickly forgave her protégé, other participants in the salon were livid. One of the more moderate responses came from Bulwer, who insisted that as a "public man" he might seem "a fair subject for public exhibition," but not at the hands of "a guest." To violate such norms of civility risked undermining the "confidence" at the "foundation" of "society." Willis's acts, Bulwer warned, "have done great disservice to your countrymen," for "in future we shall shrink from many [American] claimants on our hospitality, lest they should become the infringers of its rights."[37]

In private correspondence with Lady Blessington, Willis accepted Bulwer's criticism, acknowledging that his incivility was a violation of his hosts' "rights." In public exchanges Willis was less contrite. John Lockhart, the editor of the Tory *Quarterly Journal* who had somehow acquired the sketches and printed excerpts from them, attacked Willis for violating the privacy of his host and her guests, calling his gossipy pieces "the first example of a man creeping into your home and forthwith printing, — accurately or inaccurately, no matter which, — before your claret is dry on his lips, — unrestrained *table-talk on delicate subjects, and capable of compromising individuals.*"[38] For Lockhart's attack to have force, he had to depict Lady Blessington's salon as a domestic space — "your home" — a point accentuated by his repetition of the second person possessive pronoun: "your home," "your claret." Willis implicitly refused to accept this characterization of the salon. He expressed his regret, publicly and privately, for causing personal offense, referring to some unflattering descriptions of salon participants as "some remarks on individuals which I would recall at some cost." However, he insisted in the preface to the first London edition of his collected columns — which he rushed out to prevent further pirating of his material — that "the only instance in which a quotation by me from the conversation of distinguished men gave the least offense in England was the one remark by Moore, the poet, at a dinner party, on the subject of O'Connell."[39] In the account, Thomas Moore, the Irish lyric poet, had berated Daniel O'Connell, the Irish nationalist leader, for lack of manliness and gentility in refusing to accept his opponents' challenges to duel them. Willis was sorry, it seems, not so much for his violation of private conversation as he was for the publicizing of a conflict that had national and international political implications. Publicizing the ostensibly personal conversations of the public figures at these dinners, he must have realized, was his forte; to apologize for that kind of indiscretion would be to make most of his career seem illegitimate.

Willis's attitude toward his act of international incivility thus stands in contradistinction to that of Martin Delany. As we saw in Chapter 2, Delany's calculated incivility was a strategy to reveal American claims to civility as merely national norms, which could be trumped by his appeal to humanity and masculinity: *"I am a man."* Willis, in contrast, started out assuming that he could appeal to the safety of nationality but retreated when he realized that the print public sphere crossed national borders. As we will see later in this chapter, Willis's commitment to nationalist norms went farther than at first it might appear.

The accusations of incivility leveled at Willis also ironically resemble those later faced by—and perhaps courted by—Fanny Fern in regard to her thinly veiled portrayals of her brother and in-laws.[40] Reviews from the *New York Times* to the *Protestant Episcopal Quarterly Review* attacked Fern as "unfilial" and not "womanly" because of her indecorous public airing of her domestic grievances. Even Hawthorne's famous appreciation of *Ruth Hall* drew on the idea that Fern had violated a gendered boundary between the personal and the public, first condemning those women writers who "write like emasculated men" and contrasting them with Fern, who "come[s] before the public stark naked, as it were."[41] In a later expansion on these comments Hawthorne phantasmatically stripped Fern still further, calling the novel "[c]ertainly not an exhibition to please Nat Willis nor one to suit the finikin, this spectacle of Fanny Fern in little more than her bare bones, her heart pulsating visibly and indecently in its cage of ribs. Still, there are ribs and there is a heart. Here is not merely silk and suavity and surface."[42] In this last sentence Hawthorne might have meant to contrast Fern with the sartorial style of either a lady or a dandy, an ambiguity both symptomatic and double-edged. While both Fern and Willis transgressed the gendered boundary between personal and public, they crossed that border in different directions and to different effects, differences that can perhaps be limned in the contrasting images of Fern left naked by her public performance of personal life while Willis was fully, even excessively, clothed.

Paul Fane *and the Publication of Personality*

This metaphorics of nakedness took on complex overtones for Willis himself. While traveling in Italy, where he sent dispatches home to the *Mirror* and toyed with the idea of becoming a sculptor, Willis wrote in a private letter: "I think of returning to naked America with daily increasing repugnance. I love my country, but the ornamental is my vocation and of this she has none."[43] In another letter three years later he echoed this statement, writing that "I am proud to *be* an American, but as a literary man, I would rather live in England."[44] Such proto-Jamesian sentiments are played out most fully in Willis's only novel, *Paul Fane,* whose eponymous protagonist "give[s] up, at last, that misplaced Americanism of trying to be an artist here" and decides, in the opening chapter, to travel to Italy to study and practice portrait painting.[45]

Though his admirers had often urged him to apply his talents to a longer narrative form, Willis turned to the novel only after his sister's success with *Ruth Hall*.[46] Working in this genre, and writing a novel at least as autobiographical as his sister's, gave Willis the opportunity to continue his project of publicizing personal life, his own and that of others. Indeed, he announces that intention on the title page—the novel's full title is *Paul Fane; or, Parts of a Life Else Untold: A Novel*—thus immediately indicating that for him, the novel was the ideal genre in which to display and perform the publication of personal life, life that otherwise would remain "untold."

The narrative opens with its eponymous protagonist secretively trying to enter a domestic space, tapping at the "closely shuttered window" of a house that turns out to be his own (9). Throughout the narrative Paul peers and pries into spaces that are figured as domestic, intimate, or both. He repeatedly enters into others' home lives and family affairs, arranges the marriages of his friends and former lovers, and probes the personalities of all around him. But he is not portrayed as a bore or a busybody; in fact, this aspect of his character is depicted in terms familiar to us from the women's sentimental novels discussed in Chapter 4, through a rhetoric of sympathy. This rhetoric is used to describe both his own identity and his relations to others. As in women's fiction, the sympathetic nature of the protagonist organizes a constellation of contradictory character traits: he intervenes actively in others' lives and yet is strangely passive in his own; he is reticent and yet is simultaneously a performative, dandiacal figure; he is self-aware, even self-absorbed, and yet can be utterly "absorbed" in a painting, a scene, or in others' lives; he is passionate, even erotic, and yet strives toward what Willis calls "disinterestedness" in relation to hetero-sexual romance. And, as I have noted, he needs to escape the confines of the United States to develop his artistic talents, and yet he insists that he has an "American soul and brain, as well as [an] American heart, taste, and temper" (395).

In the novel's opening scene, Willis presents sympathy in its conven-tionally feminine form. Paul's mother responds to the tapping at her win-dow and lets him in, and the two confer in the attic, out of earshot of Paul's father, who plays no role in the novel other than to oppose Paul's artis-tic pursuits. His mother, though, is all sympathy. Every night when Paul comes home they retire to the attic, a place "where their voices would be unheard, and where the son's history of his day, and mother's tender sym-pathy and counsel, could be freely exchanged. To learn by heart each leaf of her boy's mind, as it was written and turned over, was the indispens-able happiness of each day to that friend-mother" (10). Sympathy here has all the positive powers it possessed throughout sentimental culture: it is produced in "freely exchanged" personal narratives, as in Washingtonian temperance meetings; it is a medium of transparent communication, as in Delany's politics of affect; it enables one subject to read—even "to learn by heart"—the character of another subject, as if it were a book ("each leaf of her boy's mind, as it was written and turned over"), just as Alger's boys can be read by their mentors.

After setting up sympathy as a maternal characteristic in the opening pages, in the rest of the novel the author associates it most closely with Paul himself. Later, "the peculiarity of Paul's nature" is explained as "his dispo-sition wholly to forget what impression he might himself make, when once interested to absorb the meaning or sweetness of another's mind," a dis-position that endears him to his mother, to the young American woman, Mary Evenden, with whom he has grown up like brother and sister, and especially to the subjects of the portraits he paints when he gets to Italy (237–38). Paul's character as well as his artistic talent derive from his ability to read the value and nature of a personality from the person's features, and again this capacity is described in the language of sympathy. As he establishes himself as a successful portrait painter in Florence, he gradually becomes known as an artist with an uncanny ability to probe to the depths of his subject's character. Once he gets access to this "inner character," he is able to paint "a portrait of inner and more true resemblance" (227). Sympathy again becomes a form of experience, an affective basis for the reading of character that ambiguates the distinction between inner character and outer experience.

The most dramatic such encounter between Paul and a subject occurs when he is commissioned to produce a portrait of a woman named Winifred Ashly. For reasons not entirely clear, he has decided not to reveal a slight prior connection to her family, and so has taken on Mary Evenden's last name in her absence. As Mr. Evenden, he spends days vainly trying to capture his model's essence in a crayon sketch. Much to his dismay, Winifred remains immune to Paul's probing gaze; "her un-emotional current of reserve and coldness" does not respond to his efforts to read her character sympathetically (222). Because of this lack of reciprocity, "Paul had none but mechanical powers to bring to his work," but he nonetheless manages over several days to produce something that "approached a likeness" (223). But just as he is on the verge of renouncing this portrait, he arrives one morning to find Winifred playing the piano and watches her face in a mirror, spellbound. While she plays, her face is transformed as if it "were an outer mask that had become miraculously transparent, revealing another and a strangely unimagined face beneath it" (226). Her music is pure affective expression—"[I]t seemed like an improvisation of thoughts dropping upon the keys"—and on her face is registered "what seemed a complete, yet unconscious abandonment to utterance of feeling," to the point that "the warm softness of a tear unforbidden" is visible (227). This vision of a previously impervious face, revealed in a mirror to be the mask for deep, personal emotions, inspires Paul to start anew on the portrait. His decision is not to reproduce Winifred's posture at the piano perfectly, which "would have seemed affected, to English eyes, as a literal portrait," but instead to create the "inner and more true" depiction of her character, "which was now to be embodied in the expression—a wholly different character, of which the self-same lineaments were to be the presence and language" (229).

Willis here deploys the amalgam of sentimental and Romantic tropes that had pervaded his writing since his early "Unwritten Poetry" and "Unwritten Music," narrativizing aesthetic principles that value the spontaneous and unaffected as authentic expressions of character because they cannot be feigned—to make the obvious pun on Paul's last name, which Willis nowhere makes explicitly. Playing out the sentimental logic of sympathy still further, the affective exchange in the sessions becomes increasingly reciprocal, as they both enter a state of "self-forgetfulness." A lengthy discussion ensues, turning quickly from a theory of aesthetics to a theory of personality. Paul bewilders Winifred by applying his "theory of two or more souls inhabiting one body" to her, addressing her as "*both* the Misses Ashly" and "bowing ceremoniously as if to two persons" (231). Paul had developed his theory of personality earlier in the novel in his interactions with Mary Evenden. Throughout his childhood, he had existed with almost as much "vagueness of boundary" as James's Miss Birdseye, living in such proximity to Mary that she "stood almost in the relation of a sister" whose "habitual happiness was to mirror his own inner nature" in an "exchange of thoughts and sympathies" (23, 26). "It was a peculiar friendship," Willis asserts, and his effort to explain it produces some of the most peculiar passages in the novel. He insists, again, that "the possibility of love had not given the alarm to either heart," but that they were "sacredly dear to each other—the link, whatever it might be, all the more pure and precious that it had never been named nor measured." Then, as throughout the novel, what seems to be an intersubjective relationship is explained as if it were an aspect of Paul's own character. "Paul had a favorite theory of two or more souls inhabiting one body, and it was mainly fed and strengthened by the perfectly single-hearted exclusiveness with which Mary Evenden maintained a recognition only of his inner nature." The most straightforward way of explaining Mary's feelings would be to say that she sees only Paul's good side, but Willis takes this idea and pushes it farther: "To her and to his mother he was veritably one manner of man, and to his common acquaintances he was just as veritably another; and the two, separately described, would hardly have been thought reconcilable. It was Paul's riddle of human nature—not that he was in any way contradictory or other than single-minded to himself; but that, with daily conduct and manners as studiously truthful and natural as he could jealously and almost resentfully make them, he was to different eyes still so different" (24). Though he plays multiple characters for different audiences, each is "studiously truthful and natural"; none are feigned. This characterization nicely condenses Willis's take on the dandy figure: his subjectivity is thoroughly audience-oriented, but that performativity does not diminish his authenticity. Paul is just as "veritably one manner of man" as he is "veritably another."

Winifred Ashly takes slight offense at the application of this theory to herself, quite reasonably objecting to the idea that her "general look and manners" are less pleasant or attractive than what he is trying to (re)produce in his painting. Paul, "evading the personality by a general remark," goes on talking about the multiplicity of character. Interestingly, Willis here uses the word "personality" in a sense that was quickly becoming archaic, as the expression or publication of a personal insult. Paul's "general remark," though, concerns the more modern notion of personality as "the totality of qualities and traits, as of character or behavior, that are peculiar to a specific person," or "the pattern of collective character, behavioral, temperamental, emotional, and mental traits of a person."[47] He asserts that "to every character of any depth or variety, there is an inner as well as an outer nature—the character being none the less estimable because these are apparently very different." Which nature is interior and which is exterior, however, turns out to be entirely arbitrary: "Probably it is an accident of education or circumstances which of the two puts its stamp upon the features and manners" (232).

Winifred demurs again, arguing that "there would surely be more dignity in an exterior that was a frank and full expression of the whole character." In response to this desire to be self-identical, Paul extends his argument still further, if only to "apologize to her for herself." His comment also reveals the extent to which Willis sees "personality" as a form of subjectivity wholly oriented to an audience. "That would be true," Paul replies, "if the bad world we live in gave a frank and full response to this whole expression" (232). Again Winifred bemoans the fact that "such concealment" can prevent "mutual recognition . . . simply because the manners give no clue to the character." But Paul is unrelenting in his complex form of antiessentialism, insisting that although "chance (as we have found today) may reveal the secret . . . even if to the quicker sense that could best appreciate it, there be no betrayal of the hidden nature, by sympathy or physiognomy. And what a luxury, after all, to have an inner character, for those who are intimate with us, of which the world knows nothing! How delightful to have even different looks and manners for the few by whom we are understood or the one to whom the heart is given!" (233).

What is "delightful" about the multiplicity of character, it turns out, is that it allows for the creation of the category of intimacy. It is important to recognize, though, that intimacy here is not entirely authentic or foundational for the self, though it is certainly a pleasurable "luxury." It is, as we have seen, relatively arbitrary which aspect of one's character occupies the position of interiority and "which of the two puts its stamp upon the features and manners." As Winifred says to Paul, "I do not know whether my own inner countenance, as you are pleased to consider it, is preferable to the outer and usual one. We might easily differ, in our opinion of it, though I suppose you will scarcely allow my judgment, even of my own face, to be more correct than yours, who have studied it so much" (233). In other words, even self-knowledge turns out, in *Paul Fane,* to be a matter of taste, an aesthetic question.

Paul confirms Winifred's presentiment, asserting that "curiously enough, we are better judges of any face than of our own." Again, this is because personality—even if we consider the term as representing one's "inner countenance"—is a performance for an audience. "There are few things people are more mistaken about than the impression their faces make on others," Paul says. He does concede that one can judge the *"fidelity"* of a representation of the self, because even such a self-relation—a gaze upon a portrait of your self—is a mediated relation between a performer and an audience that can be judged by one's affective response. "[T]here is a certain *feel,* independent of the eye, which infallibly recognizes resemblance. When you look upon your own portrait, you know whether you were ever conscious of what is there portrayed" (234). But to remain consistent, Paul relativizes even this affective self-relation, insisting that "this does not decide the choice between the becomingness of different expressions which are equally true, nor, between the comparative desireableness of the inner and outer countenances of which we were speaking" (234).

Through Paul, Willis reproduces and simultaneously complicates the claims about the relation between appearance and identity that had been developed in contemporaneous pseudosciences such as physiognomy and phrenology. Paul then puts these claims to the test by showing Winifred the not quite complete portrait of her on his easel, confidently announcing, "Let me introduce you to yourself!" He tells her that this sketch, when complete, "will represent you—if not truly—at least as reflected in the mirror of my present eyes" (234). With this peculiarly protomodernist claim, Paul unveils the sketch. "It was," in the narrator's words, "by no means a literal likeness of the lady who now stood before it." But it does meet the sensational or affective criteria that Paul has set up for a portrait; it bears a "resemblance to what she felt true" or "the likeness of which she *felt* to be herself" (235; emphasis in original).

Willis here presents his readers with his own allegory of sentimental representation, comparable to the allegory of sentimental performance discussed in Chapter 4. Sympathy, for Willis, is the prerequisite for the representation of character. It is also, of course, a medium of affective exchange. Paul leaves Winifred to look at his sketch, which he calls "your other self," in order to "compare it with the original—an original which it will require solitude to see truly" (235–36). And when he returns the next day, her "inner countenance" has been externalized. From then on, she plays on the piano while he sketches. The music itself becomes the medium in which her "other self" can come to the fore, in which she can perform her personality. Indeed, "She thought music!" (237).[48]

What Willis calls Paul's "absorbent" nature allows him to enter into the other's heart. Two weeks later, Winifred writes him a letter proposing marriage, offering him her fortune to support his art, all because he has revealed her "inner self." "I wish," she bluntly asserts, "to belong to my first discoverer" (241). However, throughout the novel Paul refuses to allow aesthetic and sentimental sympathy to mutate into heterosexual romance, at least in his own life. Instead of taking up Winifred's proposal, he deflects it in two ways. First, he reveals that the "Mr. Evenden" to whom she had addressed the letter does not exist, but he does not yet disclose his true name. Then—despite disingenuously claiming to have an "aversion to meddling with other people's disposal of their hearts"—he deftly matches her up with another character whose personality he has accurately read, his friend Tetherly. He then shows Tetherly the painting. Paul has represented Winifred's "inner countenance" so successfully that Tetherly is able to read it immediately, so much so that he becomes "very evidently absorbed by the picture before him" (245).

Completing his mediation of the affective exchange, Paul writes a letter to Winifred. Consistent with the logic of sympathy and representation that pervades the novel, Paul explains that if she and Tetherly had met without the mediation of the letter and the painting, they "would each take a wholly erroneous impression of the other . . . the veiled countenance and qualities of each, being (if I am not mistaken) just that of which the other might be most appreciative." Romantic compatibility is here figured as a performance in which each actor is an "appreciative" audience for that which remains "veiled" in the other's performance. Elsewhere described as promulgating a "peculiar religion of appreciation," here Paul himself takes up the role of the mediator between actor and audience, for "even with the most open eyes, two human countenances may require an interpreter to exchange language understandingly" (331, 247). Paul compares this mediation to his earlier introduction of Winifred to her "other self," assuring her that if she allows Tetherly "a genial acting out of his better and more confident self" he will change "as effectually as did the portrait of Miss Ashly under my suddenly enlightened and wholly reinspired pencil" (247). And indeed, once the two do meet, they gradually fall in love and are ultimately married.

Indifferent Intimacy

I have analyzed this peculiarly triangulated romance in some detail because it illuminates several facets of Willis's project for the publication of personality. We have seen that for Willis personality is defined and constituted by the contrast between interiority and exteriority, but also that neither feature of the self is necessarily more true or authentic. Interiority and exteriority are, it seems, arbitrary signifiers; it is "an accident of education or circumstances" which aspect of character appears on one's face. Paul and Winifred call each aspect a "countenance"—a surface or outward appearance, a face—implying that both are oriented outward, toward a viewer or audience that participates in this "peculiar religion of appreciation." "Translating" personality to this appreciative audience is, of course, the role of sympathy, the affective mediation that allows one to see through the "veil" to whichever "countenance" happens to be the "inner" one. More specifically, in *Paul Fane* it is the sympathetic *artist* who performs this mediation; Winifred Ashly is introduced first to "her other self" and then to her future husband, in each case through the mediation of Paul's sympathetic and aesthetic capabilities, and Paul takes on the role of translating the personalities of Tetherly and several other characters, whether their "introduction" is directed toward interlocutors or, as in Winifred's case, to themselves.

The fact that Paul performs these introductions under a false name brings up an aspect of his character that I have not yet emphasized. His pseudonymousness here is indicative of a kind of self-abstraction that Willis calls either "indifference" or "disinterestedness," both terms that are meant to account for Paul's character as well as his artistic talent. "Disinterestedness" comes up specifically to describe Paul's attitude toward heterosexual romance. We have already seen him inadvertently inspire Winifred Ashly to propose marriage, and that his surprisingly rational response is "to attempt a transfer, to Tetherly, of what [he] was to refuse for himself" (245). Even more striking is a more traditional romantic triangle later in the novel, when Paul falls in love with a young Englishwoman named Sybil Paleford, who returns his affections. However, when he discovers that she already has a more appropriate suitor, Winifred's nephew Arthur Ashly, he produces another work of art that externalizes a character's "inner countenance." Through a complex set of machinations Paul has produced a portrait of Arthur as a gift for Sybil, "throwing a new and more favorable light upon the character and features of his rival" (325). Although Arthur is in fact absent for most of this rivalry, as Paul puts it, the "portrait and I came into competition" in his absence. Paul watches as his sympathetic representation of Arthur awakens an affection that might not otherwise have come to light: "[H]is own unclasping of that locked book, and his own laying open of the hidden leaves of character, had induced her to read with new eyes, and with approval unfelt before!" (327).

The conflict comes to a head when Paul is accused of wooing Sybil despite knowing of "Arthur's passion" for her. Paul never denies being attracted to Sybil, but he insists that he has been simultaneously representing Arthur's interests in his absence by painting the portrait. His accuser is understandably bemused by this claim. "I did not think you—I do not think any human being in fact—capable of disinterestedness toward a rival in love" (346). But she does not yet know Paul. Indeed, he offers to retire from the field to give Arthur "a fair trial" at wooing Sybil. Once again, with the aid of a portrait, Paul is able to "transfer" a woman's affections from himself toward someone else. This time is a little different, since he is in love with Sybil himself, and he is aware that she is "not indifferent" to him. Yet in this scenario Paul once more acts as a mediator, abstracting his own desires through the "disinterestedness" his artistic role allows him.

Such disinterestedness is Paul's ideal throughout the novel, especially in relation to romance. Early in the story, soon after arriving in Italy, he writes to his mother that he has "no intimates." This lack of personal connections allows him to maintain his disinterested stance in relation to others; as he continues in the same letter, "It might be different if I had intimacies, but as I said before, I have none—my attention, up to the present time, having enough to do to be general only—wholly engrossed, that is to say, with being civil enough to pass muster while I observe merely" (51–52). This state of self-abstraction is necessary for his artistic evolution, which proceeds, he asserts, "by a *consciousness intellectual only*. The body, with all its perfected beauty, is forgotten in the soul" (52). He associates this bodily beauty with the heterosexual relation to Mary Evenden that he renounced by traveling to Italy; such desire, it seems, is in conflict with his artistic development. Though in the course of the novel he develops close friendships and even falls in love once, these affective states seem not to be in tension with his disinterested pose.

Paul's "disinterestedness" is developed most fully in his relationship with an artist he meets shortly after he arrives in Italy. At a party at the Palefords' home he meets a woman identified throughout the novel as the Princess C——, who offers to bring him to the studio of "a young sculptor, Signor Valerio, in whom she was interested" (135).[49] When he arrives at the studio, he sees "a person in the costume of an artist" and is shocked to hear the princess's voice. Signor Valerio is in fact the princess herself in male garb. Like Paul, she keeps her artistic identity secret, and they discuss at some length the virtues of producing art in private. "How are you content with secrecy?" he asks, but she rejoins that "it is the contrary that seems wonderful to me . . . how genius, particularly artistic genius, can consent to promiscuous publicity." Such "genius," she says, "which is very feminine in its instincts," should "reserve its beauties for the few" (141). The artist should create works only for a select and intimate audience, not for the masses.

To illustrate this point about audience, and to debate the gendering of artistic genius, the two discuss a sculpture the princess has made of Antinoüs as "Indifference." To Paul's surprise, the princess has made Indifference an androgynous male: "One of your sex," as she puts it, "with the beauty of ours." He is, then, a hybrid character not unlike Fern's Apollo Hyacinth. Like the mythological Hyacinth, Antinoüs was loved and lost by an older man, Hadrian, who raised him to the level of a god after his death, placing a statue of the youth in the central square of every town in the empire. Ironically, in the midst of these references to public male-male love, the reason the princess gives for this choice of subjects is that in "spite of our self-love, it is a law of nature to love our opposites. Antinoüs was the type of Indifference because, being beautiful like a woman, he loved no woman." Antinoüs embodies a "perfection of equipoise" between masculinity and femininity, she continues, and because of this "was passionless" (143–44).[50] Paul protests the implications of her artwork, saying that "in the excessive beauty of this creation, you have made Indifference more attractive than it is in real life." But the princess replies with a somewhat tendentiously heteronormative account of Hadrian's love for Antinoüs, arguing, consistent with her insistence on human beings' "nature to love our opposites," that "[w]e are not told what passion was inspired by the masculine attractions of Antinoüs—mythology stopping only to chronicle the passion inspired by his feminine attractions" (144).

Paul's reply untactfully undermines the princess's theory of natural bisexuality by remarking that "on a woman all masculinities sit ungracefully," prompting her to point to her own masculine attire. To avoid the embarrassment of an implied insult, Paul invokes the distinction between the interior and the exterior self once again, insisting that because she is an artist, "it is of little importance how your outward person is attired; but I must still own that I have seen your highness dressed more becomingly" (145). Here again his theory of personality allows him to evade even the possibility of heterosexual desire; like the princess's reading of the Antinoüs myth, he is able to concentrate on one gendered half of her self. By the end of his stay, "Paul ceased to find fault with the male costume of the gifted woman. . . . In the glow of her genius he forgot, and almost made Paul forget, the woman and the princess" (148–49).

All this gender-bending and cross-dressing allows Paul to have what can perhaps best be described as a chaste homosocial romance with a woman. Consistent with the more conventional triangulated romances elsewhere in the novel, romance is here conceived of as a performance for an audience. As he writes in another letter to his mother, he "need[s] to be followed very closely by some loving and willing appreciator." While he "needs the delicacy and watchful devotion of a woman," he also wants "the well-balanced and unimpulsive judgment of a man." As he explains, " 'Signor Valerio' is just this friend to me," providing "immediate recognition." This ideal audience is a replacement for a more abstract public: "My genius . . . does not depend on the deferred or unheard approval of a distant public, but has its reward while the glow of performance is still warm" (208). This relationship between performer and audience is made possible by the ungendering mediation of creativity, "this intimacy of common pursuits . . . a sort of *fraternity* of Art between us which makes her male attire seem natural" (209, emphasis in original).

This "fraternity" with a woman in male attire excites Paul in his "indifferent" way; it is, he says to his mother, "even more absorbing than a love would be—a friendship without passion, and better than a passion." He acknowledges the "danger in such an intimacy, for the princess is very lovely as a woman," but to give in to such a "tempting human passion" as a sexual or romantic relationship would be to divide "the else completely united hearts" of Paul and the princess (209). While he asserts that "this slender and soft-eyed youth, who looks over my shoulder as I draw, is the romance of my present life," he describes with pride his ability to look upon her nude sculpture of Hermione, which greatly resembles herself, and "without a thought of indelicacy, criticise and admire all its graces and proportions" (209). In sum, Paul's "disinterestedness" seems to be a heightened state of sexual tension, which—again prefiguring a psychoanalytic notion of sublimation—arouses his artistic "genius."

While this fraternal romance depends on an imaginary bond between the masculine aspects of each character, Willis does assert a gendered difference at the level of artistic creativity. Paul, as we have seen, possesses a talent for representing the "inner countenance" of others. In contrast, the princess projects an aspect of her *self* onto each of her creations. Paul sees, and she ultimately acknowledges, that the features of her sculptures all resemble her own. In regard to her rendering of Hermione, she insists that "the likeness to myself in feature, if any there be, is unintentional . . . though the feeling embodied in it is, I will venture to tell you, a memory of my own" (145). Upon further scrutiny, he sees in the Antinoüs sculpture as well "proofs of the fascinating artist's unconscious reproduction of herself." And this phrase is especially apt, for while Paul *represents* others, the woman artist's role, though highly praised, is *reproduction*. The princess is given some classically Romantic lines about her art: "It is natural of course . . . that one's own nature, whatever it be, should impress itself on the model as one works. It is the escape, indeed, of a fermenting identity, which might else, I think, become an agony" (147). She relies on art, she says, to "slake this thirst for self-transfusion." Her art is expressive in a way that corresponds to Paul's sublimation, but with a gendered difference. Whereas for Paul artistic production substitutes for heterosexual romance, for the princess it is a replacement for the "love or maternity—perhaps family cares or charity—[that] may be the escape valve for other women. I have tried these, each in its turn, but they were not enough. Without the something more—deeper and stronger even than love—which this impassioned study of Art gives to me, I have a prisoner within my inmost soul, who would madden with solitary confinement" (148). Evident in the princess's rhetoric is the fact that Willis sees the "indifference" Paul aspires toward, the sublimation that makes artistic production possible, as something of a strain. Indeed, in one scene in which Paul consciously tries to displace his desire into a work of art—when he reveals the painting of

Arthur Ashly to the object of his desire, Sybil Paleford—he actually faints, unable to sustain the tension that made him able to produce the flattering image of his rival (247).

Paul loses consciousness because he is trying to represent too much. His painting, he has claimed, has represented the interests and desires of Arthur; at the same time, Paul wants to represent himself, to perform his own identity. "[H]e made one struggle to seem as he had been gathering strength to seem at that crisis—but it was too late. Around him swam all the objects in the room—furniture, people, windows—and Paul fell senseless to the floor" (325). Paul's romantic conflicts only proliferate as the novel progresses, until we are told in the final pages of "[h]is adoption of a style of Art peculiarly his own, his doubtful success for a while, his marriage to Miss Mary Evenden, and his struggles with poverty and misappreciation (her love and completeness of sympathy forming the whole sunshine of his life)" (401). But all this, Willis says, is a matter of public record; the purpose of the novel has been to describe the "*trainings of his heart and pride, as well as his pencil* . . . those secret mouldings of his genius and character '*which were else untold*'; but, by the reader's acquaintance with which, he will be enabled to comprehend the impulses to Fane's artistic career and style, as well as the motives for some peculiarities in his life and manners" (492). These latter "peculiarities" are left undescribed; they, as well, must be matters of public record.

National Personality

All of these abrupt resolutions appear briefly in the last two pages of the novel. Willis goes into much more detail, however, describing the resolution of the conflict that opened the novel but seemed to be forgotten for most of it: the question of Paul's nationalist sentiments. The resolution of this conflict ends up subsuming all the more personal, romantic, and sexual dilemmas that pile up until chapter 34. At this point Paul is in England, the novel's three English women (two of whom are married) have at one point or another confessed their love for him, they are all at a party, and he is in a giddy but anguished state.

Paul resolves his erotic dilemma by deciding to become a national subject. As throughout the novel, sentiments are expressed through letters interpolated into the text. Making up most of the penultimate chapter is a letter from the Princess C——, whom the narrator describes as "the most intimate friend he had found in Europe" (386–87). She inveighs against his suddenly nationalist sentiments, arguing that "[i]f there were any great question at stake—any call on your patriotism—it might be different. Were the 'stars and stripes' in danger, or were your countrymen likely to starve or become paganized, without you, there might be reason in flying home. . . . So, why desert the temple where your genius has its fitting pedestal, to go back to the cave where at best you will only serve your country by seeming as patriotically unhewn as the stones around you" (387–88). It is thus left to the princess to voice the argument that was initially Paul's own. Above all, she says, his audience-oriented personality will be unsatisfied in the United States. For him "there must be *discriminating appreciation* in the very atmosphere. You must be conscious of appreciative eyes, always waiting for what you do. . . . With nothing but hurry and money-making around you, are you to feel sympathy, or breathe freely?" (388).

Rather than replying to the princess, Paul answers these questions in a letter to his mother that opens the final chapter. All these years in Europe have produced a national subject, one who feels his nationalism in his sentiments. "I think my own country is *my mind's* native air," he writes. "I find my American soul and brain, as well as my American heart, taste, and temper, pining for America to breathe in" (395). He recounts his artistic accomplishments and, in oblique terms, his romantic conquests and subjects his mother to a long disquisition on the vices of European class hierarchies. And although he acknowledges all he has learned from art and artists in Europe, he claims that "in America [the artist] is the tent pitched in the desert, with the sunshine and air all around him. I feel the want of this singleness and free fame" (399). In short, Paul becomes a national subject by expressing sentiments that contradict almost everything he has valued during the rest of the novel: the collaborative dynamic in the studio with the princess, his access to high society, his free-floating social position, the "appreciative" audience he has developed for his work. In their place, he says, he is "coming home, dearest mother, to be happy in American liberty—the liberty not only of sinking to where, by the laws of specific gravity, I belong, but of being looked at, after I get to that level, *through one pair of eyes at a time*" (397–98). By this odd phrase he means "to be judged of by the simple individual opinion, without class condescension, class servility, or class prejudice," a classlessness that "seems to me to be American only" (398). Indifference and disinterestedness in relation to aesthetic taste and class position, it turns out, are not just individual traits; they are aspects of American national character.

As if to underscore the nationalist conclusion of the novel, immediately following its last page are advertisements for Scribner's *Cyclopedia of American Literature,* touted as "An Important National Work." And indeed, Willis seems to have aspired in *Paul Fane* to reconcile his project of publicizing personality with "national work," narrating the creation of a nationalist personality. Through his poetry and his magazine work, Willis had earlier deployed the rhetoric of intimacy in a public forum, inviting readers into his garret, his romantic and erotic life, and the homes of the rich and famous. In *Paul Fane,* he essayed a genre that could fulfill this intimate ideal. The novel is in its very nature, after all, an invasion of privacy, a fictionally intimate sphere that is constituted by the reading public's desire to violate and penetrate that intimacy just as Paul's painting allows Tetherly to "penetrate . . . the main-spring of the lady's character." His protagonist is a fantasy version of the dandy persona he had created, a man who is able to enter into any number of intimate spheres by sympathetically reading the character of those spheres' occupants. Paul is all too successful in this project; starting out in Europe as a man with "no intimacies," he ends up with too many affective connections, which he somewhat unconvincingly replaces with nationalist sentiments. Even the cursory mention of his eventual marriage to Mary Evenden entails the disavowal of affect; he writes to his mother that "for her I felt no passion at home, and I feel none now." But he has a "presentiment" that even though he has learned of "the incompleteness of all love," Mary might eventually provide him with a love at the intellectual level, what he calls "the *mind's love*" that "is the best worth securing and living for" (399). With love portrayed as such a coldly rational sentiment, with the protagonist's most passionate affect directed at the nation rather than his future wife, it is no wonder that in the last sentence of the novel Willis feels the need to apologize that *Paul Fane* "has not turned out to be as much of a 'romance' as was expected" (402).

James's Dandies

I began this chapter with a discussion of Henry James because in several novels across his career, James deployed the dandy figure to articulate many of the same contradictions embodied in *Paul Fane*. Rather than resolving these contradictions with the somewhat unconvincing nationalist sentiments that conclude Willis's novel, James explored the denationalizing and degendering potential of the aesthetic, and of the dandy's masculine embodiment of that category. In the earliest of these novels, *Roderick Hudson* (1875), he even associates the dandy's aesthetic power to trouble gender and national identities with Willis himself and then juxtaposes him with the name of a woman most associated with nationalist sentimentalism: Lydia Huntley Sigourney. After the central consciousness of the novel, Rowland Mallet, has brought the sculptor Roderick Hudson from Massachusetts to Italy to develop his aesthetic sensibility, Rowland spends time with a woman painter by the name of Augusta Blanchard. Blanchard takes on properly sentimental subjects in her work: "Flowers . . . were her speciality, and though her touch was a little old-fashioned and finical, she painted them with remarkable skill."[51] Recall that Hawthorne used the word "finikin" to describe those like "Nat Willis" who would not be pleased by the "spectacle" of a naked Fanny Fern, betraying a connection between the aesthetics of the dandy and the prudishness of the female sentimentalist.[52] Here Blanchard's "finical" style is unnerving to Rowland's fine sensibilities for similarly gendered reasons: "She talked in a sweet soft voice, used language at times a trifle superfine, and made literary allusions. These had often a patriotic strain, and Rowland had more than once been treated to quotations from Mrs Sigourney in the cork-woods of Monte Mario, and from Mr Willis among the ruins of Veii."[53] Here, as in the quotation from Hawthorne, Willis's name is placed in apposition to that of a woman writer characterized as a sentimentalist. This time, though, both are examples of the "patriotic strain" of the "literary allusions," evidence that the early James may have read Willis's dandyism as performing the kind of "national work" gestured toward at the conclusion of *Paul Fane*.[54]

An America characterized by sentimental femininity and dandified masculinity is a queer nation indeed, and the barely triangulated romance between Rowland and Roderick that occupies most of *Roderick Hudson* is among James's queerest narratives. In *The Princess Casamassima* and *The Tragic Muse,* James seemingly detaches the problematic of the dandified man from the American national context, instead playing out conflicts between art and politics, masculinity and theatricality, public and private, in a British and European setting. At this stage in his career, though, James still saw his novels set in Britain as meditations on American problems; by living in London, he wrote, "I lose nothing at all . . . for London is fast becoming an American city—and our national character is vivid and familiar there, in every sort of example and in higher relief and saliency than it is at home."[55] Like Willis, who wanted to *be* American while living somewhere else, James saw national identity as mobile and hybridized—though what unified this hybrid nationality for James (but not for Willis) was race. James wrote at this time that "I can't look at the English-American world, or feel about them, any more, save as a big Anglo-Saxon total, destined to such an amount of melting together that an insistence on their differences becomes more and more idle and pedantic; and that the melting together will come the faster the more one takes it for granted. . . . I aspire to write in such a way that it would be impossible to an outsider to say whether I am at a given moment an American writing about England or an Englishman writing about America."[56]

The Princess Casamassima (1886) and *The Tragic Muse* (1890) are two of the novels that James wrote from this ambiguated national perspective, and both contain important dandy figures. I want to make a few brief observations about these figures and their problematic public performances of masculinity and then conclude with an anecdote from James's *Autobiography* that will serve as a comment on the historical shifts in the meaning of public and national manhood that I think he is registering here.[57] In *The Tragic Muse*, Nick Dormer is torn between two versions of masculinity. The first, insisted upon by his mother and his fiancée, is that of the public man like his late father, the politician who will stand for election to Parliament and represent his district, an unappealing area called Harsh. The second, offered by his best friend, the dandy and aesthete Gabriel Nash, is the life of a painter. Much of the novel turns on a pun that James and his characters reiterate throughout: Nick has to choose between "representation" in the political sense and the "representation" of painted portraiture, which Nick calls "a kind of 'representation' with which [his constituents] would scarce have been satisfied."[58] Nash, the purest dandy and aesthete in James's novels, is also the character with the least "vagueness of boundary" to his personality; as Nick says of him, "He doesn't shade off into other people; he's as neat as an outline cut out of paper with scissors."[59] And yet the attempt to represent him threatens to destroy this individuality: when Nick tries to paint him, Nash disappears, having "melted back into the elements," even as the unfinished painting, á la Dorian Gray, has "begun an odd tendency to fade gradually from the canvas, for all the world as in some delicate Hawthorne tale—and making the surface indistinct and bare of all resemblance to the model. Of course the moral of the Hawthorne tale would be that his personage would come back in quaint confidence on the day his last projected shadow should have vanished."[60]

In short, Nash represents the contradictory nature of the dandy in James's theatricalized and aestheticized world, where public and private are both performative states, not separate spheres. The dandy is a man who performs his sentiments publicly; as Nash proudly proclaims, "All my behaviour consists of my feelings."[61] Throughout *The Princess Casamassima*, the novel immediately preceding *The Tragic Muse*, Hyacinth Robinson struggles for a way of reconciling his "behaviour" and his "feelings." Indeed, his narrative dilemma revolves around a pun almost as explicit as Nick's. Instead of "representation," the word is "act," which is used repeatedly to refer to the possibility that Hyacinth will follow through on his promise to assassinate a duke but is also invoked in the various theatrical settings in which he finds himself, and which distract him from his political commitment.

Hyacinth embodies at least as many contradictions as does Paul Fane: he is of noble and French origin but was brought up in the British working class; he is a fearless revolutionary with slight features continually described as "feminine"; he is politically committed to the destruction of class privilege but affectively invested in aesthetic pleasures that he sees as dependent on class distinction. Like Paul Fane, he translates his passions between aesthetic, political, and class registers, though with far less personal success. Throughout the novel Hyacinth searches for a stage on which to perform his conflicting sentiments, whether a social circle in which he can exercise his aesthetic sensibility or a political gesture through which he can publicize the revolutionary conspiracy he believes is on the verge of bursting forth to the world. But his conflicting commitments lead him to an equally paradoxical act of narcissistic violence: he kills himself rather than assassinating the duke. Like Nick Dormer, he chooses aesthetic representation over political representation, painting over Parliament, but because he is not an artist himself and does not see his craft of bookbinding as equal to the artistry he has seen on his travels on the Continent, his only option is to prevent the destruction of the class privilege that is, for him, the prerequisite for aesthetic beauty.[62]

The Princess Casamassima—like *The Bostonians* and *The Tragic Muse*—is about a man attempting to act publicly. The contradictory, even impossible choices faced by Hyacinth are contrasted with the political and gendered certainty of Eustache Poupin, the owner of the bookbinder's shop where Hyacinth works. Poupin is "a Republican of the old-fashioned sort, of the note of 1848, humanitary and idealistic, infinitely addicted to fraternity and equality."[63] Hyacinth's guardians ask that the boy be made, "if you can, what the Frenchman is," a line that refers in context to the occupation of bookbinder but connotes as well the form of republican masculinity embodied by this veteran of the Paris Commune, who speaks of the events of 1789 as if he had experienced them firsthand.[64] Placing the novel's only truly political acts in the past relegates to history its imagined synonymy between masculinity and publicity; the only masculine "act" or "representation" James can imagine here bears a remarkable resemblance to the virtuous, disinterested male citizen of republican ideology. Gabriel Nash even invokes such republican rhetoric, however ironically, when at the end of *The Tragic Muse* he compliments Nick Dormer on the "disinterestedness of your attitude, the persistence of your effort, the piety, the beauty, in short the edification of the whole spectacle."[65] For James as for Willis, public masculinity requires a self-abstraction or "disinterestedness" that he represents as unsustainable in the present.

Perhaps the most interesting moment at which James placed public masculinity in the past was an occasion when he imagined it almost naked. In a very odd passage in his memoir, *Notes of a Son and Brother,* he describes the effect on him of a story told by his father. Much to James's surprise, his father had been "an early comrade" of Edwin Forrest, the American Shakespearean actor known for his very physical, melodramatically gestural style and his booming voice. Henry Sr. described to his son "an occasion, which must have been betimes in the morning, of his calling on the great tragedian, a man of enormous build and strength, [when] the latter, fresh and dripping from the bath, had entered the room absolutely upside down, or by the rare gymnastic feat of throwing his heels into the air and walking, as with strides, on his hands." What is remarkable about this scene, James writes, is "less the direct illustration of the mighty mountebank than of its being delightful on the part of a domestic character we so respected to have had, with everything else, a Bohemian past too." For James, this tale threw the "domestic character" of his father into a new light. First he wondered why Henry Sr. had so casually violated the private domesticity of a public man—"the glory of the footlights and the idol of the town." Then he imagined his father as having lived in the company of dandies, comparing this story to things he had read in the "diaries and memoirs . . . of the giftedly idle and the fashionably great, the Byrons, the Bulwers, the Pelhams, the Coningsbys, or even, for a nearer vividness perhaps, the N. P. Willises? — of all of whom it was somehow more characteristic than anything else, to the imagination, that they always began their day in some such fashion." [66]

Locating Willis in this glorious past of naked national manhood was an especially ironic gesture because in the period to which it refers Willis and Forrest were in fact publicly and even violently opposed to one another. Willis had been briefly allied with Forrest when he had taken the American actor's side in the conflict with the English Shakespearian William Macready that culminated in the Astor Place riot. But in June of 1850 the actor, suspecting that Willis had seduced his wife, Catherine Sinclair Forrest, came upon the author in Washington Square Park and flogged him with a whip. The assault was only the most dramatic gesture in another drama of publicized personalities, which culminated a year and a half later in a sensational divorce trial. Willis was one of eight men who, in a servant's deposition that Forrest himself may have leaked to the press, were alleged to have had affairs with Catherine Forrest; others included the blackface performer George Jamieson, "Samuel Marsden Raymond, a bewhiskered Whig merchant and lawyer subsequently described as 'inclined to fashionable dandyism,' " and Willis's brother Richard. [67]

Willis — with the support of his wife, Cornelia — took the side of Catherine in this scandalous trial, printing defenses of the wife and attacks on the husband in both the *New York Herald*, the paper that had printed the original allegations of adultery, and which throughout the affair sided against "Mr. Nincom Poop Willis," and his own *Home Journal*. [68] From Forrest's point of view Willis's public stand added insult to injury, and it must have fueled his rage. But by most accounts the attack in the park helped turn public opinion against Forrest, especially when Willis's version of events — that he was assaulted, without warning, from behind, and that Forrest's bodyguards prevented others from intervening — held sway in much of the press. For Willis to appear as the wronged man in this incident, he had to portray himself as a passive victim, to take on the effeminate characteristics that his detractors had attributed to him over the years. Baker cites critics who mocked him as "Namby-Pamby Willis" and as "an impersonal passive verb — a pronoun of the feminine gender," noting that even though Willis was two inches taller than Forrest, he was depicted in cartoons and words as "a man *half his size.*" The always slightly sickly Willis was far more frail than the bodybuilding Forrest, but Baker is right to say that "it seems that Willis shrank physically in the estimation of many in part so that his assailant might shrink morally."[69] Edwin Forrest's relentless counterattacks on Willis and his "coterie of male dandies" thus may have fed into the perception that the Washington Square incident was not a fair fight.[70] And when Forrest's lawyer John Van Buren—the son of the former president—repeatedly questioned Willis's manhood in the trial, the judge reprimanded him for such personal remarks, perhaps further damaging his client's case, which he ultimately lost completely.[71]

In associating Forrest with Willis and a set of dandy figures, James clearly conflated what had once been two opposed forms of performative masculinity. His fantasy of his father's friendships with actors and dandies implies that the tensions he explored in his dandy novels were, again, re-solvable only in the past. Interestingly, in James's memoir the anecdote about the naked performer introduces a letter from Henry James Sr. that I cited in Chapter 3 because of its reference to Horatio Alger, another man whose works locate authentic public masculinity in the ideals of republican ideology. Henry Sr. complained that Alger, who was then writing a biog-raphy of Forrest, similarly violated a boundary between public and private by talking all too freely of his dismissal from the ministry for homosexual pederasty, "which," the father commented, "he in fact appears to enjoy as a subject of conversation."[72]

Like the figure of the dandy, this autobiographical anecdote stages, me-diates, and condenses the problematics of theatricality, public masculinity, and personality that I have been discussing. It also locates their origins in the days of Nathaniel P. Willis. Unlike the later "domestic" incarna-tion of his father—and unlike the critics of Willis, including Fanny Fern—James seems to take some pleasure in representing masculinity as theatricalized and performative, even if such masculinity is represented as problematic, contradictory, almost impossible, as tenuous as a man walk-ing on his hands, which he calls "an extraordinary performance if kept up for more than a second or two."[73] Both the memoir and the novels betray a desire for a different performance or representation of manhood, evincing that desire as a nostalgia for an earlier form of masculinity overlaid with a homoeroticism and aestheticism that both seem rooted in literary and sexual-political discourses of the later part of the century. For James, masculinity verges on a palpably queer theatricality, though it is traversed by what I can not resist calling performance anxiety. Both the pleasure and the anxiety of this aestheticized masculinity are represented in the unresolved paradoxes of the dandy figure, from Fern's Apollo Hyacinth, through his model, Nathaniel Parker Willis, to James's Hyacinth Robinson.

In 1852, just as the dandy, editor, and poet Nathaniel Parker Willis's assault charges against the virile actor Edwin Forrest were being resolved, a sixteen-year-old Samuel Langhorne Clemens published his first sketch, "The Dandy Frightening the Squatter." The story depicts a fight as thoroughly theatrical—and almost as uneven—as that between Willis and Forrest two years earlier in Washington Square Park and portrays antagonists resembling those adversaries. Set in Hannibal, Missouri, "[a]bout thirteen years ago," the story features "a spruce young dandy, with a killing moustache, &c." who wishes to garner the attention of the female passengers aboard the steamboat on which he is a passenger. Near where the boat is moored, he spies a "tall, brawny woodsman" and decides that if he can frighten this man, it will be most impressive to his audience. The dandy takes up a knife and two pistols and "[t]hus equipped, strode on shore, with an air which seemed to say—'The hopes of a nation depend on me.'" Brandishing the pistols, he threatens the larger man, but the squatter "planted his huge fist directly between the eyes of his astonished antagonist, who, in a moment, was floundering in the turbid waters of the Mississippi."[1]

As one would expect of such a character, the dandy consciously performs his masculinity for an audience, "to bring himself into notice." In an effort to "mak[e] an impression on the hearts of the young ladies on board, he thought he must perform some heroic deed." He displays his ersatz heroism not only in his unprovoked assault, but also by uttering a line drawn, it would appear, from his reading of western stories or novels: "Found you at last, have I? You are the very man I've been looking for these three weeks! Say your prayers! . . . [Y]ou'll make a capital barn door, and I shall drill the keyhole myself!"[2] The humor here, as in many of Twain's early writings, depends on a reversal of expectations; this dandy's performance is entirely unsuccessful. Not only is the squatter physically superior to the dandy, but he bests his assailant by taking up the assailant's own theatrical fiction: "I say, yeou, next time yeou come around drillin' key-holes, don't forget yer old acquaintances!" The squatter's performance entirely wins over his audience, as the last line of the story is "The ladies unanimously voted the knife and pistols to the victor."[3]

I want to make two points about this slight sketch that began Mark Twain's literary career. The first is thematic. Here, as throughout his work, Twain correlates masculine superiority with theatricality; the dandy, contrary to the expectation of his character type, simply does not put on as effective a performance as does the squatter. In the latter character, where one would expect to find simplicity and straightforwardness, perhaps associated with authenticity, there is instead crude but effective wit, a performance that pleases "the ladies." These strains of audience-oriented masculinity persist throughout Twain's works, from the western humor of the "Jumping Frog" sketches through virtually all the characters in a work like *The Adventures of Huckleberry Finn* and even to the later writings. Twain's other successful fictional creation, the Mark Twain persona itself, was also characterized by such performativity. Especially in his most flamboyant phases on the lecture circuit in his all-white suit, Twain bears a close though complex relation to the dandy figure analyzed in Chapter 5.

The second point is literary-historical. Twain published "The Dandy Frightening the Squatter" not in a local Hannibal newspaper, but in the *Carpet-Bag,* a Boston paper edited by Benjamin P. Shillaber. Shillaber's "Ike Partington" tales, which first began to appear in book form in 1854, are credited as major literary sources for Twain's boys and, along with "Peck's Bad Boy," inaugurated the subgenre known as the "bad-boy book."[4] The bad-boy book also has antecedents in the antebellum adventure stories of Ned Buntline, Tom Sawyer's favorite author.[5] This chapter focuses on what might be called the mainstreaming of the bad boy, the period when the more crude and disruptive figure exemplified by Shillaber's and Peck's protagonists was taken up by relatively genteel writers who wrote books of this genre in the last decades of the nineteenth century, including Thomas Bailey Aldrich (*The Story of a Bad Boy,* 1869), Twain (*The Adventures of Tom Sawyer,* 1876), Charles Dudley Warner (*Being a Boy,* 1877), and William Dean Howells (*A Boy's Town,* 1890).[6] In their stories, these writers seem to have wanted to combine what is engaging about each of the figures in Twain's sketch: the flamboyant, audience-oriented performativity of the dandy and the decisive, unambiguous masculinity of the squatter. Like

Henry James in the autobiographical anecdote about his father and Edwin Forrest cited at the end of Chapter 5, these authors located this appealingly hybrid form of masculinity in the past, in their own boyhoods.

Rather than speculating about psychobiographical explanations for this phenomenon, I want to discuss what it implies about shifting understandings of the reading public in the later nineteenth century. The question of *Tom Sawyer*'s audience in particular has been an open one since even before the novel's publication, when Twain and Howells exchanged a series of letters about whether the book should be addressed to boys, to men, or to an unspecified general public. In his preface to the novel, Twain seems to choose the last of these options, writing, "Although my book is intended mainly for the entertainment of boys and girls, I hope it will not be shunned by men and women on that account."[7] Only a few pages later, however, the narrator seems to narrow this open address, remarking that "the reader probably remembers how to [whistle] if he has ever been a boy" (5). Similarly, Twain repeatedly and vociferously denied ever having written a book for boys, claiming to "write for grown-ups who have *been* boys."[8] Contemporary reviewers questioned the sincerity of Twain's claim to address a general audience as well as his desire primarily to address boys and girls. An anonymous writer in the *Athenaeum* quoted the sentence from the preface cited above, musing that "[q]uestions of intention are always difficult to decide. The book . . . does not seem to us calculated to carry out the intention here expressed." And a *New York Times* reviewer wondered parenthetically whether "the book really is intended for boys and girls."[9] The novel's ambiguity of address structured virtually every public response to it in its time.

Critics generally have attempted either to resolve this ambiguity, usually by designating *Tom Sawyer* a boys' book—as opposed to *The Adventures of Huckleberry Finn,* which they claim is clearly written for adults—or to assert that the earlier book's ambiguity of address is a mark of its failure, again in contrast with the clear and consistent voice of *Huck Finn.*[10] But *Tom Sawyer*'s ambiguity is no accident; it is typical of the bad-boy genre and was explicitly planned by Twain and Howells. Twain came to conceive of *Tom Sawyer* in these terms shortly before finishing the book's final draft, taking up the idea that the novel's address to boys could function in part as a lure for adult readers. In July 1875 he had insisted in a letter to Howells that the novel "is *not* a boy's book, at all. It will only be read by adults. It is only written for adults." But by November he acceded to Howells's suggestion that he address adult readers by pretending to write for children. "I think you ought to treat it explicitly *as* a boy's story," Howells wrote, because "[g]rown-ups will enjoy it just as much if you do." Two days later, Twain acquiesced, writing back that "Mrs. Clemens decides with you that the book should issue as a book for boys, pure & simple—& so do I."[11]

This ambivalent logic is played out in other examples of the genre as well. Howells's *A Boy's Town,* for instance, was originally published in a children's magazine and in its book form retained the subtitle *Described for "Harper's Young People."* These facts, as well as Howells's reference on the first page to "the boys who read *Harper's Young People,*" indicate an intended audience of boys. But the same sentence includes a knowing jibe at other boy books; Howells states that his book contains "no very exciting adventures or thread-bare escapes; perhaps I mean hair breadth escapes; but it is the same thing—they have been used so often."[12] Similar knowing jokes throughout the book, combined with the fact that its style and tone are obviously designed to appeal to nostalgic older men, indicate that Howells still believed his claim, made fourteen years earlier, that an adult audience could be constituted through an overt address to boys. The novels' overt address to boys functions as a lure for "grown-ups who have *been* boys," interpellating men without quite naming them. Instead of directly addressing adult men, the books systematically produce and exploit ambiguities about the gender and age of their audience, nonetheless presuming that their readers are capable of enjoying certain kinds of identifications with a boy.

Throughout this book I have been using Louis Althusser's term "interpellation" to designate the modes of address that constitute a subject precisely by making it identify itself *as* the subject that is being addressed while simultaneously making it identify *with* a represented subject position that it (mis)recognizes as its own.[13] Thus a genre, such as the sentimental novel, that addresses its audience as gendered subjects helps to reinscribe in each reader's subjectivity his or her status as a gendered subject. The bad-boy book complicates this model, interpellating readers as men by addressing them as boys.[14] The genre, as we will see, stages and restages a crisis of masculinity, offering as a pleasurable point of identification a figure who apparently puts into question culturally valorized masculine ideals like individuality, autonomy, and self-possession. The goal of this chapter, then, is twofold. First, I will work through the logic of such identification, analyzing how a genre could address nineteenth-century men by telling them "a boy's story." We will see that the forms of identification modeled in the bad-boy book reinscribe the masculine character of the public sphere, even though they represent the relation between masculinity and publicity quite differently than did antebellum writers concerned with such a relation, such as the temperance authors discussed in Chapter 1 or the black nationalist authors in Chapter 2. By the end of the chapter I will also argue that this identification with a boy—a figure both the same as and different from an adult male reader—functions as an interpellation of a heterosexualized masculine subject, thereby emphasizing as well the heteronormativity of the public sphere.

Masculinity and Identification

We have seen that in nineteenth-century writings on the moral and psychological effects of reading, as well as in fiction itself, readerly identification was largely conceived of through the sentimental discourse of sympathy. Sympathy was defined as an ostensibly selfless or other-oriented affective bond between reader and text, a bond that was exemplified and modeled for the reader in the intensely emotional cathexes between characters depicted in much women's fiction, for instance.[15] Sympathy was not consistently conceived of as an exclusively female form of affect, but in this period it almost always had at least some feminizing connotations. Didactic fiction for boys was especially liable to be perceived as feminizing, not only because it was frequently written by women but because it assumed that its readers would identify sympathetically in the same emulative way readers of *The Wide Wide World* did. Horatio Alger's novels, as we have seen, could be said to "emasculate" their readers, despite their emphasis on "frank" and "manly" boys, because they aimed overtly to evoke the reader's sympathy, because they explicitly asked their readers to emulate their characters, and because their street-boy heroes are rewarded morally and financially only when they appear to lose themselves in a sympathetic identification with an even less fortunate boy.[16]

The bad-boy book, in contrast, places an aggressive and aggrandized self at the center of its web of identifications. Tom Sawyer is typical of bad boys in that he takes great pleasure in creating a scene, often planning his pranks and games with what he calls "the theatrical gorgeousness of the thing" in mind (116). Tom is particularly skilled at transforming others—sometimes his gang of boys, sometimes the whole town—into spectators of his adventures, an audience for his theatrical spectacles.[17] All the world may not be a stage for Tom, but often the entire public sphere is a theater. For example, when he rises in the courtroom to reveal the true murderer of Dr. Robinson, his listeners are spellbound: "Tom began—hesitatingly at first, but as he warmed to his subject his words flowed more and more easily; in a little while every sound ceased but his own voice; every eye fixed itself upon him; with parted lips and bated breath the audience hung upon his words, taking no note of time, rapt in the ghastly fascinations of the tale. The strain upon pent emotion reached its climax when the boy said . . ." (172).

When Tom here describes the murder he witnessed, as when he tells the story of his and Becky's ordeals in the cave or his discovery of a treasure, the reader—who already knows the events of the story—is in a position to identify simultaneously with Tom's cognitive ascendance over his audience and that diegetic audience's absorption in the narration of his tale. This form of identification, based in a combination of knowledge and disavowal, is not unique; it characterizes, for instance, the detective genre that Twain both used and burlesqued in *Huckleberry Finn, Tom Sawyer, Detective,* and *Pudd'nhead Wilson*.[18] The story's hermeneutic enigma is unfolded simultaneously through narration and performance, and readers enjoy the epistemological pleasures of both narrative forms at once.

Tom's triumphantly theatrical scenes always revolve around a dramatic *self*-display, as when he seems to return from the grave to the applause of the entire town, for example. This tendency is not characteristic only of Tom's personality, however. Early in the novel, when Judge Thatcher visits the Sunday school classroom, Tom may be (temporarily) the most successful performer in the room when, to everyone's surprise, he presents to the superintendent the tickets that signal that he has memorized a thousand verses of scripture, entitling him to the prize of a forty-cent Bible. But he is not the only performer; Twain emphasizes that everyone in the room was "showing off," putting those two words in quotation marks seven times in one paragraph. In this scene, every individual is simultaneously performer and audience; even the instigator of the special occasion, the judge himself, "warmed himself in the sun of his own grandeur—for he was 'showing off,' too" (34).

All the bad-boy books presume that this audience-orientation is an aspect of everyone's personality, and especially of the character of boys. But while it is clear that these boys' most prominent trait is their desire to attract attention to themselves, it is difficult to provide a positive description of the "self" Tom Sawyer or any other bad-boy protagonist possesses. The books assert far more emphatically what a boy is *not*, and what a boy does *not* do. A "real boy," Howells says in *A Boy's Town*, has no love for flowers, never appears in the parlor when his mother has company, nor, most important, does he feel or express sympathy. These are all traits of girls, or worse, what he calls "girl-boys." Sympathy differentiates girls from boys and makes the former inappropriate interpreters of spectacles like the make-believe circus put on by the boys in Howells's book. "[E]ven as spectators [girls] were a little *too* despicable," he writes, "they did not know anything; they had no sense; if a fellow got hurt they cried."[19] Sympathetic identification induced by the display or depiction of suffering, characteristic of women's sentimental novels and didactic children's fiction, is anathema to a "real boy." Instead, "if another boy gets hurt they laugh, because it is funny to see him hop or hear him yell."[20]

Boys, then, respond to fiction (and theatrical performances) in exactly the opposite way from girls. When girls cry, boys laugh; when girls invest themselves emotionally, boys distance themselves. This opposition is quite rigorous, leading Howells to assert that boys are largely incapable of any emotional version of friendship, of any affective connection even to the other boys who inhabit the semiautonomous Boy's Town: "I very much doubt whether small boys understand friendship, or can feel it as they do afterwards, in its tenderness and unselfishness."[21] Warner remarks somewhat sarcastically that the attachments formed in boyhood are "fervent, if not enduring," but he never describes a close friendship between the protagonist of *Being a Boy* and another boy.[22]

Lacking the capacity for friendship, incessantly disavowing any desire to sympathize with others, boys appear to be atavistically presocial in these books. Indeed, judging by his statements in *A Boy's Town*, Howells's concept of "boy-nature" is equivalent to "savagery," and the "world" boys inhabit resembles nothing more than a state of precivilization.[23] "Everywhere and always the world of boys is outside of the laws that govern grown-up communities," Howells says; a boy obeys his world's unwritten laws "instinctively," like "the far-off savages from whom his customs seem mostly to have come."[24] Charles Dudley Warner seems to have agreed, stating that "[e]very boy who is good for anything is a natural savage."[25]

Boys' "savagery" and apparent presocial nature are means by which their world and their character are differentiated from the domestic and feminizing space depicted in sentimental novels and didactic boys' fiction. As in Henry James's *Speech and Manners of American Women,* cited in Chapter 5, the social field has been thoroughly feminized in the bad-boy books. It is women in general, and mothers in particular, who limit boys' fantasies and threaten to suppress their savagery, to "sivilize" them, as Huck Finn says. The boy's freedom is not noticeably constrained by the patriarchal authority of a father figure like Captain Nutter in Aldrich's *Story of a Bad Boy,* who responds to the boy's wildness by reminiscing about his own boyhood. Rather, as Howells says, "[t]he mother represented the family sovereignty."[26] Howells's later boy book, *The Flight of Pony Baker,* consists entirely of a set of reasons why the young boy Pony is justified in running away from home to join a mythical tribe of Indians, listing the many enjoyable things that Pony's overprotective mother proscribed, such as swimming in the pond all day and owning a gun.[27] Other boy books also envisioned an escape to "savagery" as an alternative to domesticity; Twain's own unfinished *Huck Finn and Tom Sawyer among the Indians* (1884) is similarly framed.[28]

It is, of course, not surprising that boys' responses and reading practices were defined in opposition to those of girls. But in the bad-boy book boys are just as emphatically opposed to men. While these books define the "savagery" of boy-nature in opposition to feminine domesticity, sentimentality, and sympathy, they also parody the valorization of reading as virtuous publicity characteristic of books like Alger's. Unlike the Alger boy, who thinks of literacy as a sign of virtue, Tom Sawyer wants to think of it as an instrumental skill, the value of which can be judged by its consequences rather than its reflection of the boy's moral qualities. Hence Tom expresses no interest in the reading and memorization exercises of his Sunday school until he conceives of the desire to impress Becky Thatcher. Then he trades in the yellow tickets that are meant to signify literate accomplishment but actually represent his profits from tricking his friends into whitewashing a fence. In exchange for his supposed reading, he receives Becky's admiration as well as a Bible, although the latter is withdrawn when his fraud is uncovered. Far more consciously and deliberately than the Alger boy, Tom Sawyer uses the apparent virtue of literacy for personal profit.

Like all the humor in the novel, the parody of Alger's virtuous publicity cuts both ways. For instance, when Tom tries to recite Patrick Henry's "Give me liberty or give me death" speech at a school assembly—an oration that would have given Alger an opportunity to associate literacy, republican virtue, and public performance [29] — he is "seized" by a "ghastly stage-fright" and unable to continue. Once again, Tom's performativity, which seems designed to demonstrate his self-possession, serves equally to illustrate its limits.

The bad boy seems systematically to negate the traits valued in nineteenth-century advice books for boys and young men, including individuality, autonomy, and self-possession.[30] Boys in these books even lack any meaningful distinctiveness; as Howells says, "All boys are a good deal alike."[31] The protagonist of Charles Dudley Warner's *Being a Boy,* for example, is continually described as "typical" and "normal." Warner writes in his preface that "[t]here was no attempt at the biography of any particular boy; the experiences given were common to the boyhood of the time and place."[32] The photographs in one edition, approved by Warner, depict events that happen to a boy named John in the narrative, but they are quite clearly not all pictures of the same boy. They, like the book's title, underscore that the book's subject is not John's particularity but his typicality, what Howells and Warner both refer to as "the nature of boys," "boy-nature," or "the boy-mind."

Twain declares in *Tom Sawyer*'s preface that Tom "is a combination of the characteristics of three boys whom I knew, and therefore belongs to the composite order of architecture" (xvii).[33] At first glance this seems an innocuous statement of a realistic writer's method of constructing a character, representing a typical but still individualized identity made up of diverse "characteristics." The phrase is part of the novel's claim to verisimilitude — "Huck Finn is drawn from life; Tom Sawyer also, but not from an individual" — and is thus consistent with the bad-boy book's claim to represent the reality of boyhood. As Howells wrote in his review of the first prominent example of the genre, Thomas Bailey Aldrich's *Story of a Bad Boy,* the bad-boy book's realism is its distinguishing characteristic. "No one else seems to have thought of telling the story of a boy's life, with so great desire to show what a boy's life is, and so little purpose of teaching what it should be."[34] And Aldrich himself claims to have invented the term "bad boy" as a synonym for "real boy" in order to "distinguish myself from those faultless young gentlemen who generally figure in narratives of this kind."[35] But in *A Boy's Town* Howells raises the possibility that a real boy *is* a "composite" or plural subject, and that the subject's origin in multiplicity may not culminate in a larger unity:

Every boy is two or three boys, or twenty or thirty different kinds of boys in one; he is all the time living many lives and forming many characters; but it is a good thing if he can keep one life and one character when he gets to be a man. He may turn out to be like an onion when he is grown up, and be nothing but hulls, that you keep peeling off, one after another, till you think you have got down to the heart, at last, and then you have got down to nothing. . . . All the boys may have been like my boy in the Boy's Town, in having each an inward being that was not the least like their outward being, but that somehow seemed to be their real self, whether it truly was so or not.[36]

The constitutive multiplicity of boyhood character and the contingency of the boy's accession to adulthood are quite startling in this passage. It is perhaps as peculiar an understanding of individual subjectivity as is Paul Fane's "favorite theory," cited in Chapter 5, "of two or more souls inhabiting one body," and it raises many of the same issues. A boy, for Howells, is not a singular and distinct individual; he is an agglomeration of "many characters," of "twenty or thirty" other boys. "To be a man" consists in the ability to condense this multiplicity into "one life and one character." The attainment of such coherence and singularity is "a good thing," but the nostalgic tone of *A Boy's Town* and the image of some men as hollow sets of "hulls" makes the path to adult masculinity seem a complex, risky, and possibly fraudulent process and portrays manhood as an only partly desirable state. Even the assertion that a boy's veiled "inward being" is his "real self" is qualified by the phrase "somehow seemed," and this qualification is underscored when the final phrase questions the "truth" of this "real self." Distinctions between singularity and multiplicity, particularity and generality, interiority and exterior appearance are apparently foreign to "the nature of boys," even though nineteenth-century advice for young men usually assumed that these same distinctions are essential for the bourgeois individual's participation in contractual exchange and the masculine public sphere.[37]

This image of manhood as plural and radically contingent is evidence of conflicting tendencies in the male subjectivity imagined and addressed by the bad-boy book. On the one hand, the reader is encouraged to desire the self-mastery and theatricality figured in Tom's most dramatic scenes, when he is able to manipulate the entire town of St. Petersburg into enthusiastic participation in his own spectacles. At the same time, the reader is expected to take vicarious pleasure in the boy's freedom from the ego constraints of masculine individuality. The boy's appeal to a reader is also a source of anxiety, however, for the risk—and pleasure—of identifying with a boy is that in asserting an analogy or coincidence with such a multiple and fragmented figure, the reader may give up his own sense of singularity, coherence, and self-possession. Howells's figure of failed adult masculinity, the set of "hulls" with nothing at the center, sets out concisely the poles between which the bad-boy book's reader is meant to situate himself: masculine character may be an irreducible multiplicity or it may be no character at all. Howells acknowledges that the transcendence of this opposition may never occur, that the ideals of unity and coherent self-possession are always in tension with the fantasies of multiplicity and fluid subjectivity associated with boyhood.

Even Tom Sawyer's most attractive and seemingly masterful characteristic—his theatricality—has as its most common subtext a radical threat to his individuality. Tom repeatedly imagines how theatrically effective his own death would be as a way of attracting attention to himself. Each time he stages or fantasizes a death or disappearance he transforms the arousal of sympathy into a form of mastery and even violent revenge. After Aunt Polly has punished him unjustly, "he pictured himself lying sick unto death and his aunt bending over him beseeching one little forgiving word, but he would turn his face to the wall, and die with that word unsaid. Ah, how would she feel then?" (23). He wants to display his mastery over an audience by evoking its sympathy: "[S]he would be sorry some day—maybe when it was too late," he thinks when Becky rejects him (64). However, like Eva in *Uncle Tom's Cabin* or any other dying sentimental heroine, he exerts his power most effectively through a theatricalization of his own self-negation. Twain expresses the paradox of Tom's position succinctly when he writes, "Ah, if he could only die *temporarily*" (64).

Although Tom's death fantasies are usually planned as manipulative and masterful hoaxes, they have a peculiar tendency to turn back on themselves, to transform him into the tearful, sentimental spectator he means to produce. Tom's theatricalized subjectivity is especially narcissistic because it is based in a sympathetic identification in which he has colonized both roles, switching from suffering hero(ine) to sympathetic spectator at a moment's notice, oscillating between affectively absorbed audience and masterful male performer.[38] In fact, he is often the most sympathetic spectator of his own performances. Fantasizing his own death, "[h]e so worked upon his feelings with the pathos of these dreams that he had to keep swallowing, he was so like to choke; and his eyes swam in a blur of water" (22–23). And the image of Becky discovering his death "brought such an agony of pleasurable suffering that he worked it over and over again in his mind and set it up in new and varied lights till he worked it threadbare" (24). As he hides under Aunt Polly's bed, watching the scene of mourning he has created by running away to Jackson's Island, his emotions reach a climax: "Tom was snuffling, now, himself—and more in pity of himself than anybody else" (116). Although he is tempted to relieve his aunt's agony by coming out from under the bed—"and the theatrical gorgeousness of the thing appealed strongly to his nature"—he prefers the form of theatricality he has planned, the dramatic appearance at his own funeral service, so he "resisted and lay still" (116–17).

Whereas at some moments it is clear that Tom wishes to "die temporarily" as the ultimate expression of his power over his audience, at others his death drive appears as a result of having no audience to perform for. He expresses this wish in the few scenes in which he is entirely solitary, cut off from his domestic life by his aunt's punishment, from his romantic life by Becky's whims, and from his male friends by his own melancholy. "He wandered far from the accustomed haunts of boys, and sought desolate places that were in harmony with his spirit" (23). For Tom, whose very identity depends on his being the center of attention, solitude brings out a potentially fatal form of his constitutive theatricality. He sits by the river, "wishing, all the while, that he could only be drowned, all at once and unconsciously, without undergoing the uncomfortable routine devised by nature.... He wondered if *she* [Becky] would pity him if she knew? Would she cry, and wish that she had a right to put her arms around his neck and comfort him? Or would she turn coldly away like all the hollow world? ... At last he rose up sighing, and departed in the darkness" (24).

Both the sentimental death scene and Tom's imaginary reworkings of it rely on the assumption that a female "audience"—in this case, both Becky and Aunt Polly—responds sympathetically. Tom is even able to confirm this when he sneaks back to his aunt's house to observe the women family members grieving and his cousin Sid's envy. But Tom's audience is never only female, for one aim of his fantasy is to separate him from the feminized private sphere epitomized by the deathbed scene. While he hides under Aunt Polly's bed to observe her mourning, the theatricality of his own position is evident only to himself and the novel's readers; the women in the scene are excluded from the audience. This passage does more than mock the sentimental death scene; it rewrites the conventions by excluding women (and the "good boy" figure, Sid) from the web of identifications that characterizes it. Whereas the sentimental reader is positioned as a sympathetic spectator to the angelic character's death, identified as much with the sinners gathered around her bed as with the dying girl herself, Twain's reader is positioned under the bed with Tom, sharing his cognitive and affective ascendance over his female audience and even the almost supernatural ability to enjoy his own mourning and funeral.

In identifying with Tom's desire to die "temporarily," with a consciously theatricalized sympathy, Twain's audience is again differentiated from a sympathetic, feminine readership. Instead of disavowing the theatricality of Tom's position, Twain underscores it, figuring the character's position—and, by extension, the identifying reader's—as an active, masterful performer rather than a passive, affective spectator. Tom's theatricality always seems to entail his own absorption in the scenario he has constructed. Indeed, the oscillation between theatricality and absorption, "agony" and "pleasurable suffering," sympathy and distance, performer and spectator is Tom's defining characteristic; it motivates his actions and drives the novel's plot. The anxiety at the center of the genre is, then, the possibility that an identification with a protagonist whose masculinity and individuality are always destabilized by self-absorption might destabilize the masculinity and individuality of the reader as well.

Like the sentimental novel, which registers nineteenth-century limits of female individuality in its recurrent images of death and self-effacement, the bad-boy book's model of theatricalized masculine individuality is predicated on self-negation.[39] Even as the boy's theatrical self-mastery is asserted, he repeatedly fantasizes his own nonexistence, wallowing in perversely pleasurable fantasies of death and disappearance that are apparently designed to place him back at the center of attention. In his death fantasies, Tom's desire is to enact the same kind of sympathetic identification that sentimental death scenes evoke in women's fiction. Tom's performances of sympathy are strikingly effective; they produce tears and forgiveness from his Aunt Polly, and often a wider adulation from the rest of St. Petersburg. But the fluidity and reversibility of roles in a scene like this one—the way death turns into life, performer into spectator, activity into immobility, sadism into masochism—entail the possibility that his fake death will become a real loss of individuality, that Tom will become the sentimental heroine and/or reader whose role is so often parodied in Twain's fiction. In the process of mastering his audience, he risks losing himself in his own performance.

A Bad Boy and Others; or, Masculine Self-Possession

What does it mean to identify with such a boy, to experience an affective analogy or coincidence with someone whose masculinity and individuality seem always to be in crisis? Variants of this question helped motivate the explosion in the 1870s of articles and conferences on the reading of boys and young men, a discourse that almost replaced the worries over women's reading that had pervaded literary criticism in the first half of the century.[40] In Chapter 3 I discussed some of these debates as they pertained to Horatio Alger's fiction and the question of whether it should properly take a place in the public library. There, though, I analyzed them primarily as debates about the shape of the public sphere; here I will look at them as debates about theories of identification, about how readers, boys in particular, affectively insert themselves in what they read. It is worth reiterating, however, that one point of this book is that debates about the public sphere and debates about theories of identification are almost always closely linked, that one debate often turns into the other. Those cultural arbiters for whom so much was at stake in such an apparently marginal activity as the reading of boys believed something that Habermas argues in *The Structural Transformation of the Public Sphere*. For them, as for Habermas, fiction plays a role in creating a public sphere by modeling forms of identification that constitute the potential citizen's character as public. Despite—or actually because of—the novel's generic concern with psychological interiority, intimacy, domesticity, and privacy, novels work to constitute audience-oriented subjectivity.[41]

Perhaps no subgenre was more aware of its own role in creating such public personality than the bad-boy book, which after all took as its project the explanation of how mischievous, self-absorbed, often criminal "bad boys" could grow up to be respectable public and cultural figures like William Dean Howells and Charles Dudley Warner. So, before looking at contemporary criticism of bad-boy books and the identifications they figure and provoke, it is important to note that the novels themselves often revolve around the question of readerly identification. Literary bad boys are themselves constituted by what they read. As Lionel Trilling has observed, Tom Sawyer's mind has "literary furnishings"; he is constructed out of the texts he encounters:[42] the *Arabian Nights, Don Quixote,* sensational boys' adventure stories by popular authors like Ned Buntline, and other sources.[43] The "composite architecture" of boyhood is apparently built of books.

The protagonists of Howells's *A Boy's Town* and Charles Dudley Warner's *Being a Boy* are similarly attached to fiction. Howells asserts that even a boy's "inward being" comes from his reading: "While he was joyfully sharing the wild sports and conforming to the savage usages of the boy's world about him, he was dwelling in a wholly different world within him, whose wonders no one else knew. . . . It was all vague and vast, and it came out of the books that he read, and that filled his soul with their witchery."[44] By Howells's account, "the nature of boys" includes an unquenchable desire to apply what they have read to their lives. In his *Atlantic* review of *Tom Sawyer* he remarks approvingly that "though every boy has wild and fantastic dreams, this boy cannot rest till he has somehow realized them."[45] He argues that this relation to fiction or fantasy, though somewhat extreme in Tom's case, is typical of "the boy-mind." As if to prove his own point, fourteen years later Howells again used the word "realize" to describe his own bad boy, who "was not different from other boys in his desire to localize, to realize, what he read."[46]

Boys in these texts clearly invest themselves quite intensely in the fiction they consume. Howells describes his boy's affective investment in his reading as constituting what little interiority his character possesses—"the world within him"—as well as his "outward" behavior. Referring to the exotic stories his protagonist is fond of reading, Howells says: "He was always contriving in fancy scenes and encounters of the greatest splendor, in which he bore a chief part. Inwardly he was all thrones, principalities, and powers, the foe of tyrants, the friend of good emperors. . . . [O]utwardly he was an incorrigible little sloven, who suffered in all social exigencies from the direst bashfulness, and wished nothing so much as to shrink out of the sight of men if they spoke to him."[47] It is a boy's nature, Howells asserts, to assimilate what he reads into his subjectivity, "inwardly" to become the protagonist of a book, a play, a story. Howells, like other writers of the time, represented boys' reading as a form of incorporation, an almost literal absorption into and of the book and its protagonist.[48]

The effects of such reading are, for these fictional boys, unstable. A boy's character is constituted by his incorporations, by the "thrones, principalities, and powers" that make up his "inward" self. At the same time, it is the multiplicity of these identifications that makes it difficult and perhaps even undesirable to consolidate the "many lives" and "many characters" of boyhood into the "one life and one character" of manhood. Even more than the "absorbent" eponymous protagonist of Willis's *Paul Fane,* the bad boy exhibits a paradoxically public form of interiority. His incorporative nature inverts the normative masculine relation to the public realm; his virtuousness, heroic nature, and publicness are entirely "inward" characteristics, while "outwardly" he wishes to "shrink out of the sight of men." And without his compulsion to identify, the boy ceases to exist. As Howells writes, "I dare say this was not quite a wholesome frame of mind for a boy of ten years; but I do not defend it; I only portray it.... At any rate, it was a phase of being that could not have been prevented without literally destroying him."[49] Even though the boy's drive to identify disrupts the putative singularity of male subjectivity, its absence is equated with the effacement of the self.

The precariousness and ambiguous moral valence of this figuration of reading and subjectivity are nowhere more evident than in the writings of another adult reader of bad-boy books, the moral crusader and professional censor Anthony Comstock.[50] Comstock's 1883 book *Traps for the Young* is a compendium of evils threatening to seduce nineteenth-century youth from the path of virtue, including bad-boy books and adventure fiction for boys.[51] From its first paragraph, *Traps for the Young* conceives of readerly subjectivity through a confused but relentless metaphorics of assimilation and absorption. "Each birth begins a history," Comstock announces in the book's first sentence, and he makes clear that this history is a written one. "The pages are filled out, one by one, by the records of daily life. The mind is the source of action. Thoughts are the aliment upon which it feeds. We assimilate what we read. The pages of printed matter become our companions. Memory unites them indissolubly, so that, unlike an enemy, we cannot get away from them."[52]

For Comstock, you are what you read. A boy *is* a book, and his "companions" are so fully incorporated into himself that they can be described as the "pages" of his own book.[53] The language of the passage—"the aliment upon which it feeds," "we assimilate what we read"—metaphorizes both reading and intersubjective relations in general as forms of incorporation.

As we have seen, this is not an uncommon way to represent the reader's relation to a text; Comstock could have drawn it from the novels themselves as easily as from the Lockean tabula rasa rhetoric he is obviously deploying. But his equation of book and reader makes this textual absorption curiously reciprocal, as if there were no difference between the "pages" of the individual's "daily life," the "pages" that represent other people, and the "pages of printed matter" that he or she reads. For Comstock, inherent in the process of reading is the possibility that the distinctions between self and other, text and reader, experiential history and fictional story will be ambiguated. This blurring of boundaries, he makes clear, is what makes it essential to control what children read, and what makes the unconstrained drive to identify so dangerous in bad-boy books.

In Comstock's theory of reading, these incorporative identifications absorb readers into a fictional "world," thus threatening to lure a boy away from the direct path to an ideally singular, coherent, and morally upright manhood. This absorption and consequent de-individuation is figured in Comstock's writing as the transformation of bonds between boys and books into bonds between boys and other boys. In short, absorbed boy readers are incorporated into gangs. *Traps for the Young* is filled with stories of and interviews with young criminals who cite bad-boy books and sensational story-papers as the inspiration for their formation of "gangs of boy bandits." "[C]lassical literature," explains one boy, "didn't seem to belong to my real life, but these stories did." This boy—the son of a judge, and therefore presumed to be well read—attributes his life of crime to his identification with the heroes of these stories: "They were boys like myself who did these wonderful things . . . and they lived in a world like ours."[54]

These boys' minds, like Tom Sawyer's, have "literary furnishings." In fact, the writers of bad-boy books seem to share Comstock's assumption that boys' absorption in their reading leads to the formation of criminal, or at least mischievous, gangs. The narrative structure of the main anecdotes in *The Adventures of Tom Sawyer* is virtually identical to that of Comstock's cautionary anecdotes, and the books' accounts of the consequences of reading are strikingly similar as well. Whatever Tom reads—boys' adventure stories, *Don Quixote,* or history books—he interprets as a model for action, and his first step in "realizing" what he reads is always to reconstitute "Tom Sawyer's Gang."[55] "[O]f course there's got to be a Gang," he exclaims, "or else there wouldn't be any style about it" (243). In the course of Tom's adventures, his gang becomes pirates, holy crusaders, treasure hunters, conspirators, abolitionists, and other unsavory imaginary groups. The identities of bad-boy protagonists are always inextricably tied to their membership in groups like the gang in Aldrich's novel, the "Rivermouth Centipedes," as if a boy's central fantasy were to see himself as one of the legs of a single organism.

Of course, Comstock condemns the gangs he depicts, while bad-boy books revel in them. But both discourses recognize the seductiveness of gang-formation as essential to the popular pleasures of reading. For Comstock, the gang draws a boy away from honesty and public virtue. This is precisely the appeal of the gang for the bad-boy hero and his reader; it initiates him into an all-male world in which boys can constitute their own identities, write their own "pages," without the constraints of adult, properly public masculinity.[56] At the beginning of *The Story of a Bad Boy,* Tom Bailey is extremely anxious about his social standing in the new town he has moved to, but his acceptance into a secret club indicates that he has achieved a newly stable position. The pleasures of being a part of Tom's gang of robbers are even enough to motivate Huck Finn to submit to the Widow Douglas's confining care at the end of *Tom Sawyer.* "Well," he says, "I'll go back to the widder for a month and tackle it and see if I can come to stand it, if you'll let me b'long to the gang, Tom" (259).

The idea that boyhood mischief could be linked to respectable public manhood was by no means a new one in the late nineteenth century. Early in Benjamin Franklin's *Autobiography* he describes an incident that "shows an early projecting public Spirit, tho' not then justly conducted," in which he and some other boys steal some stones from a building site to make into a wharf in a nearby salt marsh. What seems to me to be different in the bad-boy book is the way it offers the homosocial identification of the gang as an end in itself, without the external "projecting public spirit" materialized and metaphorized by Franklin's wharf. In this genre, the boy's identity is presented as most complete when he has become part of a gang. The book's reader is invited to join as well, to participate in a homosocial identification. Howells explicitly interpellates his reader with this offer: "[T]he reader can be a boy with him there on the intimate terms which are the only terms of true friendship."[57] In the bad-boy book as well as in the discourses condemning it, both the pleasure and the danger of identifying with a boy derive from the multiplicity and unfixity of the unstable object of that identification. A reader who is not necessarily a boy can "be a boy with" the protagonist, who is himself made up of "twenty or thirty" boys. The gang, then, can represent both the source and the result of that multiplicity. The pleasure of "being a boy" is to negate, or at least defer, the reduction to "one life and one character." And the pleasures of reading the bad-boy book lie in the fantasy of accompanying the protagonist in this simultaneous self-negation and self-constitution. I use the word "pleasure" here with every intention of evoking its erotic connotations, for in the bad-boy book identification is significantly sexualized. The genre represents masculinity as a pleasurable form of self-possession, defined in direct and explicit opposition to the self-negation of feminine sympathy. The bad-boy book's characteristic form of identification is just as powerfully gendered as sentimental sympathy, but in the process reading is linked to sexuality.

I am not claiming that bad-boy books are erotic because they detail the romantic agonies of boys as young as eight, nor because they depict the homoerotic relations Leslie Fiedler has analyzed in *The Adventures of Huckleberry Finn*.[58] Rather, the genre works to address a masculine readership through the sexual identifications it figures and provokes. One scene in *The Adventures of Tom Sawyer* may illustrate this point. At the beginning of chapter 20, Tom Sawyer attempts to apologize to Becky Thatcher for an early hostile act but is haughtily spurned. Tom's wish for reconciliation is quickly transformed into a desire that combines and equates violence and a gender reversal: he "moped into the school-yard wishing she were a boy, and imagining how he would trounce her if she were" (148). A few minutes later, he returns to the classroom, surprising Becky in the act of stealing a peek at the book that the schoolmaster pores over every day. This book, for the children, contains an inaccessible but fascinating secret: "Every boy and girl had a theory about the nature of that book; but no two theories were alike, and there was no way of getting at the facts in the case" (148). Twain's phrasing here recalls Freud's account of children's attempts to discern the secrets of sexual difference and reproduction, and this is exactly what the book contains: it is a book of anatomy, featuring "a handsomely engraved and colored frontispiece—a human figure, stark naked" (148).[59]

Becky, for whom "the title-page—Professor somebody's 'Anatomy'" means nothing, opens to the image of the naked body just as Tom looks over her shoulder. For a brief, disruptive moment, an act of reading is shared by both genders on equal terms—something that rarely happens in nineteenth-century American fiction. And what they read together is an image that could only have been perceived by Twain's readers as sexual; indeed, Howells and Twain's wife, Olivia Clemens, convinced Twain to censor this scene because of its sexual connotations.[60] Tom "caught a glimpse of the picture," and in her attempt to conceal it from him Becky "had the hard luck to tear the pictured page half down the middle" (149).

What follows is a drama simultaneously sexual, visual, epistemological, and interpretive. In tears, Becky scolds Tom for "sneak[ing] up on a person and look[ing] at what they're looking at," while Tom retorts, "How could *I* know you was looking at anything?" Becky tries to assert her superior knowledge—she has seen another boy spill ink on Tom's spelling book, which is sure to get Tom punished—by responding "*I* know something that's going to happen. You just wait and you'll see!" Each child then goes on to fantasize about the punishment the other will receive, a "licking" from the schoolmaster. Tom goes on to imagine the scene of Becky's discovery and punishment in some detail, but his initial sadistic pleasure in the idea of Becky being whipped is contaminated by an involuntary sympathy: "Considering all things, he did not want to pity her, and yet it was all he could do to help it. He could get up no exultation that was really worthy of the name" (149). Then, after the teacher's discovery of the torn illustration, Tom falsely but heroically claims responsibility, drawing upon himself his second whipping that day in order to prevent Becky from having to endure the first "licking" of her life. Identification has turned a desire into its opposite, transforming a sadistic fantasy into a masochistic reality, in which Tom undergoes what Twain refers to as "pleasurable suffering." The most immediate consequence of Tom's selfless act is the revival of Becky's affections for him; in fact, she does not spurn him again for the rest of the book. But the price of this affection is a temporary and painful loss of self. Tom's substitution of his own body for that of a girl leads to both a literal and a figurative violation of his bodily integrity, as he "gather[s] his dismembered faculties" and receives "the most merciless flaying that even Mr. Dobbins had ever administered" (152). The sexual ambiguity of the act of reading and the moral ambiguity of Tom's "heroic lie" lead to an act of extreme violence, as if the teacher's role were to enforce the gender difference pictured in the anatomy book.

What is most interesting about this scene is the way it constructs a connection between sexuality, reading, and a fluidity of gender roles resulting from an act of male sympathy. An act of reading shared by both sexes—looking at an image of a naked body whose gender is never specified—leads to an act of male homosocial violence that itself borders on the erotic; the master "seemed to take a vindictive pleasure" in whipping the boy, and Tom is "dismembered" by the punishment. Like so much else in the novel, however, this scene serves to constitute Tom's masculinity. The effects of the schoolmaster's acts are precisely the opposite of their intentions; the adult man's "vindictive pleasure" transforms Tom's transgressions into virtues, and the boy's "dismemberment" leads to his heroization. At the end of the book, Becky's father compares Tom's "noble lie" to George Washington and the cherry tree and offers to send Tom to West Point and law school, thus doubly prefiguring the boy's potential positioning in some of the most masculine sectors of the public sphere.[61] The scene also solidifies the relationship between Tom and Becky; the chapter concludes when Tom falls asleep "with Becky's latest words lingering dreamily in his ear—'Tom, how *could* you be so noble!'" (152).

The contradiction between the homosocial violence of the scene and its heterosexual outcome is only apparent, of course. As Eve Kosofsky Sedgwick and others have argued, homosocial bonds—economic, political, and personal ties between men—are often essential underpinnings for both compulsory heterosexuality and the exclusion of women from power, even when this homosociality is itself an eroticized, violent, or asymmetrical relation of power.[62] Here Sedgwick's point is demonstrated by Tom's almost magical transformation of the power relations in the situation. The master's exertion of power and Tom's violent emasculation ultimately serve to confirm the boy's masculine virtue and to solidify his position in a relationship that it is only slightly anachronistic to call heterosexual. One of the rare moments when the novel represents a normative, moral, discrete masculinity occurs as a direct result of the eroticized disintegration of the boy's body.

Thus the bad-boy book's pleasures rely on an uneasy proximity between masculine individuality and its dissolution, on the almost explicit claim that radical self-loss is the prerequisite for the attainment of normative masculinity. The genre offers several ways of containing the risk that an identification with such an unstable position may lead to a loss of self, of affirming the reader's difference from the character undergoing these experiences while evoking an equivalential identification with him. C. B. Macpherson has aptly described the Lockean model of subjectivity as "possessive individualism," and the novels draw on a rhetoric of possession and self-possession in their characterization of their protagonists. However, it is rarely the boy's own self-possession that is asserted. Howells, for instance, insulates adult male readers from his boy's constitutive instability by figuring the relation between boy and reader as one of ownership. In order to emphasize that the hero of *A Boy's Town* is "merely and exactly an ordinary boy," Howells says early in the book, "For convenience, I shall call this boy, my boy; but I hope he might have been almost anybody's boy."[63] In fact, the character remains nameless throughout the novel; he is never referred to as anything but "my boy."

The epithet posits ownership as the man's relation to his former self, possession as a way of asserting the continuity of manhood with boyhood. But the singularity and self-possession of both men and boys are again problematized by this sentence's qualifications—"I hope he might have been almost anybody's boy"—and by the assertion of ownership between two subjects who are both the same as and different from one another. This dynamic of equivalence and difference—evident as well in the photographs in Warner's *Being a Boy*—is central to the way the genre constitutes and addresses its audience by inducing an identification with a boy. The bad-boy book images a form of masculine identity constituted out of the tension between norms of masculine individuality and boyhood's alleged dissolution of identity. But while this instability and its reiteration produce the pleasures of the genre, the novels' narrative trajectories imply that the tension is unsustainable. In the end, the destabilizing characteristics of boyhood subjectivity are projected onto others. Through this process of projection, bad-boy books transform the multiplicity, contingency, and instability of their male protagonists into a version of the singularity, autonomy, and self-possession that, they assume, their readers have always already possessed.

Becky Thatcher is the screen for such a projection toward the end of *The Adventures of Tom Sawyer*. The chapters in which Becky and Tom are lost in McDougal's cave—the only episode in which adventure plot and romantic plot come together—have as their subtext the projection of all of Tom's fantasies of self-negation onto Becky. While just beforehand the girl has been as active as the boys, playing "'hi-spy' and 'gully-keeper'" with Tom and the others, when they get lost in the darkness Becky suddenly seems to become the dying heroine of a sentimental novel. In what could almost be a direct reference to Eva's death in *Uncle Tom's Cabin,* Becky falls into a peaceful sleep. Tom "sat looking into her drawn face and saw it grow smooth and natural under the influence of pleasant dreams; and by and by a smile dawned and rested there." Tom is inspired by this sight much as Eva's observers are moved by the sight of the "bright, the glorious smile [that] passed over her face" in her last moments,[64] and when Becky awakens she utters a sentence that could have come from Eva: "I've seen such a beautiful country in my dream. I reckon we are going there" (227).

If this projection of Tom's death fantasies were an anomalous incident it might not be very significant. However, it marks the novel's emphatic exclusion of Becky and enables a crucial transformation in Tom. The girl is permanently reduced to a powerless, tearful figure and thoroughly marginalized for the rest of the narrative. Even when Tom tells Becky he has found the way out of the cave, she continues in her role of dying little girl, absorbing both Tom's fears and his death fantasies: "[S]he told him not to fret her with such stuff, for she was tired, and knew she was going to die, and wanted to" (235). The last time we see Becky we are told that she "did not leave her room until Sunday, and then she looked as if she had passed through a wasting illness" (236). The expulsion of Becky from the plot coincides with Tom's acquisition of traits that, though somewhat ironized, still amount to an image of stability, autonomy, and self-possession. At the same moment Tom finds the exit to the cave, he also deduces where the treasure is hidden. This leads to his becoming quite wealthy; it also signals his trajectory toward a public masculinity that may even exceed that of a Horatio Alger protagonist in both its print publicity and its road from rags to riches. Earlier, when Tom was "a glittering hero" for discovering the murderer of Dr. Robinson, "[h]is name even went into immortal print, for the village paper magnified him. There were some that believed he could be President, yet, if he escaped hanging" (173). Now he again appears in print, as "the village paper published biographical sketches" of Tom and Huck. Judge Thatcher praises Tom both for his rescue of his daughter and his earlier lie to the teacher that prevented Becky from getting a whipping, even associating him with republican virtue by comparing this lie with "George Washington's lauded Truth about the hatchet!" (255). Tom never again expresses a desire to die or experience any other feeling of self-loss. Although *The Adventures of Tom Sawyer,* unlike *The Adventures of Huckleberry Finn,* is usually interpreted as lacking an emphasis on a boy's emotional or moral growth, Tom does develop a degree of virtuous publicity and financial and affective autonomy that he lacked earlier in the book. He has become an exemplar of nineteenth-century ideals of middle-class public masculinity and audience-oriented subjectivity.

By projecting Tom's self-negating traits onto Becky and then expunging her from his world, Twain formulates a relatively stable representation of masculine individuality and reasserts conventional representations of gender roles with a vengeance. The boy acquires his individuality and autonomy only when he has definitively rejected the girl. And Twain does more than marginalize Becky from the plot; he incorporates that act of containment and exclusion into the renewed fantasy of "Tom Sawyer's Gang" that serves as the novel's conclusion. Toward the end of the book, standing at the spot where he and Becky had escaped from the cave, Tom describes the glories of life in a gang of robbers, reveling in the prospect of kidnapping, extortion, and murder. "Only you don't kill the women," he tells Huck. "You shut up the women, but you don't kill them. . . . Well the women get to loving you, and after they've been in the cave a week or two weeks they stop crying and after that you couldn't get them to leave. If you drove them out they'd turn right around and come back. It's so in all the books" (244). "It's so" in *The Adventures of Tom Sawyer* as well. Tom has once again merged his reading with his life, referring here both to boys' adventure stories and his own experience with Becky in the cave, where she cried for days, became meek and dependent, and refused to leave.

This dynamic is exemplified in condensed form in Twain's unpublished "Boy's Manuscript" of 1868. The story is written as if it were the diary of a young boy by the name of William T. Rogers and is clearly the antecedent to the Becky Thatcher plot in *The Adventures of Tom Sawyer,* following the same pattern of heterosexual attraction and violent rejection. It outlines the vicissitudes of Billy's affections for a girl named Amy. Billy's attempts to get Amy's attention run the same gamut as Tom's theatrical gestures, including the staging of a torchlight procession by her house and the sentence, written in a letter: "I love you to destruction Amy and I can't live if you don't come back."[65] Such statements of self-negation characterize Billy's courtship methods and are backed up by a failed suicide attempt.

Billy's actions, like Tom's, have ambiguous effects and connotations; although his aborted poisoning attracts Amy's sympathy, it also makes him quite ill and leads him to be portrayed as the bedridden, usually female, invalid in a sentimental novel. As Billy writes, "I had lost all interest in things, and didn't care whether I lived or died."[66] But almost immediately the emotionality of the scene is projected onto Amy, who rushes to his bedside and sheds enough tears for the both of them.

Toward the end of "Boy's Manuscript," Billy announces that he definitively rejects not only Amy but girls in general. If heterosexual marriage turns out to be compulsory, he says, he will "hunt up a wife" in a manner that projects his own anxieties about individuality, anonymity, and even his desire for death onto his object of choice: "I would just go in amongst a crowd of girls and say 'Eggs, cheese, butter, bread / Stick, stock, stone— DEAD!' and take the one it lit on just the same as if I was choosing up for fox or baste or three-cornered cat or hide'n'whoop or anything like that." He describes this decision as his first assertion of individuality and autonomy. "I'm thankful that I'm free," Billy proclaims. "I've come to myself. I'll never love another girl again. There's no dependence in them."[67]

The violent expulsion and containment of the girl—anticipated and condensed in Billy's shout of "DEAD!" at the end of his rhyme—provide both closure for the boys' stories and suture for the their potentially fragmented subjectivity. This closure comes at the expense of both the girl and, more surprisingly, everything that makes the boy an attractive site of identification—that is, the distance from normative masculine individuality that makes him appealing—thus raising the question of why a novel whose pleasures and cultural work depend on an identification with a boy would conclude by negating everything appealing about its protagonist.[68]

Heterosexual Interpellation

The telos of the bad-boy book is its own protagonist's existence, an affirmation of boyhood's difference from adult manhood. But the purpose is not, of course, to construct boy-nature as entirely antithetical to or distant from manhood. While the stories never narrate their heroes' maturation to adulthood, they refer humorously though sincerely to the idea that bad boys often grow up to be good men. Warner describes one boy who compulsively stole pies from his mother's pantry, "who afterwards grew up to be a selectman, and brushed his hair straight up like General Jackson, and went to the legislature."[69] Aldrich notes in passing that one of his more mischievous friends has grown up to be "a judge, sedate and wise," and that the others "are rather elderly boys by this time—lawyers, merchants, sea-captains, soldiers, authors, what not."[70]

The conclusion to *The Adventures of Tom Sawyer* reveals a self-consciousness about the contradictions in this dynamic: "So endeth this chronicle," Twain writes. "It being strictly a history of a *boy,* it must stop here; the story could not go much further without becoming the history of a *man.* When one writes a novel about grown people, he knows exactly where to stop—that is, with a marriage; but when he writes of juveniles, he must stop where he best can" (260). Twain seems to be placing boys and men in contradistinction to one another, but the paragraph's underlying opposition is between a *history* of a boy and a *history* of a man. The distinction asserted is not primarily one of generation, but one of genre and, ultimately, gender. For it was not merely novels "about grown people" that conventionally ended in marriage, it was primarily novels about women.[71] At least since Leslie Fiedler's 1948 essay on *Huckleberry Finn* and his expansion of his thesis in *Love and Death in the American Novel,* it has been clear that one element distinguishing the boys' books— which Fiedler claims make up the mainstream of the American canon from Cooper to Hemingway—from the sentimental tradition is the boy's aversion to sexual and romantic desires for girls, or at least to marriage. But it is misleading to call this phenomenon, with Fiedler, an evasion of heterosexuality. Indeed, it is more plausible to conceive of bad-boy books as participating in the construction or reconstruction of sexualities, both hetero- and homo-, as *identities,* and as embodying and enforcing these identities through and in individuals rather than institutions like marriage. Boy books construct identificatory identities, structuring gender and sexuality through the identifications figured in their plots. They represent the practices and pleasures of reading as constitutive of gendered sexual identity.

Despite Twain's claim in *Tom Sawyer*'s preface that the book addresses all ages and genders, the bad-boy book's disavowal of a target audience is in fact the genre's way of interpellating a specific audience. The genre's distinction between boy-nature and self-identical, self-possessed individuality moves the reader toward a masculinity that it assumes the reader already possesses and yet represents as being constitutively in crisis. In its images of homosocial violence, its fantasies of de-individuation, and the unstable, multiple identifications figured in the male gang, the genre bears the traces of the work—the repression as well as the production of fantasies—necessary for the construction of a heterosexualized male identity based on the violent exclusion of women. Paradoxically, but surprisingly powerfully, the novels imagine a masculine individuality that is not rooted in a singular and stable male identity, and a heterosexuality that does not require women.

The bad-boy books thus deploy and contain the risky pleasures of identifying with a boy. Although it appears to open up a playful, less stringently gendered position for its audience, the genre models and produces identifications that interpellate readers as masculine, heterosexualized subjects. *The Adventures of Tom Sawyer* itself can be read as a series of such interpellations. Its opening words are in fact a failed hailing, as Aunt Polly cries out "Tom!" and "You Tom!" but receives "no answer" to this attempt to address Tom as the self-identical subject of her disciplinary gaze (1). Similarly, in the scene where he is unable to recite the requested Bible verses in front of Judge Thatcher, the teacher has to coax him to refer to himself by his full name, Thomas Sawyer. And when he first meets Becky Thatcher, she says that she knows his name, "Thomas Sawyer," but he replies, "That's the name they lick me by. I'm Tom, when I'm good. You call me Tom, will you" (55). Just as the Horatio Alger hero changes his name to fit his station in life—Ragged Dick becomes Dick and then Richard Hunter—Tom Sawyer changes his name depending on his relation to the public sphere. I think it is safe to assume that when his "biographical sketch" is published, he appears as "Thomas Sawyer," and that the bank account in which he places his share of the treasure is also under his full, adult, public name. Even if Twain chooses not to narrate the final stages of his boy's accession to full public masculinity, he is no less oriented in a public direction than is the Alger protagonist. Indeed, he supplements the Alger hero's inadvertent performativity with a conscious and calculated theatricality, epitomizing an "audience-oriented subjectivity."

Even though the narrative of *The Adventures of Tom Sawyer* ends with its female character relegated to silence and its male protagonist wealthy and publicly virtuous, it does not fully resolve all the contradictions inherent in the attempt to interpellate an audience though its identification with a boy. The provisional nature of Huck Finn's assimilation into society— marked most prominently by the cache of guns and ammunition he and Tom have hidden in the cave—signals the possibility that both the narrative and the reader's identification with the boys' instability may pick up again. On the one hand, this openness is a canny marketing move on Twain's part, for it remobilizes the reader's pleasure in one of the more unstable aspects of boy-nature, the identification with the gang, and allies that attachment with the desire for a sequel. At the same time, the promise of more plot is inseparable from those aspects of boy-nature that both constitute and destabilize masculine individuality. The pleasures and dangers of identifying with a boy are thus infinitely repeatable, as are their contributions to the self-fashioning of a masculine subjectivity oriented to an audience.

CODA TOWARD A HISTORY
OF IDENTIFICATION

The first chapter of this book opens with a description of a growing social movement; the final chapter concludes with fantasies of fictional boys.
In the book's opening section, novels are engaged in political change, the
construction of counterpublics, and the articulation of relationships between the state and the market; by its end, literature plays a role in middle-
class masculine self-fashioning. Described in this way, *Public Sentiments*
could be misread as one more title in the list of laments about the decline of public culture in the United States, wherein the radical democratic
potential of the early American novel is gradually supplanted by the atom-
izing individualism of mass culture or the psychologism associated with
aestheticism and modernism. But my intention was not to tell that kind
of story. Nor is this book meant to narrate a political declension from
artisan republicanism's civic engagement to liberalism's more stable but
less democratic possessive individualism. *Public Sentiments* is not a literary
version of *The Fall of Public Man* set in the United States, and despite its
engagement with Habermas's arguments and terminology, it is no *Structural Transformation of the Public Sphere,* in which a heroic if limited bourgeois publicity is eviscerated by "the social-psychological liquidation" of
the public sphere's political function, brought about by mass culture and
mass politics.

Such stories undeniably have some explanatory power for U.S. literary and cultural history in the nineteenth century and beyond. It is especially tempting to narrate the history of the public sphere as a decline if,
like Habermas, we take the public sphere to be a singular entity, if we assume a civic republican model as its normative form, and if we describe the
way increased participation in public culture and the rise of mass-cultural
forms have undermined the qualities of public life that we see as essential
to its political efficacy. I do not premise my argument on these norms, although the story I tell here does describe shifts in the social role of the novel
that parallel shifts in the relationship between the literary public and the
political public, and some of my terminology is drawn from such narra-

tives of decline. For instance, I have found it quite useful to use Habermas's concept of "audience-oriented subjectivity," as well as Sennett's claim that "personality entered the public sphere" in the course of the nineteenth century, in order to describe shifts in the social meaning of the dandy, the spectacularization of the author experienced by Louisa May Alcott displaying herself on a stage at Vassar, and the authorial celebrity courted, in different ways, by Fanny Fern and Mark Twain.

However, the nonchronological ordering of the chapters of *Public Sentiments* is meant to suggest that the relationship between the literary public and the political public in the United States is best accounted for through a less linear narrative, one characterized by uneven development rather than steady decline. This sense of unevenness is in part a result of trying to keep two concepts in mind at once, the two indicated, once again, by this book's title. My goal has been to tell the history of the public sphere—especially though not exclusively the literary public sphere—as a history of public sentiments. I discussed in the Introduction the close historical and conceptual connections between these terms: the way publicity, despite Habermas's emphasis on "rational-critical discourse," has always had a crucially affective component, and the way sentiment, despite its association with individuality, intimacy, and interiority, has always been oriented toward an audience. And the analyses in every chapter have, I hope, borne out the claim that publicity and sentimentality are reciprocal discursive constructions.

One consequence of this conjunction between sentiment and publicity is that the history and theory of a public sphere is, in important and unavoidable ways, a history and theory of identification. In a sense, there is nothing new about this assertion; indeed, I describe in the Introduction Habermas's assertion that the form of subjectivity characteristic of bourgeois publicity—the "privateness oriented to an audience"—has its origins in the forms of identification modeled in and elicited by "the psychological novel." Seldom, though, have those forms of identification been sufficiently historically specified. *Public Sentiments* takes a few steps in that direction, most notably in its exploration of what I have called "the logic of sympathy." Very early in the process of researching and writing this book I came to the realization that sympathy was a key word in nineteenth-century American understandings of the social, political, and cultural implications of the sentimental structure of feeling. And of course I have not been alone in that discovery; even if they have not put it in precisely these terms, many of the richest recent studies of nineteenth-century American culture have contributed to the understanding of sympathy's multifarious meanings.

My interest throughout has been to identify and unpack the logic of sympathy as it plays out in each text, each genre, each institution of the public sphere, each social movement, each debate over the social meaning of reading. As such, my main effort has been to derive from these texts and discourses themselves an understanding of nineteenth-century theories of interpellation and identification. Each chapter has located in its archive a somewhat different logic of sympathy; indeed, it would be odd—not to mention inaccurate—to claim that temperance novelists, black nationalist activists, female sentimentalists, and children's writers deployed identical modes of addressing and constituting their various audiences. However, certain commonalities, certain thematics, certain key words have emerged across several of these chapters, making for unexpected and, I hope, illuminating connections. The Washingtonian theory of corporeal and social transformation through sympathetic identification, for instance, turns out in many ways to resemble female sentimental novelists' consistent assumption that the representation of suffering and sympathy would interpellate their readers in an affectively transformative way. Several of the writers I have discussed placed strong emphasis on the risk that excessive and uncontrolled sympathy may lead to dangerous imitation, a fear expressed by the public librarian talking about the Irish reader of boy's fiction, by Anthony Comstock in *Traps for the Young,* and by the writers of boys' fiction themselves. Martin Delany and Horatio Alger placed a premium on communicative transparency as being essential to their otherwise quite different projects for the construction of public spheres. Public librarians shared with Henry James a concern that the forms of reading that make for a coherent public sphere were being replaced by a homogeneous form of mass-cultural consumption. And theories of sentimental sympathy as different as those of the Washingtonians, Alger, Alcott, and Twain all linked the effectivity of sympathetic identification with a theatricalized performativity that we see most clearly in representations of the dandy from Fern to Willis to James.

Other trajectories through the material I have amassed and analyzed here could undoubtedly be traced, as could connections to a still larger archive of cultural texts. Instead—even though the emphasis in most of this book has been on grounding my account of interpellation and identification in the texts and their historical circumstances—I would like to conclude by commenting on some of the theoretical, methodological, and political implications of the history of sentimental sympathy outlined here. One set of implications has to do with the argument at the end of the last chapter about the construction of what I call "identificatory identities" through the process of interpellation. In the essay on "Ideology and Ideological State Apparatuses" in which he develops the concept of interpellation, Louis Althusser illustrates the conjunction of interpellation and identification with an anecdote. Althusser claims that a police officer calling out, "Hey, you there!" almost inevitably ("nine times out of ten") gets a response from the right person, who unconsciously "recognizes that the hail was 'really' addressed to hi, and that 'it was *really him* who was hailed' (and not someone else)." The hailed pedestrian, because of this recognition, turns around. "By this mere one-hundred-and-eighty-degree physical conversion," Althusser writes, "he becomes a *subject*."[1] By addressing the pedestrian as subject to the law, the police officer elicits the person's identification with that subject-position, and thus the interpellation and its corresponding identification constitute the individual's subjectivity. In an almost mathematical equation, interpellation and identification add up to identity.

I would like to return to Twain's unfinished "Boy's Manuscript" to cite an oddly parallel anecdote that may add some specificity to Althusser's account of ideological interpellation. Toward the end of the story, just before renouncing his love, Amy, along with heterosexual sentiment in general, eight-year-old Billy Rogers writes a letter that begins: "*Darling Amy*[,] I have had lots of fights and I love you all the same. I have changed my dog which his name was Bull and now his name is Amy. I think its splendid and so does he I reckon because he always comes when I call him *Amy* though he'd come anyhow ruther than be walloped, which I *would* wallop him if he didn't." Billy then goes on to apologize for the crudeness of the drawing he has enclosed, which is a picture of himself. "[T]he horable thing which its got in its hand is you though not so pretty by a long sight," he romantically writes, concluding his description with another apology: "I didn't mean to put only one eye in your face but there wasnt room."[2]

Twain's little tale contains all the elements of the bad-boy book's simultaneous parody and enactment of masculine identity-formation as I discussed it in Chapter 6. A simultaneous identification and distanciation, enforced by violence and projection onto a "horable" other, characterizes the genre as a whole. More broadly, though, the tale usefully brings to the surface the power differential implicit in Althusser's choice to personify ideology in the form of a police officer. Still more pertinently, it whimsically but effectively foregrounds the instability at the core of the process of producing an identity out of an identification. Billy's "hailing" of his dog with Amy's name interpellates it through a forceful attribution of a gendered identity, albeit one that goes against the dog's biological sex.[3] Of course, for Billy's "hailing" to be effective, the dog need not *identify* with the gendered identity it is assigned nor act like Billy's girlfriend; he need only come when called. Perhaps most important, the real subject of Billy's gendering interpellation in this letter is not the dog, but Amy, who gets figured here as docile enough to be held in Billy's hand and who, he wishes, would come when called "Amy," just as the dog does. The only slightly displaced threat of violence toward the girl is evident. And ultimately, as in many bad-boy books and in much of Twain's humor in general, the reader is interpellated not by a straightforward identification with a protagonist, but because of the cognitive asymmetry between reader and character; the humor of the tale relies on the reader's awareness of the backhandedness of Billy's tribute to Amy.

We should not put too much theoretical weight on this humorous anecdote, but it is worth noting that even in this slight tale there are gaps between interpellation and identification, gaps that are here sutured by humor, the conventions of the genre, and the acknowledged distance between an adult reader and a barely literate boy narrator. Such disjunctions are not peculiar to this story; they may be indicative of an aporia in the process of interpellation itself, a gap between the act of "hailing" and the act of identification that is its proper response. Althusser suggests as much in his emphasis that ideological interpellation is always based in misrecognition, and when he invokes Lacanian imagery in his argument that the interpellative structure of ideology is a "duplicate mirror-structure."[4] For Althusser, though, the "doubly speculary" structure of ideology guarantees that the "mutual recognition" of the hailed subject and the interpellating ideology—the pedestrian and the police officer—is experienced by the subject as a *self*-recognition. In other words, for Althusser, interpellation guarantees that identification is experienced as identity.

In the narratives I have analyzed in these pages—all obviously more complex than the anecdotes from Twain and Althusser—such gaps are still more notable precisely because each cultural form claims to map its identificatory structure onto a stable identity. In every variation on nineteenth-century sentimental experience I have encountered, sympathetic reading is conceived of as a practice constitutive of categories of identity. The particular forms of whiteness and masculinity interpellated by Washingtonian rhetoric, for instance, were not simple iterations of identity categories always already in place; the process of production of the categories themselves is visible in the communicative exchanges figured in both experience meetings and temperance novels. In a different but comparable way, Martin Delany worked throughout his career to articulate his audiences' identifications into a complexly synthetic black or "colored" identity. Sympathy, in all its variants, serves a structurally similar function throughout the nineteenth century. The authors of bad-boy books, whose ostensible purpose bears little resemblance to those of Washingtonians or black nationalists, still deploy sympathetic identification in their plots in order to structure categories of gender and sexuality.

As in the anecdote from the "Boy's Manuscript," visible in each of these cultural forms are disjunctions between identification and identity. In the bad-boy book, for instance, identification with an adolescent boy constitutes not an adolescent subject position for the reader, but a respectable adult manhood. Each chapter of *Public Sentiments* identifies such a disjunction at the core of sympathy's logic, such as the disparity between print fantasies and personhood in Alger's novels, or that between domesticity's ideology of femininity and women's fiction's generic imperatives of narrative and character. This disjunction is perhaps most visible in the Washingtonian scenarios I described, where the listeners' or readers' emotional identification with a violent, bloated, red-faced narrator and protagonist is meant to transform them into the pale, respectable, white men who are rarely figured in the narratives themselves, just as Twain and other bad-boy book authors foreclosed the representation of their protagonists' respectable adulthood even as their novels insist that such is their characters' destiny.

In each case, it is not so much a particular identity or subject position that is reproduced in the reader's act of identification as it is the transformative process of identification itself. By analyzing these processes of identification in specific political, institutional, and textual locations, I have tried to flesh out Diana Fuss's important claim that "identification has a history," that "identification is neither a historically universal concept nor a politically innocent one."[5] What I have described as the sentimental structure of feeling contains an originary form of the "politics of identification" that Fuss, Carla Kaplan, and others have analyzed as a site of important and ongoing debate in feminist theory and practice.[6] At stake in these debates is the question of whether basing political solidarity on identification risks the denial, disavowal, or negation of all differences other than the one that forms the basis of the identification, of whether a feminist politics of identification necessarily entails ignoring, for example, differences of race and class. An examination of the nineteenth-century politics of sympathy demonstrates that writers in that period and earlier were concerned with remarkably comparable subjective and political problematics, that such risks are implicit in the logic of sympathy itself.

It might be more accurate to say that what is (re)produced in the logic of sympathy is not identification, but affect itself. To cite Theodore Parker's description of the sympathetic writer or orator one last time: "Feeling, he must make others feel."[7] This phrase remains the most concise general account of the structure of identification in a sentimental structure of feeling, in part because it acknowledges the circularity of sentimental interpellation. Affect is by this account both the origin of the sentimental act (the orator's "feeling," but more broadly, the sentimental axiom, dating back to Scottish Common Sense philosophy, that the ability to feel another's pain is definitional of human subjectivity) and its outcome (whatever it is that the "others feel"). And the two verbs in Parker's slogan nicely acknowledge a constitutive tension within sentimentalism. The main action of the sentence is coercive; the speaker "make[s] others" share his or her feelings, while at the same time the word "must" redounds upon the subject of the sentence, compelling him or her into an act of interpellation.

The rhetorical and political power of the sentimental politics of affect can be limned in the conjunction of reciprocity and coercion evident in Parker's phrase. Making this conjunction visible can serve as a corrective to a sentimental fantasy that underpinned some of the more political nineteenth-century deployments of sympathetic identification and that is sometimes visible in more contemporary manifestations of the politics of identification: the fantasy that affect can be the ground and site of noncoercive communicative exchange in the public sphere. This fantasy is a powerful one, and it is often politically productive; it operated in antebellum reform movements from temperance to abolition, and it has operated in the "politics of identification" that Carla Kaplan analyzes in feminism since the 1970s and the "politics of affect" that Ann Cvetkovich attributes to early 1990s AIDS activism.[8] However, like America's founding fantasy that self-abstraction, disembodiment, disinterestedness, and reason could guarantee the noncoerciveness of a democratic public sphere—a fantasy to which the politics of affect is clearly a response—it can also be dangerous, especially if those who wish to "make others feel" as they do fail to recognize the element of coercion in the affective medium of their communication. What remains to be seen is whether it is a fantasy we can or should do without, whether we can yet imagine a politics or a culture characterized by something other than a sentimental structure of feeling.

NOTES

Introduction

1 The term "cultural work" is adapted from Jane Tompkins, *Sensational Designs: The Cultural Work of American Fiction, 1790–1860* (New York: Oxford University Press, 1985).

2 Raymond Williams, *Keywords: A Vocabulary of Culture and Society,* rev. ed. (New York: Oxford University Press, 1983), 281.

3 Celia W. Dugger, "Kashmir War, Shown on TV, Rallies India's Unity," *New York Times,* 18 July 1999, final national edition, sec. 1, p. 4.

4 Williams goes on to say that the words "sentiment" and "sentimental" were by the seventeenth century used to denote "both opinion and emotion." Williams, *Keywords,* 281.

5 See, for instance, G. J. Barker-Benfield, *The Culture of Sensibility: Sex and Society in Eighteenth-Century Britain* (Chicago: University of Chicago Press, 1992); Janet Todd, *Sensibility: An Introduction* (London: Methuen, 1986); Ann Jessie Van Sant, *Eighteenth-Century Sensibility and the Novel: The Senses in Social Context* (Cambridge: Cambridge University Press, 1993); David Marshall, *The Surprising Effects of Sympathy: Marivaux, Diderot, Rousseau, and Mary Shelley* (Chicago: University of Chicago Press, 1988). The implications of this development in an American cultural context have become a focus recently in works such as Julia A. Stern, *The Plight of Feeling: Sympathy and Dissent in the Early American Novel* (Chicago: University of Chicago Press, 1997); Elizabeth Barnes, *States of Sympathy: Seduction and Democracy in the American Novel* (New York: Columbia University Press, 1997); Bruce Burgett, *Sentimental Bodies: Sex, Gender, and Citizenship in the Early Republic* (Princeton: Princeton University Press, 1998); Gregg Camfield, *Sentimental Twain: Samuel Clemens in the Maze of Moral Philosophy* (Philadelphia: University of Pennsylvania Press, 1994); and Lori Merish, *Sentimental Materialism: Gender, Commodity Culture, and Nineteenth-Century American Literature* (Durham, N.C.: Duke University Press, 2000). Julie Ellison's *Cato's Tears and the Making of Anglo-American Emotion* (Chicago: University of Chicago Press, 1999) most thoroughly outlines the transatlantic development of the culture of sentiment.

6 For a set of case studies tracing the transformation of American emotions into their twentieth-century, psychologized form, see Joel Pfister and Nancy Schnog, eds., *Inventing the Psychological: Toward a Cultural History of Emotional Life in America* (New Haven: Yale University Press, 1997).

7 Williams, *Keywords*, 281. William Empson has explored the tense but mutually constitutive relation between sentiment and sensibility in *The Structure of Complex Words* (1951; reprint, Cambridge, Mass.: Harvard University Press, 1989), 250–69.

8 Hannah Webster Foster, *The Coquette; or, The History of Eliza Wharton*, ed. Cathy Davidson (New York: Oxford University Press, 1986). For illuminating, though quite different, analyses of the forms of sentiment in *The Coquette*, see Stern, *The Plight of Feeling*, 71–151, and Burgett, *Sentimental Bodies*, 81–111.

9 Much of the best recent scholarship on early national culture and the early American novel has explored the role of the rhetoric and experience of sentiment in the prehistory of the modern psychological subject and the liberal citizen; *Public Sentiments* draws extensively on such work. In addition to those already cited, see Michael Warner, *The Letters of the Republic: Publication and the Public Sphere in Eighteenth-Century America* (Cambridge, Mass.: Harvard University Press, 1990); Shirley Samuels, *Romances of the Republic: Women, the Family, and Violence in the Literature of the Early American Nation* (New York: Oxford University Press, 1996); and Grantland S. Rice, *The Transformation of Authorship in America* (Chicago: University of Chicago Press, 1997).

10 Harriet Beecher Stowe, *Uncle Tom's Cabin* (1852; reprint, New York: Norton, 1994), 385.

11 The phrase "culture of sentiment" is drawn from Shirley Samuels, ed., *The Culture of Sentiment: Race, Gender, and Sentimentality in Nineteenth-Century America* (New York: Oxford University Press, 1992).

12 Parker goes on to gender such sympathy, asserting that "Poetry and Eloquence are twin sisters; Feeling is their mother, Thought is the father," and that "Men, oftener women, may have great warmth of feeling." Theodore Parker, *Lessons from the World of Matter and the World of Man*, vol. 14 of *The Collected Works of Theodore Parker*, ed. Rufus Leighton (London: Trübner and Company, 1872), 108–9, 113.

13 Todd, *Sensibility*, 4. David Marshall focuses on eighteenth-century sympathy's dual connotations, which persist in its nineteenth-century manifestations: "*Sympathy* . . . suggests not just feeling or the capacity for feeling but more specifically the capacity to feel the sentiments of someone else . . . *sympathie* implies a correspondence of feelings between people such as a mutual attraction or affinity; yet even in this sense it contains both an etymology and a network of eighteenth-century associations that suggest the act of entering into the sentiments of another person." Marshall, *Surprising Effects*, 3.

14 Philip Fisher, *Hard Facts: Setting and Form in the American Novel* (New York: Oxford University Press, 1985), 105.

15 Adam Smith, *The Theory of Moral Sentiments* (1759), ed. D. D. Raphael and A. L. Macfie (Oxford: Clarendon Press, 1976), 9. The subsection titled "Of Sympathy" is part of the opening section, "Of the Sense of Propriety," thus further demonstrating the prescriptive attitude philosophers of sensibility had toward emotions. For an

instructive reading of Smith, see David Marshall, *The Figure of Theater: Shaftesbury, Defoe, Adam Smith, and George Eliot* (New York: Columbia University Press, 1986).

16 Philip Fisher analyzes this passage from Rousseau in *Hard Facts,* 104–7.

17 In an article published in 1991, I used the words "equivalence" and "identity" instead of "analogy" and "coincidence" to describe this dynamic. The newer terms are, I think, clearer; they also jibe with Freud's analysis of sympathy, discussed below. For the earlier version of this point, see Glenn Hendler, "The Limits of Sympathy: Louisa May Alcott and the Sentimental Novel," *American Literary History* 3, no. 4 (Winter 1991): 685–706.

18 As several recent discussions of sentimentalism have argued, the valorization of sympathy as a model for both intersubjectivity and social relations derives largely from the writings of Adam Smith and other Scottish Common Sense philosophers. Elizabeth Barnes writes: "As Smith describes it, sympathy is more than feeling for others; it involves a projection of the self outward, so that the viewer or reader imaginatively inhabits the minds of others" (*States of Sympathy,* 20). Other critical works tracing a trajectory from Adam Smith to nineteenth-century American sentimentalism include Merish, *Sentimental Materialism,* and Camfield, *Sentimental Twain.*

19 J. Laplanche and J-B. Pontalis, *The Language of Psychoanalysis,* trans. Donald Nicholson-Smith (New York: Norton, 1973), 205.

20 Sigmund Freud, *Group Psychology and the Analysis of the Ego,* trans. James Strachey (New York: Norton, 1959), 39. For an analysis of this story, its role in the development of Freud's theory of identification, and the figure of the boarding school itself, see Diana Fuss, *Identification Papers* (New York: Routledge, 1995), 41–42, 107–34.

21 Stowe, *Uncle Tom's Cabin,* 72–73.

22 Ibid., 75.

23 Eve Kosofsky Sedgwick, *Epistemology of the Closet* (Berkeley and Los Angeles: University of California Press, 1990), 154.

24 The phrase "politics of affect" is drawn from Ann Cvetkovich, *Mixed Feelings: Feminism, Mass Culture, and Victorian Sensationalism* (New Brunswick, N.J.: Rutgers University Press, 1992), 1. My thoughts on the politics of affect in sentimentalism were very helpfully clarified by an e-mail exchange with Elizabeth Barnes.

25 Saidiya V. Hartman, *Scenes of Subjection: Terror, Slavery, and Self-Making in Nineteenth-Century America* (New York: Oxford University Press, 1997); Laura Wexler, "Tender Violence: Literary Eavesdropping, Domestic Fiction, and Educational Reform," in Samuels, *The Culture of Sentiment,* 9–38.

26 Dana D. Nelson, *The Word in Black and White: Reading "Race" in American Literature, 1638–1867* (New York: Oxford University Press, 1993), 144.

27 Those who developed the cultural practices and institutions of sentimentalism in the nineteenth century were also in the business of making these distinctions. Karen Halttunen's account of the development of the funeral industry and its conventions remains one of the most useful and careful studies of the nuances of the sentimental

structure of feeling. Karen Halttunen, *Confidence Men and Painted Women: A Study of Middle-Class Culture, 1830–1870* (New Haven: Yale University Press, 1982), 124–52.

28 Marianne Noble, "The Ecstasies of Sentimental Wounding in *Uncle Tom's Cabin*," *Yale Journal of Criticism* 10, no. 2 (1997): 304.

29 Ibid.

30 Elizabeth Barnes, "The Epistemology of the Real: A Response to Marianne Noble," *Yale Journal of Criticism* 10, no. 2 (1997): 322.

31 Barnes is wisely cautious about her assertion of communicative impenetrability, almost offering to take it back in a parenthetical query in her next sentence: "Of course this is a fact (or is it?) that sentimental writers persistently resist." Ibid.

32 Tompkins, *Sensational Designs,* 127.

33 Whether they value the sentimental novel positively or negatively, most participants in the debate over its politics characterize it in these terms: see especially Nina Baym, *Women's Fiction: A Guide to Novels by and about Women in America, 1820–1870* (Ithaca: Cornell University Press, 1978); Ann Douglas, *The Feminization of American Culture* (New York: Avon, 1977); and Tompkins, *Sensational Designs.* The essays in Mary Chapman and Glenn Hendler, eds., *Sentimental Men: Masculinity and the Politics of Affect in American Culture* (Berkeley and Los Angeles: University of California Press, 1999), challenge the aspect of this characterization that I do not take up here: the premise that sentimentalism was an exclusively or even primarily feminine rhetorical mode or structure of feeling.

34 Joel Pfister has recently suggested that the entire concept of the psychological can be viewed through the lens of Williams's concept of a structure of feeling. See "On Conceptualizing the Cultural History of Emotional and Psychological Life in America," in Pfister and Schnog, *Inventing the Psychological,* 43 n. 2.

35 Raymond Williams, *Marxism and Literature* (Oxford: Oxford University Press, 1977), 133–34, 132.

36 Ibid., 132.

37 Ibid., 133.

38 Joan W. Scott, "Experience," in *Feminists Theorize the Political,* ed. Judith Butler and Joan W. Scott (New York: Routledge, 1992), 37. Scott explicitly draws on Raymond Williams, "Experience," in *Keywords,* 126–29.

39 Parts of the preceding paragraphs are adapted from my essay "The Structure of Sentimental Experience," *Yale Journal of Criticism* 12, no. 1 (1999): 146–53.

40 Jürgen Habermas, *The Structural Transformation of the Public Sphere: An Inquiry into a Category of Bourgeois Society,* trans. Thomas Burger and Frederick Lawrence (Cambridge, Mass.: MIT Press, 1989). For good examples of work influenced by Habermas, see Mary P. Ryan, *Women in Public: Between Banners and Ballots, 1825–1880* (Baltimore: Johns Hopkins University Press, 1990); Lauren Berlant, *The Anatomy of National Fantasy: Hawthorne, Utopia, and Everyday Life* (Chicago: University of Chicago Press, 1991); Lauren Berlant, *The Queen of America Goes to Washington City:*

Essays on Sex and Citizenship (Durham, N.C.: Duke University Press, 1997); Warner, *Letters of the Republic;* Nancy Fraser, "Rethinking the Public Sphere: A Contribution to the Critique of Actually Existing Democracy," in *Habermas and the Public Sphere,* ed. Craig Calhoun (Cambridge, Mass.: MIT Press, 1992), 109–42; Linda K. Kerber, *Women of the Republic: Intellect and Ideology in Revolutionary America* (Chapel Hill: University of North Carolina Press, 1997).

41 For an admirably clear summary of Habermas's argument that also succeeds in placing it in a range of intellectual contexts, see Craig Calhoun's introduction to *Habermas and the Public Sphere,* 1–48. My account of Habermas here is indebted to Calhoun's.

42 There is no word in English that corresponds to the word in Habermas's German title, *Öffentlichkeit,* that is translated as "public sphere." In the text, the translators also use "public" (in its noun form) and "publicity" when Habermas is referring to the property of being public. Because "publicity" has other potentially confusing connotations in English, I most often use the awkward and less common word "publicness" for this latter purpose, though for the sake of consistency with the translation, "publicity" will appear when I am closely recapitulating Habermas's argument, as in this case. See Thomas Burger, "Translator's Note," in Habermas, *Structural Transformation,* xv–xvi.

43 Here, despite Habermas's later critiques of Foucault, the two are on quite similar ground; anyone familiar with the way the spectacle of the scaffold functions in the first part of *Discipline and Punish* will understand what Habermas is referring to with his concept of representative publicness. Michel Foucault, *Discipline and Punish: The Birth of the Prison,* trans. Alan Sheridan (New York: Vintage, 1979).

44 Habermas, *Structural Transformation,* xxx.

45 Ibid., 29.

46 See ibid., 31–43.

47 Ibid., xviii.

48 Michael Schudson, "Was There Ever a Public Sphere? If So, When? Reflections on the American Case," in Calhoun, *Habermas and the Public Sphere,* 143–63. Quotation is on 160.

49 Habermas, *Structural Transformation,* xviii.

50 Oscar Negt and Alexander Kluge, *Public Sphere and Experience: Toward an Analysis of the Bourgeois and Proletarian Public Sphere,* trans. Peter Labanyi, Jamie Owen Daniel, and Assenka Oksiloff (Minneapolis: University of Minnesota Press, 1993).

51 Here I diverge from Negt and Kluge, who insist on fundamental differences between the proletarian public sphere and the bourgeois public sphere. At the same time, each chapter of *Public Sentiments* delineates different formulations of particular public spheres; I do not assume that publicity takes only one form, exemplified by the European bourgeoisie. My analysis has more affinity with Miriam Hansen's important study of early cinema, where she uses the concept of a counterpublic to

designate the ethnically and economically distinct reception communities of early cinema, while still emphasizing their intimate relation to the hegemonic bourgeois public sphere and the corporate, mass-cultural instruments of publicity that structure a cultural form like cinema. See Miriam Hansen, *Babel and Babylon: Spectatorship in American Silent Film* (Cambridge, Mass.: Harvard University Press, 1991). The concept of a counterpublic has been especially fruitful for feminists; see Rita Felski, *Beyond Feminist Aesthetics: Feminist Literature and Social Change* (Cambridge, Mass.: Harvard University Press, 1989), 164–74, and Fraser, "Rethinking the Public Sphere."

52 This is another point at which Habermasian theories of the public sphere converge productively with recent work on the rise of the category of the psychological. See Pfister and Schnog, *Inventing the Psychological.*

53 Habermas, *Structural Transformation,* 211.

54 Michael Warner, "The Mass Public and the Mass Subject," in Calhoun, *Habermas and the Public Sphere,* 382. Warner draws on Benedict Anderson, *Imagined Communities: Reflections on the Origin and Spread of Nationalism,* rev. ed. (London: Verso, 1991), 1–65.

55 Warner, "Mass Public," 382.

56 Ibid., 382–83.

57 See Fraser, "Rethinking the Public Sphere." Also see Nancy Fraser, "What's Critical about Critical Theory"; Jean L. Cohen, "Critical Social Theory and Feminist Critiques: The Debate with Jürgen Habermas"; Joan B. Landes, "The Public and the Private Spheres: A Feminist Reconsideration," and Marie Fleming, "Women and the 'Public Use of Reason,'" all in *Feminists Read Habermas: Gendering the Subject of Discourse,* ed. Johanna Meehan (New York: Routledge, 1995), 21–137.

58 See, for instance, Ryan, *Women in Public.*

59 Linda K. Kerber, "Separate Spheres, Female Worlds, Women's Place: The Rhetoric of Women's History," *Journal of American History* 75 (June 1988): 39.

60 Eve Kosofsky Sedgwick, *Epistemology of the Closet* (Berkeley and Los Angeles: University of California Press, 1990), 109.

61 "Interpellation" is Louis Althusser's term to describe the way that ideology addresses and constitutes the subject, constructing identity through the very act of "hailing" the individual. Louis Althusser, *Lenin and Philosophy,* trans. Ben Brewster (New York: Monthly Review Press, 1971), 127–93. For more on this concept, see the end of Chapter 6, below, and the Coda.

62 Habermas acknowledges the first of these major omissions, and the work done by feminist critics to correct it, in an essay written nearly thirty years later in response to the publication of the eighteenth German edition of *Structural Transformation* and its translation into English in 1989. See Jürgen Habermas, "Further Reflections on the Public Sphere," trans. Thomas Burger, in Calhoun, *Habermas and the Public Sphere,* 421–61. For an effort to address the omission of racial disparities in the dis-

tribution of access to publicity, see the special issue of *Public Culture* on "The Black Public Sphere," *Public Culture* 15, no. 1 (1994).

63 Habermas, *Structural Transformation*, 56.

64 Ibid., 23.

65 Ibid., 50–51.

66 Burgett, *Sentimental Bodies*, 1.

67 Habermas, *Structural Transformation*, 43.

68 Ibid., 48.

69 Ibid., 49.

70 Ibid.

Chapter One

1 While the new temperance organizations that arose in the early 1840s took on a variety of names, the general phenomenon was known then as the Washingtonian movement, and historians still refer to it as such. The common feature of most groups' names was their reference to heroes of the revolution; Jefferson was another favorite. These names were not chosen because of any tendency among the Founding Fathers toward teetotalism; indeed, George Washington himself had set up a whiskey distillery at Mount Vernon after retiring from the presidency (W. J. Rorabaugh, *The Alcoholic Republic: An American Tradition* [Oxford: Oxford University Press, 1979], 73). The names, rather, were part of a larger tendency among artisanal and working-class movements to claim that their values were an extension of the masculine public virtue of the republicans. See David Montgomery, *Citizen Worker: The Experience of Workers in the United States with Democracy and the Free Market during the Nineteenth Century* (Cambridge: Cambridge University Press, 1993), and Eric Foner, *Free Soil, Free Labor, Free Men: The Ideology of the Republican Party before the Civil War* (New York: Oxford University Press, 1970).

2 Quoted in Milton A. Maxwell, "The Washingtonian Movement," *Quarterly Journal of Studies on Alcohol* 11 (1950): 419.

3 T[imothy] S[hay] Arthur, *Temperance Tales; or, Six Nights with the Washingtonians* (1842; reprint, 2 vols. in 1, St. Clair Shores, Mich.: Scholarly Press, 1971). Hereafter cited as *Six Nights*.

4 Abraham Lincoln, *An Address Delivered by Abraham Lincoln, Before the Springfield, Washingtonian Temperance Society, at the Second Presbyterian Church, Springfield, Illinois, On the 22d Day of February, 1842* (Springfield, Ill.: O. H. Oldroyd, 1889).

5 Walt Whitman, *Franklin Evans; or, The Inebriate* (1842), reprinted in *The Early Poems and the Fiction*, ed. Thomas L. Brasher (New York: New York University Press, 1963), 124–239. (Subsequent parenthetical references to this novel in the text are to this edition.) Michael Warner notes that although we call *Franklin Evans* a novel, its readers would more likely have seen it as a newspaper supplement or a tract; see "Whitman Drunk," in *Breaking Bounds: Whitman and American Cultural Studies*, ed. Betsy Erk-

kila and Jay Grossman (New York: Oxford University Press, 1996), 30–43. Though its first readers encountered it in the unwieldy form of a story paper, *Franklin Evans* had been advertised as a "novel, which is dedicated to the Temperance Societies and the friends of the Temperance Cause throughout the Union . . . by one of the best Novelists of this country." Despite Whitman's own claim that his story is "somewhat aside from the ordinary track of the novelist," most critics persist in referring to it as a novel. Leslie Fiedler intriguingly locates *Franklin Evans* in two novelistic traditions: the sentimental novel, on the one hand, and "the main line of American city novels . . . through Crane's *Maggie* up to the fiction of Dreiser and the 'muckrakers,'" on the other. See *Love and Death in the American Novel*, rev. ed. (New York: Anchor, 1992), 484. For the quotations from the advertisement referred to above, as well as a complete account of the text's publication history, see Brasher's notes to Whitman, *Franklin Evans*, 124–26 n. 1.

6 Walt Whitman, *The Madman* (1843), reprinted in *The Early Poems and the Fiction*, 240–43. No subsequent installments of *The Madman* have been located. Two of Whitman's pro-Washingtonian editorials are reprinted in *Walt Whitman of the "New York Aurora": Editor at Twenty-Two*, ed. Joseph Jay Rubin and Charles H. Brown (State College, Pa.: Bald Eagle Press, 1950), 35–36. The variety and extent of Whitman's literary contributions to the temperance cause put into question his later claims to have written *Franklin Evans* solely for the money, with a bottle of liquor at his side. Such comments have raised controversy about the sincerity of Whitman's devotion to temperance. Analyses by Warner and by Michael Moon wisely sidestep this debate over intentionality to argue that Whitman rehearses in his temperance writings the thematic and formal concerns that would later inform his poetry, especially the first two editions of *Leaves of Grass*. Although my concern is less to contextualize Whitman's later writings than it is to view *Franklin Evans* and other temperance writings as sites of discursive and political conflicts that were also played out in the Washingtonians' social practices, Moon's arguments about Whitman's ongoing desire "to project actual physical presence in a literary text," as well as Warner's arguments about Whitman's "sexual expressivism; and the strange conception of a public that distinguishes his poetic writing and his publishing practice," inform my analysis here. See Michael Moon, *Disseminating Whitman: Revision and Corporeality in "Leaves of Grass"* (Cambridge, Mass.: Harvard University Press, 1991), 5, and Warner, "Whitman Drunk," 31.

7 Warner, "Whitman Drunk," 34.

8 Ian R. Tyrrell, *Sobering Up: From Temperance to Prohibition in Antebellum America, 1800–1860* (Westport, Conn.: Greenwood Press, 1979), 135–51.

9 See Floyd Stovall, *The Foreground of "Leaves of Grass"* (Charlottesville: University Press of Virginia, 1974); David S. Reynolds, *Beneath the American Renaissance: The Subversive Imagination in the Age of Emerson and Melville* (Cambridge, Mass.: Har-

vard University Press, 1989) and *Walt Whitman's America: A Cultural Biography* (New York: Knopf, 1995); Robert S. Levine, *Martin Delany, Frederick Douglass, and the Politics of Representative Identity* (Chapel Hill: University of North Carolina Press, 1997), 99–143; and Moon, *Disseminating Whitman.*

10 Some of the key critical and historical texts to have developed and institutionalized the domestic/public opposition as central to an understanding of nineteenth-century American culture, especially "women's sphere" and sentimental fiction, are Nina Baym, *Woman's Fiction: A Guide to Novels by and about Women in America, 1820–1870* (Urbana: University of Illinois Press, 1993); Nancy F. Cott, *The Bonds of Womanhood: "Woman's Sphere" in New England, 1780–1835* (New Haven: Yale University Press, 1977); Carl Degler, *At Odds: Women and the Family in America from the Revolution to the Present* (New York: Oxford University Press, 1981); Ann Douglas, *The Feminization of American Culture* (New York: Avon, 1977); Mary Kelley, *Private Woman, Public Stage: Literary Domesticity in Nineteenth-Century America* (New York: Oxford University Press, 1984); Mary P. Ryan, *Cradle of the Middle Class: The Family in Oneida County, New York, 1790–1865* (Cambridge: Cambridge University Press, 1981); Mary P. Ryan, *Empire of the Mother: American Writing about Domesticity, 1830–1860* (New York: Harrington Park Press, 1985); Kathryn Kish Sklar, *Catharine Beecher: A Study in American Domesticity* (New Haven: Yale University Press, 1973); and Barbara Welter, "The Cult of True Womanhood, 1820–1860," *American Quarterly* 18 (1966): 151–74. Much recent work on American masculinity is based in this feminist work and to a large extent shares its conceptualization of the public/domestic division. See David Leverenz, *Manhood and the American Renaissance* (Ithaca: Cornell University Press, 1989); E. Anthony Rotundo, *American Manhood: Transformations in Masculinity from the Revolution to the Modern Era* (New York: Basic Books, 1993); and Michael Kimmel, *Manhood in America: A Cultural History* (New York: Free Press, 1996).

11 See, for instance, Ryan, *Cradle of the Middle Class,* and Stuart M. Blumin, *The Emergence of the Middle Class: Social Experience in the American City, 1760–1900* (Cambridge: Cambridge University Press, 1989).

12 See Michael Warner, *The Letters of the Republic: Publication and the Public Sphere in Eighteenth-Century America* (Cambridge: Harvard University Press, 1990); Elizabeth Barnes, *States of Sympathy: Seduction and Democracy in the American Novel* (New York: Columbia University Press, 1997); and Bruce Burgett, *Sentimental Bodies: Sex, Gender, and Citizenship in the Early Republic* (Princeton: Princeton University Press, 1998), among others.

13 For a set of essays that begin the process of complicating the homology described above, see Mary Chapman and Glenn Hendler, eds., *Sentimental Men: Masculinity and the Politics of Affect in American Culture* (Berkeley and Los Angeles: University of California Press, 1999).

14 Quoted in Maxwell, "Washingtonian Movement," 412.

15 Lincoln, *Address,* 7.

16 Philip Fisher, *Hard Facts: Setting and Form in the American Novel* (New York: Oxford University Press, 1985), 99.

17 For details on the class composition of Washingtonian chapters, see Tyrrell, *Sobering Up,* 162–71. He argues that the group was far from exclusively working class; it included members from various class positions, most notably artisans displaced by upheavals of rapid industrialization whose livelihood had been damaged by the depression of 1837. "What distinguished the Washingtonians of the early 1840s," Tyrrell concludes, was not a homogeneously working-class constituency, but "the relative absence of the older evangelicals and wealthy and upwardly mobile captains of industry from controlling positions in the new societies" (167). It is this relative autonomy from direct bourgeois control that makes the Washingtonian movement less easy to fit into the argument that temperance movements were a form of middle-class social control; see, for instance, Bruce Laurie, *Working People of Philadelphia, 1800–1850* (Philadelphia: Temple University Press 1980), 40–42.

18 The Washingtonians also differed from many of their predecessors in their insistence on total abstinence; most regular temperance organizations had not completely rejected wine and beer. However, the teetotalist position had been gaining strength for some time. The Washingtonians were responsible for popularizing it, but it was not their innovation; the mainstream American Temperance Society, for instance, adopted a total abstinence pledge in 1836 (Tyrrell, *Sobering Up,* 137, 144).

19 Lincoln, *Address,* 5.

20 Quoted in John Allen Krout, *The Origins of Prohibition* (New York: Alfred A. Knopf, 1925), 189.

21 Arthur, *Six Nights,* 1:93.

22 Quoted in Krout, *Origins of Prohibition,* 189.

23 Psychoanalysis has often represented sympathetic identification in much the same way and has similarly pathologized it by associating it with women. See especially Freud's discussion of sympathetic contagion at a girls' school in *Group Psychology and the Analysis of the Ego,* trans. James Strachey (New York: Norton, 1959), 38–39, discussed in the Introduction, above. Mikkel Borch-Jacobsen characterizes the affective cathexis of sympathy as prior to and underlying identification and object-choice, thus counteracting this tendency in psychoanalysis; see *The Freudian Subject,* trans. Catherine Porter (Stanford: Stanford University Press, 1988).

24 The exclusive homosociality of Washingtonian stories differentiates this from other moments in the history of the temperance narrative. Though these stories contain other stock tropes, including the long-suffering wife and the neglected but still-loving child, what has redemptive power is most often the sympathy of other men. On the power of the child in temperance fiction, see Karen Sánchez-Eppler,

"Temperance in the Bed of a Child: Incest and Social Order in Nineteenth-Century America," *American Quarterly* 47, no. 1 (March 1995): 1–33; on the figure of the wife, see Jerome Nadelhaft, "Alcohol and Wife Abuse in Antebellum Male Temperance Literature," *Canadian Review of American Studies* 25, no. 1 (Winter 1995): 15–41.

25 Quoted in Krout, *Origins of Prohibition*, 189.

26 Quoted in Rev. W. H. Daniels, ed., *The Temperance Reform and Its Great Reformers. An Illustrated History* (New York: Nelson and Phillips, 1878), 127.

27 It is important to mark here the difference between the typically oral form of Washingtonian narration and the fact that women's sentimentalism came into its own in print. Being in the same room with crying men had a somewhat different valence from sitting at home alone identifying with a sympathetic and tearful female protagonist. As we will see below, however, Washingtonian sentimentalism placed a great deal of emphasis on the print medium; its public was probably formed at least as much through its own publications and newspaper accounts of its gatherings as through men's physical presence at experience meetings. And sympathetic identification in its literary manifestations, male and female, often drew on a fantasy of physical immediacy, as if its writers half wished their readers could be physically present to share their own, and their characters', tears. For analyses of print sentimentalism that explore this dialectic of presence and absence, see Karen Sánchez-Eppler, *Touching Liberty: Abolition, Feminism, and the Politics of the Body* (Berkeley and Los Angeles: University of California Press, 1993), especially her chapter on Whitman (50–82), and Moon, *Disseminating Whitman.*

28 Shirley Samuels, introduction to *The Culture of Sentiment: Race, Gender, and Sentimentality in Nineteenth-Century America* (New York: Oxford University Press, 1992), 3; Sánchez-Eppler, *Touching Liberty,* 27.

29 Sánchez-Eppler, *Touching Liberty,* 49.

30 Ibid., 1.

31 Ibid., 49.

32 See Introduction, above, for an account of how disembodied abstraction characterizes American citizenship.

33 Jed Dannenbaum, *Drink and Disorder: Temperance Reform in Cincinnati from the Washingtonian Revival to the WCTU* (Urbana: University of Illinois Press, 1984), 44.

34 Quoted in Krout, *Origins of Prohibition*, 187.

35 Reynolds, *Beneath the American Renaissance*, 359. In *Walt Whitman's America*, Reynolds confirms that Whitman attended Gough's Washingtonian lectures in New York and in general provides more information on Whitman's connection to the temperance movement (92–97).

36 Krout, *Origins of Prohibition*, 197. Gough himself was charmingly self-deprecating about his physical strength and appearance in his *Autobiography*. See John B. Gough, *An Autobiography by John B. Gough* (Boston: privately printed, 1845). Thanks to John

Crowley for pointing me to the earlier 1845 version of Gough's *Autobiography,* in which he is much more interestingly and systematically Washingtonian in his self-presentation than in the more widely available 1870 version.

37 Moon argues persuasively that the poet's practice in the 1855 *Leaves of Grass* was to refunction, for his own literary-political purposes, contemporary discourses on the body, most notably anti-onanist and temperance discourses. The only difference I would have with this argument is that I think the "fluidity" between politics and sexuality, and between the text and the body, is present at least in potential form in Washingtonian discourse itself; I give Whitman somewhat less credit for bringing that potential out. Put another way, while Moon argues that Whitman queers temperance discourse, I argue that it was pretty queer already. See Moon, *Disseminating Whitman,* 1–87.

38 Karen Sánchez-Eppler has analyzed another sexual dynamic in nineteenth-century temperance fiction: the incestuous desire of the drunken father for his innocent daughter (and occasionally son) that, as she demonstrates, often motivates the inebriate's reform. See Sánchez-Eppler, "Temperance in the Bed of a Child." Though this dynamic is present in Washingtonian narratives, it seems to me to be less prevalent there than in the wider range of temperance fiction Sánchez-Eppler discusses. This difference may have something to do with the Washingtonians' insistence that sentimental experience be an affective exchange between men, or with the fact that their speeches and writings focus more on the depravities that precede reform than on the process of transformation or its aftermath. I discuss both the homosociality of Washingtonianism and its lack of interest in the reformed drunkard later in this chapter and address the imbrication of domesticity, sympathy, and incest in Chapter 4.

39 Whitman, *Franklin Evans,* 129; Arthur, *Six Nights,* 1:12, 33.

40 The story's tenuous link to the temperance cause was further evinced when Whitman revised and republished it in 1845 in the *American Review* as "The Death of Wind-Foot" and then republished it without additional changes later the same year in the *Crystal Fount and Rechabite Recorder.* Though there are some minor differences between the story in the novel and the later versions, in none of its incarnations is alcohol mentioned. See Brasher's note to *Franklin Evans,* 126 n. 1.

41 Arthur, *Six Nights,* 1:3.

42 In this it parallels the connection between freedom and manhood made by Frederick Douglass in his *Autobiography* as well as in his story "The Heroic Slave," analyzed in Richard Yarborough, "Race, Violence, and Manhood: The Masculine Ideal in Frederick Douglass's 'The Heroic Slave,'" in *Frederick Douglass: New Literary and Historical Essays,* ed. Eric J. Sundquist (Cambridge: Cambridge University Press, 1990), 166–88.

43 The temperance movement was at this point just beginning to invent the idea of addiction, a concept that internalizes the causes of the compulsion to drink and thus

makes its comparison with slavery less plausible. See Eve Kosofsky Sedgwick, *Tendencies* (Durham, N.C.: Duke University Press, 1993), 130–42, and Warner's use of Sedgwick's argument in "Whitman Drunk," 33–34.

44 Donald Yacovone, "The Transformation of the Black Temperance Movement, 1827–1854: An Interpretation," *Journal of the Early Republic* 8, no. 3 (Fall 1988): 290, 291. For an analysis specifically of Frederick Douglass's use of temperance rhetoric, see Levine, *Martin Delany*, 99–143.

45 *Orations of John B. Gough, with Sketch of His Life* (Toronto: William Briggs, 1886), 28.

46 For historical accounts of the social construction of working-class whiteness, see David Roediger, *The Wages of Whiteness: Race and the Making of the American Working Class* (London: Verso, 1991) and *Towards the Abolition of Whiteness: Essays on Race, Politics, and Working Class History* (London: Verso, 1994), and Noel Ignatiev, *How the Irish Became White* (New York: Routledge, 1995). Michael Omi and Howard Winant define a "racial project" as "simultaneously an interpretation, representation, or explanation of racial dynamics, and an effort to reorganize and redistribute resources along particular racial lines. Racial projects connect what race means in a particular discursive practice and the ways in which both social structures are racially *organized*, based upon that meaning." *Racial Formation in the United States: From the 1960s to the 1990s*, 2d ed. (New York: Routledge, 1994), 56.

47 Arthur, *Six Nights*, 1:58.

48 Ibid., 60.

49 Sean Wilentz, *Chants Democratic: New York City and the Rise of the American Working Class, 1788–1850* (New York: Oxford University Press, 1984), 312.

50 See my discussion of the concept of experience and its implications for the sentimental structure of feeling in the Introduction, above.

51 Eve Kosofsky Sedgwick, *Epistemology of the Closet* (Berkeley and Los Angeles: University of California Press, 1990), 142, 146.

52 Arthur, *Six Nights*, 2:82. Tyrrell cites several sources claiming that the elections of 1842 and 1844 were major causes of backsliding among Washingtonians. See *Sobering Up*, 206–7.

53 The two major debates that factionalized the Washingtonians and led to the end of their phase of the temperance movement were over the value of "Maine Laws" prohibiting the sale of alcohol, which were antithetical to the Washingtonian commitment to "moral suasion," and over the appropriateness of newly formed secret societies like the Sons of Temperance and the Good Templars, which contradicted the Washingtonians' commitment to publicity. The former debate had its counterpart in the abolitionist movement, but with quite different implications; see P. Gabrielle Foreman, "Sentimental Abolition in Douglass's Decade: Revision, Erotic Conversion, and the Politics of Witnessing in *The Heroic Slave* and *My Bondage and My Freedom*," in Chapman and Hendler, *Sentimental Men*, 149–62. Arthur, despite his early commitment to moral suasion, was an enthusiastic prohibitionist by the time

he wrote *Ten Nights in a Bar-Room* in 1854. For differing accounts of the tensions between the Washingtonians and prohibitionism, see Tyrrell, *Sobering Up,* 191–224, and Leonard U. Blumberg, "The Significance of the Alcohol Prohibitionists for the Washington Temperance Societies," *Journal of Studies on Alcohol* 41, no. 1 (1980): 37–77.

54 Both of these functions had their correlatives in women's fiction; sentimental novels often claimed to provide imaginary "companions" for women increasingly isolated in the domestic sphere, and they served up explicit warnings against deviations from domestic norms. See Chapter 4.

55 Tyrrell cites several groups whose membership lists were predominantly female and claims that in New York City "Washingtonian women usually outnumbered men at temperance functions." *Sobering Up,* 179.

56 Dannenbaum, *Drink and Disorder,* 34.

57 Quoted in Maxwell, "Washingtonian Movement," 415. There should by now be nothing surprising about such a gendering of public speech. Even though feminist historians such as Mary Ryan have identified the important symbolic roles women played in the public sphere of the 1830s and 1840s, and despite the attention garnered by speakers like the Grimké sisters and Fanny Wright, no one has seriously questioned the idea that men had a virtual monopoly on public speech in the period. See Mary P. Ryan, *Women in Public: Between Banners and Ballots, 1825–1880* (Baltimore: Johns Hopkins University Press, 1990).

58 Arthur, *Six Nights,* 2:54.

59 Ibid., 56.

60 Ibid., 60–61.

61 Ibid., 82–83.

62 Nor did Washingtonians put much stock in the power of prayer. After his first vow, Alfred prays for the strength to remain temperate, and his mother does little in the story but pray for him. But such prayers are rarely answered in Washingtonian fiction, more evidence that although the organization appropriated the forms of religious revivalism, especially Methodism, it significantly secularized those forms.

63 Jürgen Habermas, *The Structural Transformation of the Public Sphere: An Inquiry into a Category of Bourgeois Society,* trans. Thomas Burger and Frederick Lawrence (Cambridge, Mass.: MIT Press, 1989), 31–43. On the centrality of print for the constitution of a public sphere, see Warner, *Letters of the Republic,* 1–33, and Benedict Anderson, *Imagined Communities: Reflections on the Origin and Spread of Nationalism,* rev. ed. (London: Verso, 1991), 1–65.

64 See Nancy Fraser, "Rethinking the Public Sphere: A Contribution to the Critique of Actually Existing Democracy," in *Habermas and the Public Sphere,* ed. Craig Calhoun (Cambridge, Mass.: MIT Press, 1992), 109–42; Ryan, *Women in Public;* Susan G. Davis, *Parades and Power: Street Theatre in Nineteenth-Century Philadelphia* (Berkeley and Los Angeles: University of California Press, 1986); and Michael Schudson,

"Was There Ever a Public Sphere? If So, When? Reflections on the American Case," in Calhoun, *Habermas and the Public Sphere*, 143–63.

65 These and other critiques of Habermas are summarized in Nicholas Garnham, "The Media and the Public Sphere," in Calhoun, *Habermas and the Public Sphere*, 359–60. On the prevalence of rational-critical discourse in nineteenth-century American politics, Michael Schudson is concise: "The politically oriented riot was a more familiar form of political activity than learned discussion of political principles." Schudson, "Was There Ever a Public Sphere?," 160.

66 Habermas, *Structural Transformation*, 51.

67 See Chapter 4.

68 On the development of class differences in leisure, see Lawrence W. Levine, *Highbrow/Lowbrow: The Emergence of Cultural Hierarchy in America* (Cambridge, Mass.: Harvard University Press, 1988), and Kathy Peiss, *Cheap Amusements: Working Women and Leisure in Turn-of-the-Century New York* (Philadelphia: Temple University Press, 1986).

69 Tyrrell, *Sobering Up*, 177–78.

70 Brother Roger Jamison, C.S.C., *Temperance Movement in South Bend and St. Joseph County, 1830 to 1855* (M.A. thesis, University of Notre Dame, Notre Dame, Indiana, 1938), 34.

71 Tyrrell, *Sobering Up*, 178.

72 Thanks to Gloria-Jean Masciarotte for pointing out the continuity running from Watt to Armstrong, whose arguments are otherwise quite different. The argument that the novel is a middle-class form underpins Habermas's assertion that there is no proletarian public sphere; if the public sphere is almost inherently bourgeois, that trait must derive at least in part from the bourgeois character of the novel. Given that his public sphere book came out only a few years after *The Rise of the Novel*, his arguments may have been influenced by Watt's; however, he cites Altick and Leavis as his literary-historical sources.

73 First quotation is from Arthur, *Six Nights*, iii; other quotations are from Whitman, *Franklin Evans*, 126, 128.

74 Warner, *Letters of the Republic*, 154.

75 Arthur, *Six Nights*, 2:105.

76 Ibid., iii.

77 Ibid., iv; Whitman, *Franklin Evans*, 126–27.

78 On evangelism and reform, see Ryan, *Cradle of the Middle Class*; Paul Johnson, *A Shopkeeper's Millenium: Society and Revivals in Rochester, New York, 1815–1837* (New York: Hill and Wang, 1978); and Steven Mintz, *Moralists and Modernizers: America's Pre–Civil War Reformers* (Baltimore: Johns Hopkins University Press, 1995).

79 Quoted in Dannenbaum, *Drink and Disorder*, 36.

80 Warner characterizes the dream sequence as condensing the Washingtonians' "fantasy of stateless public association," but he also remarks that "[i]f it weren't so queer,

this passage would be a true nightmare of democratic totalitarianism," identifying as mitigating queerness the man's spectacular self-relation, Franklin's presence as spectator, and the "campy feudalism involved in calling John Doe the Last Vassal." Warner, "Whitman Drunk," 34. What is left out of this dialectic of stateless association and democratic totalitarianism is the racialized basis of this fantasy that I identify below: if the Last Vassal's performance is a form of camp, his claim to be a slave breaking his chains is a form of blackface.

81 The Washingtonians' appreciation for blackface minstrelsy was one of the aspects of the movement that temperance regulars saw as less than respectable. Horace Greeley campaigned in the *New York Daily Tribune* against Charley White's Kentucky Negro Minstrels, who first came to public attention performing at the Washingtonian Teetotaler's Hall. Tyrrell, *Sobering Up,* 195. For more on how the popularity of blackface minstrelsy contributed to the social construction of whiteness in the 1840s, see Eric Lott, *Love and Theft: Blackface Minstrelsy and the American Working Class* (New York: Oxford University Press, 1993).

82 Warner's account of this mechanism is concise: "Access to the public came in the whiteness and maleness that were then denied as forms of positivity, since the white male qua public person was only abstract rather than white and male. . . . Self-abstraction from male bodies confirms masculinity." Warner, "Mass Public," 382–83.

Chapter Two

1 Dorothy Sterling, *The Making of an Afro-American: Martin Robison Delany, 1812–1885* (Garden City, N.Y.: Doubleday, 1971), 42.

2 Throughout this chapter I follow the fairly standard practice of referring to "blacks" rather than "African Americans" when discussing the antebellum period. Such terminology seems consistent with Delany's own argument that without full citizenship rights even free blacks could not plausibly consider themselves part of an American nation. Occasionally, when the period's usage demands it, I use the word "Negro," as in "Negro Convention Movement."

3 Whether to designate the dominant strain in Delany's thought "black nationalism" or "Pan-Africanism" is a vexing question. Not every formulation of his ideas involved the formation of a territorial nation-state, though he used the term "nation" to describe most of his projects. Similarly, for much of his life Delany emphasized an alliance of African peoples against white hegemony, but often his alliance politics extended to all "colored people," including Asians and American Indians. Two books on Delany exemplify the different interpretations of his thought in their very titles: Victor Ullman's *Martin R. Delany: The Beginnings of Black Nationalism* (Boston: Beacon Press, 1971) and Cyril E. Griffith's *The African Dream: Martin R. Delany and the Emergence of Pan-African Thought* (University Park: Pennsylvania State University Press, 1975).

4 Sterling, *Making of an Afro-American,* 45–46. She goes on to say that Delany de-

veloped a particular expertise in Central American and Caribbean geography and proposed that club members should study Spanish. Here, perhaps, is the root of the "Black Atlantic" conceptualization of black identity evinced in the wide geographical scope of *Blake*.

5 Ullman, *Martin Delany*, 29, 27.

6 Ibid., 29–31. Quotation is on 31.

7 In Philadelphia, for instance, a white mob attacked the Moyamensing Temperance Society, which was marching to promote black temperance and to celebrate West Indian emancipation. Several days of brutal antiblack violence ensued. For a concise survey of such riots in the period, see Leonard P. Curry, *The Free Black in Urban America, 1800–1850: The Shadow of the Dream* (Chicago: University of Chicago Press, 1981), 96–111.

8 The concept of a black public sphere has been most richly documented and theorized in the special issue of *Public Culture* bearing that name (*Public Culture* 15, no. 1 [1994]), reprinted as *The Black Public Sphere: A Public Culture Book,* ed. Black Public Sphere Collective (Chicago: University of Chicago Press, 1995). Only one essay in this volume deals primarily with the nineteenth century, however, and that one almost exclusively with the Reconstruction and post-Reconstruction era. See Elsa Barkley Brown, "Negotiating and Transforming the Public Sphere: African American Political Life in the Transition from Slavery to Freedom," *Public Culture* 15 (1994): 107–46.

9 See the Introduction for a discussion of the concept of the counterpublic.

10 The twentieth-century reprint of Delany's book leaves off the last two words of his already lengthy title, *Politically Considered*. The term "political" is important because it defines the perspective from which he approaches both the object of his study — *The Colored People of the United States* — and the narrative that the title condenses — *Condition, Elevation, Emigration, and Destiny*. Martin R. Delany, *The Condition, Elevation, Emigration and Destiny of the Colored People of the United States* (1852; reprint, Baltimore: Black Classic Press, 1993).

11 Ibid., 201.

12 Throughout this book and his career, Delany was engaged in a self-conscious project of constructing his "people." The variety of strategies he took up in this construction is quite astounding, ranging from historicizing and mythologizing narratives of African and African American individual and collective pasts to the peculiar combination of biologized racialism and biblical hermeneutics of his late book *Principia of Ethnology: The Origin of Races and Color, with an Archeological Compendium of Ethiopian and Egyptian Civilization, from Years of Careful Examination and Enquiry* (Philadelphia: Harper and Brothers, 1879), reprinted as *The Origin of Races and Color* (Baltimore: Black Classic Press, 1991).

13 For a magisterial survey of the history and theory of civil society, see Jean L. Cohen and Andrew Arato, *Civil Society and Political Theory* (Cambridge, Mass.: MIT Press,

1992). On civility, see Norbert Elias, *The Civilizing Process*, vol. 1, *The History of Manners*, trans. Edmund Jephcott (New York: Pantheon, 1978), and vol. 2, *Power and Civility*, trans. Edmund Jephcott (New York: Pantheon, 1982). Thanks to Bruce Burgett for helping me formulate this conjunction of civilities.

14 Among the most suggestive of Delany's forms of participation in civil society was his lifelong commitment to Prince Hall Freemasonry. Historian Margaret C. Jacob has argued that Masonic lodges were the first civil society institutions. While she analyzes the lodges as voluntary associations, her quotation of the Grand Master of 1740 perfectly demonstrates the conjunction of this institutional meaning of "civility" with its connotations of proper behavior: "[T]he Order of Freemasons exists to form men, agreeable men, good citizens, good subjects." *Living the Enlightenment: Freemasonry and Politics in Eighteenth-Century Europe* (New York: Oxford University Press, 1991), 7. Gesturing toward an even larger claim about Freemasonry's role in the formation of civil society, Habermas invokes "Lessing's famous statement about Freemasonry, which at that time was a broader European phenomenon: it was just as old as bourgeois society—'if indeed bourgeois society is not merely the offspring of Freemasonry.'" Jürgen Habermas, *The Structural Transformation of the Public Sphere: An Inquiry into a Category of Bourgeois Society*, trans. Thomas Burger and Frederick Lawrence (Cambridge, Mass.: MIT Press, 1989), 35. For histories of black Freemasonry focusing on the Prince Hall lodges in which Delany was active, see Loretta J. Williams, *Black Freemasonry and Middle-Class Realities* (Columbia: University of Missouri Press, 1980), and William A. Muraskin, *Middle-Class Blacks in a White Society: Prince Hall Freemasonry in America* (Berkeley and Los Angeles: University of California Press, 1975). For an analysis of Delany's published work on the topic, *The Origin and Objects of Ancient Freemasonry*, see Robert S. Levine, *Martin Delany, Frederick Douglass, and the Politics of Representative Identity* (Chapel Hill: University of North Carolina Press, 1997), 8–11. On the implications of Delany's Freemasonry, see Maurice Wallace, "'Are We Men?': Prince Hall, Martin Delany, and the Masculine Ideal in Black Freemasonry, 1775–1865," *American Literary History* 9, no. 3 (Fall 1997): 396–424.

15 The movement tended to view the franchise as the measure of blacks' potential access to the political public, a view that Delany criticized. In many states, of course, free blacks had never had the right to vote, while in others (including Pennsylvania) that right was revoked in the early decades of the nineteenth century. The first Negro Convention in Pennsylvania was called "with the specific purpose of calling attention to the recent disfranchisement of blacks within the state and to suggest means of regaining the suffrage." Philip S. Foner and George E. Walker, eds., *Proceedings of the Black State Conventions, 1840–1865*, vol. 1, *New York, Pennsylvania, Indiana, Michigan, Ohio* (Philadelphia: Temple University Press, 1979), 104.

16 Howard Holman Bell, *A Survey of the Negro Convention Movement, 1830–1861* (New York: Arno Press and the New York Times, 1969), 3.

17 On the history of the antebellum black press, see Frankie Hutton, *The Early Black Press in America, 1827–1860* (Westport, Conn.: Greenwood Press, 1993). For a useful set of selections from the black press in the period, see Martin E. Dann, ed., *The Black Press, 1827–1890: The Quest for National Identity* (New York: G. P. Putnam's Sons, 1971).

18 Bell, *Survey*, 96.

19 Ibid., 5.

20 Levine, *Martin Delany*.

21 Habermas, *Structural Transformation*, 37.

22 Delany, *Condition*, 169.

23 For a biography of Delany that focuses on the emigrationist aspects of his thought, see Griffith, *African Dream*.

24 Levine, *Martin Delany*, 91–93.

25 *Proceedings of the National Convention of Colored People; Held at Cleveland, Ohio, on Thursday, Friday and Saturday, the 24th, 25th, and 26th of August, 1854* (Pittsburgh: A. A. Anderson, 1854), 8.

26 Ibid.

27 Ibid., 33.

28 Delany continues his etymology: "*Hostis,* a public — and sometimes — private enemy; and *Peregrinus,* an *alien, stranger,* or *foreigner.*" Ibid., 34.

29 Ibid. Delany then goes on to make a distinction that comes up again years later in *Blake:* a distinction between "suffrage" and the "franchise." The former is a revokable "privilege" to vote for whites, "a mere permission, a thing suffered to be done." Delany says some blacks have confused this "suffrage" with the franchise, which he defines as an "*inherent* and *inviolate*" right not only to vote but to maintain what he calls "the *sovereign principle* which composes the *true basis* of his liberty." Ibid., 27.

30 Ibid., 35. This was an important point to Delany, which he reiterated in many speeches as well as in *Blake*. Here he emphasizes it by continuing, "To suppose otherwise is . . . [the] delusion [that] reveals the true secret of the power which holds in peaceable subjection, all the oppressed in every part of the world." Ibid.

31 "Declaration of Sentiments," in ibid., 26.

32 Ibid., 24.

33 Gregg D. Crane, "The Lexicon of Rights, Power, and Community in *Blake:* Martin R. Delany's Dissent from *Dred Scott,*" *American Literature* 68, no. 3 (September 1996): 544.

34 "Declaration of Sentiments," in *Proceedings,* 26.

35 Ibid., 27.

36 Delany, *Condition*, 203.

37 Ernest Renan, "What Is a Nation?," trans. Martin Thom, in *Nation and Narration,* ed. Homi Bhabha (New York, Routledge, 1990), 18.

38 Claudia Tate, *Domestic Allegories of Political Desire: The Black Heroine's Text at the Turn of the Century* (New York: Oxford University Press, 1992).

39 Delany, "A Project for an Expedition of Adventure to the Eastern Coast of Africa," appendix to *Condition*, 209–10.

40 Ibid., 210.

41 Ibid.

42 Kevin K. Gaines, *Uplifting the Race: Black Leadership, Politics, and Culture in the Twentieth Century* (Chapel Hill: University of North Carolina Press, 1996), 84. The conspiratorial and the elitist were perhaps most closely conjoined in Delany's participation in Freemasonry. In a discussion of Delany's *Origin and Objects of Ancient Freemasonry,* Levine argues plausibly that it "[a]nticipat[es] Du Bois's elitist notion of the Talented Tenth." Levine, *Martin Delany,* 9.

43 Delany's scientific interests were not limited to the social sciences; for instance, he published an article on comets and invented a device to help trains ascend inclines. Some of his biographers attribute at least part of Delany's alienation from the United States to his inability to get a patent for this invention because of his race.

44 Ullman, *Martin Delany,* 238.

45 Robert Levine suggestively uses the term "transnational" to connect Delany's Masonic involvement with his antislavery activities, arguing that "[h]is transnational vision . . . speaks not only to a Masonic sense of the ways in which fraternal and civilized ideals can cross national ideologies and boundaries, but also to a pragmatic sense that only by putting such ideals into practice in a particular place can blacks mount an effective challenge to U.S. slave culture . . . a Masonic transnationalism, an Afrocentric pride, and a pragmatics of nation and place." Levine, *Martin Delany,* 96. In the same spirit, I use the term "transnational" rather than "international" below to describe the incident at the Statistical Congress, understanding the former to refer to relations between norms of civility—between civilizations—and the latter to refer to relations between nation-states.

46 Sterling, *Making of an Afro-American,* 212.

47 Frank A. Rollin [Frances E. Rollin Whipper], *Life and Public Services of Martin R. Delany* (1868; reprint, New York: Arno Press and the New York Times, 1969), 119. Rollin's biography includes transcriptions of conversations with Delany.

48 Quoted in ibid., 123.

49 Lauren Berlant, *The Queen of America Goes to Washington City: Essays on Sex and Citizenship* (Durham, N.C.: Duke University Press, 1997), 2.

50 Sterling, *Making of an Afro-American,* 214–15.

51 Ibid., 215.

52 Ibid., 217.

53 Martin R. Delany, *Blake; or, The Huts of America* (Boston: Beacon Press, 1970). All subsequent references to this novel will be cited parenthetically in the text.

54 The above information and quotations are drawn from Levine, *Martin Delany,* 178–79.

55 Paul Gilroy, *The Black Atlantic: Modernity and Double Consciousness* (Cambridge, Mass.: Harvard University Press, 1993), 19–40.

56 Eric J. Sundquist, *To Wake the Nations: Race in the Making of American Literature* (Cambridge, Mass.: Harvard University Press, 1993), 190.

57 This scene of political misrecognition bears comparison to the moment in Harriet Jacobs's *Incidents in the Life of a Slave Girl* when she describes a "poor, ignorant [black] woman [who] thought that America was governed by a Queen, to whom the President was subordinate," and who had sent word to the president to free all the slaves. As Lauren Berlant points out in her analysis of *Incidents,* Jacobs presents this scene as a mirror image of the structure of ignorance that she calls the "state of civilization in the late nineteenth century of the United States." Delany and Jacobs thus have in common the rhetorical strategy of criticizing white America by claiming that it is characterized by incivility. See Berlant, *Queen of America,* 225–26.

58 Levine discusses temperance thematics as a link between Delany and Douglass in *Martin Delany,* 99–143.

59 This discussion parallels Delany's mild comments on the African slavery he came across in his Niger Valley explorations. See Martin R. Delany, *Official Report of the Niger Valley Exploring Party* (1860), reprinted in *Search for a Place: Black Separatism and Africa,* ed. Howard Bell (Ann Arbor: University of Michigan Press, 1969), 85–86.

60 Robert Reid-Pharr analyzes this passage as an "appeal for the economic, political, and cultural unity of 'The Black Community,'" underscoring Delany's black nationalism by replacing the possessive pronoun in "their eyes" with "The New African's." While I agree with Reid-Pharr that this natural communication is part of Delany's "model for how the many disparate peoples of the African diaspora might be interpellated as blacks, or more parochially as African Americans," I think it is a stretch to use this passage to support his thesis that "Blake/Delany is able to deny—without seeming to—the necessity of the abused, pitiful slave in the process of community formation," since the antecedent for "their" is in fact "the most stupid among the slaves." Delany's vanguardist elitism is certainly evident here, but this is clearly one of the moments where his protagonist has a more expansive notion of the revolutionary black counterpublic than the author himself usually evinced. See Robert Reid-Pharr, "Violent Ambiguity: Martin Delany, Bourgeois Sadomasochism, and the Production of a Black National Masculinity," in *Representing Black Men,* ed. Marcellus Blount and George P. Cunningham (New York: Routledge, 1996), 86, 90.

61 Sundquist, *To Wake the Nations,* 197.

62 Sundquist analyzes this scene, as well as the "King's Day" jubilee, in some detail in ibid., 210–21.

63 The title of the song is not given, nor is Cinque's name mentioned, but Eric Sundquist points out that the poem reproduced in the novel is James M. Whitfield's "To Cinque," from *America and Other Poems* (Buffalo: James S. Leavitt, 1853), 20–21. Several of the poems read by or ascribed to the character Placido are from Whitfield's book, which itself was dedicated to Delany. See Sundquist, *To Wake the Nations,* 203–4.

64 Nancy Fraser, "Rethinking the Public Sphere: A Contribution to the Critique of Actually Existing Democracy," in *Habermas and the Public Sphere,* ed. Craig Calhoun (Cambridge, Mass.: MIT Press, 1992), 109–42.

65 He writes in "The Destiny of the Colored Race" that "the great issue, sooner or later, upon which must be disputed the world's destiny, will be a question of black and white, and every individual will be called upon for his identity with one or the other." *Proceedings,* 40–41.

Chapter Three

1 Horatio Alger Jr., *Ragged Dick; or, Street Life in New York* (1868), reprinted in *Ragged Dick and Struggling Upward* (New York: Penguin, 1985), 21, 28, 22. All subsequent references to the novel are to this edition and will be cited parenthetically in the text.

2 See Frederick Law Olmsted, *Central Park as a Work of Art and as a Great Municipal Enterprise, 1853–1895,* vol. 2 of *Forty Years of Landscape Architecture: Being the Professional Papers of Frederick Law Olmsted, Senior,* ed. Frederick Law Olmsted Jr. and Theodora Kimball (New York: G. P. Putnam's Sons, 1928), and *Landscape into Cityscape: Frederick Law Olmsted's Plans for a Greater New York City,* ed. Albert Fein (Ithaca: Cornell University Press, 1968). A useful account of Olmsted's conflicts with commercial and political interests is Elizabeth Barlow, *Frederick Law Olmsted's New York* (New York: Praeger Publishers, 1972). The analyses I draw on most extensively here are those in Alan Trachtenberg, *The Incorporation of America: Culture and Society in the Gilded Age* (New York: Hill and Wang, 1982), 101–47; Lawrence W. Levine, *Highbrow/Lowbrow: The Emergence of Cultural Hierarchy in America* (Cambridge, Mass.: Harvard University Press, 1988), 200–219; Thomas Bender, *Toward an Urban Vision: Ideas and Institutions in Nineteenth-Century America* (Lexington: University Press of Kentucky, 1975); and Roy Rosenzweig and Elizabeth Blackmar, *The Park and the People: A History of Central Park* (Ithaca: Cornell University Press, 1992). See also Eric Homberger, *Scenes from the Life of a City: Corruption and Conscience in Old New York* (New Haven: Yale University Press, 1994), and Witold Rybczynski, *A Clearing in the Distance: Frederick Law Olmsted and America in the Nineteenth Century* (New York: Scribner, 1999).

3 Quoted in Trachtenberg, *Incorporation of America,* 147.

4 Quoted in Levine, *Highbrow/Lowbrow,* 202.

5 Olmsted, *Central Park,* 464, 410.

6 Levine, *Highbrow/Lowbrow,* 202–3; Olmsted, *Central Park,* 247–48.

7 Olmsted fought another such battle at the 1893 Columbian Exposition, trying unsuccessfully to keep his "Wooded Island" free of commercial activity; see Neil Harris, *Cultural Excursions: Marketing Appetites and Cultural Tastes in Modern America* (Chicago: University of Chicago Press, 1990), 121–22. Thomas Bender, in *Intellect and Public Life: Essays on the Social History of Academic Intellectuals in the United States* (Baltimore: Johns Hopkins University Press, 1993), and William R. Taylor, in *In Pursuit of Gotham: Culture and Commerce in New York* (New York: Oxford University Press, 1992), provide useful historical accounts of shifting definitions of the public in the United States.

8 See David I. Macleod, *Building Character in the American Boy: The Boy Scouts, YMCA, and Their Forerunners, 1870–1920* (Madison: University of Wisconsin Press, 1983).

9 Indeed, historians of childhood argue that adolescence itself was invented in this period. See, for instance, Joseph F. Kett, *Rites of Passage: Adolescence in America, 1790 to the Present* (New York: Basic Books, 1977).

10 For an analysis of the way Alger negotiated the public-private split in his writing career, see Carol Nackenoff, *The Fictional Republic: Horatio Alger and American Political Discourse* (New York: Oxford University Press, 1994).

11 See the Introduction.

12 In her revisionary analysis of the use in women's history of the notion of separate spheres, Kerber writes that "political systems and systems of gender relations are reciprocal social constructions." Linda K. Kerber, "Separate Spheres, Female Worlds, Women's Place: The Rhetoric of Women's History," *Journal of American History* 75 (June 1988): 39.

13 "Editorial Notes," *Library Journal* 4, nos. 9–10 (September–October 1879): 367. Subsequent references to this special issue will be cited simply as *Library Journal*.

14 Higginson in 1864 had written one of the earliest positive reviews of Alger's first full novel, *Frank's Campaign, or, The Farm and the Camp* (1864; New York: Hurst and Company, n.d.). In 1877 Clarke denounced the " 'endless reams' of drivel poured forth by Horatio Alger Jr., and Oliver Optic"; one Alger biography speculates that Alger named one of his villains Clarke shortly thereafter "in oblique reply" to the attack. See Gary Scharnhorst and Jack Bales, *The Lost Life of Horatio Alger, Jr.* (Bloomington: Indiana University Press, 1985), 63, 118.

15 S. S. Green, "Sensational Fiction in Public Libraries," *Library Journal*, 347.

16 T. W. Higginson, "Address of T. W. Higginson," ibid., 357.

17 William P. Atkinson, "Address of Prof. Wm. P. Atkinson," ibid., 361.

18 James Freeman Clarke, "Address of James Freeman Clarke," ibid., 356.

19 Green, "Sensational Fiction," 349.

20 Charles Francis Adams Jr., "Fiction in Public Libraries and Educational Catalogues," *Library Journal*, 334.

21 Green, "Sensational Fiction," 349. It is, of course, significant that the readers Higgin-

son describes as "taking possession" of the continent from "wild Indians" are of "the Anglo-American race," while those whom Green sees as needing to learn their limitations are Irish. *Only an Irish Boy,* one of the few Alger novels foregrounding a protagonist's non-Anglo ethnicity, had appeared serially in the *New York Weekly* in 1874, five years before the Boston conference. Horatio Alger Jr., *Only an Irish Boy; or, Andy Burke's Fortunes* (New York: Hurst and Company, n.d.).

22 Clarke, "Address," 356.

23 Adams, "Fiction," 331.

24 Ibid., 337.

25 Ibid., 331. Emphasis added.

26 Both definitions are part of the *Oxford English Dictionary* entry under "pander."

27 Horatio Alger Jr., *Julius; or, The Street Boy Out West* (1874), reprinted in *Strive and Succeed: Two Novels by Horatio Alger* (New York: Holt, Rinehart, and Winston, 1967), 22.

28 As historians of literacy have shown, literacy is always more than a statistical fact or practical skill; it has cultural meanings that shift geographically and historically. See Harvey J. Graff, ed., *Literacy and Social Development in the West: A Reader* (New York: Cambridge University Press, 1981); Harvey J. Graff, *The Legacies of Literacy: Continuities and Contradictions in Western Culture and Society* (Bloomington: Indiana University Press, 1987); Harvey J. Graff, *The Literacy Myth: Literacy and Social Structure in the Nineteenth-Century City* (New York: Academic Press, 1979); Michael Warner, *The Letters of the Republic: Publication and the Public Sphere in Eighteenth-Century America* (Cambridge, Mass.: Harvard University Press, 1990); and several of the essays in Cathy N. Davidson, ed., *Reading in America: Literature and Social History* (Baltimore: Johns Hopkins University Press, 1989).

29 Horatio Alger Jr., *Phil, the Fiddler; or, The Young Street Musician* (1872), reprinted in *Struggling Upward and Other Works* (New York: Bonanza Books, 1945), 305.

30 Scharnhorst and Bales, *Lost Life*, 96–97.

31 Alger, *Phil, the Fiddler*, 282, 301.

32 Horatio Alger Jr., *Struggling Upward; or, Luke Larkin's Luck* (1890), reprinted in *Struggling Upward and Other Works*, 96.

33 For a discussion of transparency of character as an ideal of sincerity, see Karen Halttunen, *Confidence Men and Painted Women: A Study of Middle-Class Culture* (New Haven: Yale University Press, 1982), 33–55.

34 Horatio Alger Jr., *Jed, the Poorhouse Boy* (1892), reprinted in *Struggling Upward and Other Works*, 522.

35 Horatio Alger Jr., *Silas Snobden's Office Boy* (1889/90; reprint, Garden City, N.Y.: Doubleday, 1973), 91.

36 Horatio Alger Jr., *The Store Boy; or, The Fortunes of Ben Barclay* (1887), reprinted in *Strive and Succeed: Two Novels by Horatio Alger* (Holt, Rinehart, and Winston, 1967), 34.

37 Alger, *Julius,* 35–36; Horatio Alger Jr., *The World Before Him* (1880), reprinted in *Adrift in New York and The World Before Him,* ed. William Coyle (New York: Odyssey Press, 1966), 229.

38 Alger, *The Store Boy,* 140.

39 John Cawelti, *Apostles of the Self-Made Man: Changing Concepts of Success in America* (Chicago: University of Chicago Press, 1965). This nostalgia provides another rhetorical parallel between Alger and Olmsted, whose earliest writings were published under the Jeffersonian pseudonyms of "Yeoman" and "An American Farmer" and made recourse to an agrarian republican model of the public sphere predicated on a separation between the cultural and the commercial. See Barlow, *Frederick Law Olmsted's New York,* 7.

40 David Paul Nord, "A Republican Literature: Magazine Reading and Readers in Late Eighteenth-Century New York," in Davidson, *Reading in America,* 115. For a discussion of the meaning of this association for women, see Linda K. Kerber, *Women of the Republic: Intellect and Ideology in Revolutionary America* (Chapel Hill: University of North Carolina Press, 1980), 235–64.

41 Warner, *Letters of the Republic,* 123. Warner also notes the continuity between Washington's rhetoric and Alger's.

42 Alger, *The World Before Him,* 234.

43 For more on the relationship between letter-writing and the public sphere, see Chapter 4. On pleasure at seeing one's name in print, see Brian Massumi, foreword to *A Thousand Plateaus: Capitalism and Schizophrenia,* by Gilles Deleuze and Félix Guattari, trans. Brian Massumi (Minneapolis: University of Minnesota Press, 1987), xviii.

44 Beginning with *Ragged Dick,* Alger's publishing contracts were usually for series of four to eight novels; hence the six-volume Ragged Dick series was followed by *Luck and Pluck; or, John Oakley's Inheritance,* which initiated the eight-book Luck and Pluck series. For useful information about Alger publication history, see Ralph D. Gardner, "Road to Success: The Bibliography of the Works of Horatio Alger," in *Horatio Alger; or, The American Hero Era* (New York: Arco Publishing Company, 1974), 353–495.

45 Alger, *The World Before Him,* 233.

46 Nathaniel West's hilariously vicious parody-pastiche of Alger, *A Cool Million; The Dismantling of Lemuel Pitkin* (New York: Covici, Friede, 1934), is based on the idea that Alger's formula universalizes the con game, making the world into a big con.

47 Horatio Alger Jr., *Adrift in New York* (1889), reprinted in *Adrift in New York and The World Before Him,* 81, 144.

48 Halttunen, *Confidence Men and Painted Women,* 204.

49 In his literary advice book *Books and Reading,* Yale president Noah Porter digresses slightly to perform a literary analysis that shows how pervasive was the aversion to such "posing for sympathy." Comparing Byron's Manfred to Shakespeare's Hamlet, Porter condemns the former for publicizing his story for misleading ends. "His

guilt he does not hide, he spreads it abroad for public gaze, but rather to incite the sympathy of lookers-on than in the spirit of confession and shame." Porter goes on to express his disapproval of Byron because "there are many who sympathize with Manfred to the end, and suffer no recoil of horror," while "no reader would care to change places" with Lady Macbeth. Noah Porter, *Books and Reading; or, What Books Shall I Read and How Shall I Read Them?* (1870; New York: Scribner's, 1882), 86–87. Boy book writers other than Alger also subscribed wholeheartedly to this distinction. The preface to Oliver Optic's *Desk and Debit* announces that in this book, "as in its predecessors, evil-minded characters are introduced, to show the contrast between vice and virtue," but "the writer has no fear that his readers will love, respect or admire" the story's villains. Oliver Optic [William Taylor Adams], *Desk and Debit; or, The Catastrophes of a Clerk* (Boston: Lee and Shepard, 1871).

50 Alger, *Mark the Match Boy; or, Richard Hunter's Ward* (1869), reprinted in *Ragged Dick and Mark the Match Boy: Two Novels by Horatio Alger* (New York: Collier, 1962), 250–53.

51 Alger, *Ragged Dick,* 3; *Julius,* 1–12. The performance in *Julius* is not described as blackface minstrelsy, though some performers are obviously working-class Irish Americans who, according to historians of minstrelsy, might have put on such a performance. Instead of emphasizing the racial or ethnic heritage of this performance, Alger instead focuses on class distinctions, contrasting "the classic drama or the opera, as brought out at the Academy" with "this rude performance." Julius's enjoyment of this show demonstrates that "[t]hough he is my hero I have no desire to represent him as more refined or better educated than the majority of his companions" (10).

52 Alger, *Jed, the Poorhouse Boy,* 445.

53 Alger, *The Store Boy,* 98.

54 Horatio Alger Jr., *A Fancy of Hers* (1892), reprinted in *A Fancy of Hers/The Disagreeable Woman* (New York: Van Nostrand Reinhold, 1981), 58.

55 Horatio Alger Jr., *Tattered Tom; or, The Story of a Street Arab* (Boston: Loring, 1871). Michael Moon discusses the latter tale briefly, arguing that Tom's restoration to her rich mother and "her long-lost genteel, feminine identity" is the only example of an Alger protagonist who "does not 'rise' as a consequence of her demonstrably enterprising and honest behavior." See Michael Moon, " 'The Gentle Boy from the Dangerous Classes': Pederasty, Domesticity, and Capitalism in Horatio Alger," *Representations* 19 (Summer 1987): 95–97. In fact, several of Alger's books culminate in the hero's succeeding because of the discovery that he is of genteel or even noble descent, rather than because of his behavior; see, for instance, *Adrift in New York.* What differentiates Tom's rise is that, like Mabel in *A Fancy of Hers,* she rises to a place explicitly figured as *out* of the public eye.

56 Arthur Penn, *The Home Library* (New York: Appleton's Home Books, 1883), 15. In

one novel, Alger's protagonist purchases "'Appleton's Railway Guide', which af-
forded him all the information he required." Alger, *The Store Boy,* 129.

57 Porter, *Books and Reading,* 360. S. S. Green, the Worcester librarian quoted above,
recommends Porter's text as a guide to proper literary choices. Green, "Sensational
Fiction," 346.

58 Charles Thwing, *The Reading of Books: Its Pleasures, Profits, and Perils* (Boston: Lee
and Shepard, 1883), 121.

59 Ibid., 121–22.

60 Charles F. Richardson, *The Choice of Books* (New York: Useful Knowledge Publishing
Company, 1883), 165.

61 Thwing, *Reading of Books,* 124–25.

62 Porter, *Books and Reading,* 361.

63 Ibid., 8.

64 Quoted in Levine, *Highbrow/Lowbrow,* 186.

65 Porter, *Books and Reading,* 97–98.

66 Kate Gannett Wells, "The Responsibility of Parents in the Selection of Reading for
the Young," *Library Journal,* 329.

67 Porter, *Books and Reading,* 5.

68 Penn, *Home Library,* 25.

69 Those volumes that include a section on "some choice books for boys" seldom if ever
place any of Alger's fiction on their lists, although one recommends his biography of
James Garfield (*From Canal Boy to President, or, The Boyhood and Manhood of James A.
Garfield* [New York: John R. Anderson and Company, 1881]) and praises Alger as
"another sympathetic writer for boys." Mary Alice Caller, *A Literary Guide for Home
and School* (New York: C. E. Merrill, 1892), 131.

70 Penn, *Home Library,* 28.

71 It is unfortunately all too easy to see how these tensions resonate with current debates
about the changing role of mass culture in the public sphere. To choose an obvious
but nonetheless tempting target, I would like to cite a paragraph from the chapter
on music in Allan Bloom's *The Closing of the American Mind* (New York: Simon and
Schuster, 1987):

> Picture a thirteen-year-old boy sitting in the living room of his family home doing
> his math assignment while wearing his Walkman headphones or watching MTV.
> He enjoys the liberties hard won over centuries by the alliance of philosophic
> genius and political heroism, consecrated by the blood of martyrs; he is provided
> with comfort and leisure by the most productive economy ever known to man-
> kind; science has penetrated the secrets of nature in order to provide him with
> the marvelous, lifelike electronic sound and image reproduction he is enjoying.
> And in what does progress culminate? A pubescent child whose body throbs
> with orgasmic rhythms; whose feelings are made articulate in hymns to the joys

of onanism or the killing of parents; whose ambition is to win fame and wealth in imitating the drag-queen who makes the music. In short, life is made into a nonstop, commercially prepackaged masturbational fantasy. (74–75)

Like his counterparts at the turn of the last century, Bloom tries to exert cultural authority precisely by claiming that mass culture has stripped men like himself of all such authority, which now presumably rests in the hands of "drag-queens." Bloom tries to control what we read and how we read it by putting forward a dystopian image of cultural reception, an image he juxtaposes with his own utopian vision of an enlightened, exclusively male public sphere, described in a chapter he names "Our Virtue." One implication of my argument is that such attempts can never really succeed because of how closely they are bound up with the phenomena they decry. Bloom expresses a fear of commodification in an extremely well-marketed, successful book, condenses his anxieties in the picture of a boy taking erotic pleasure in the supposedly passive consumption of mass culture, and opposes this scandalously homoerotic image to a male homosocial Enlightenment utopia. Like Porter and Alger, Bloom claims that his ideal of masculine public virtue can counter the threats of mass culture, but he fails to recognize that the discourses he opposes to one another have been inextricably intertwined for more than a century.

72 Porter, *Books and Reading,* 72–73.

73 This analysis of the contradictions in Porter's theorization of reading owes a great deal to conversations with Gerald Graff. Graff discusses Porter's ideas about literature and teaching in *Professing Literature: An Institutional History* (Chicago: University of Chicago Press, 1987).

74 Porter, *Books and Reading,* 33.

75 Ibid., 230–31.

76 Ibid., 232, 41.

77 Here I am drawing on recent historical scholarship on the construction and reproduction of masculinity and manliness in the nineteenth century, much of which is ably synthesized in the opening chapter of Gail Bederman, *Manliness and Civilization: A Cultural History of Gender and Race in the United States, 1880–1917* (Chicago: University of Chicago Press, 1995), 1–44. See also E. Anthony Rotundo, *American Manhood: Transformations in Masculinity from the Revolution to the Modern Era* (New York: Basic Books, 1993); Joe L. Dubbert, *A Man's Place: Masculinity in Transition* (Englewood Cliffs, N.J.: Prentice-Hall, 1979); Peter Filene, *Him/Her/Self* (New York: New American Library, 1975); and Michael S. Kimmel, *Manhood in America: A Cultural History* (New York: Free Press, 1996).

78 Porter, *Books and Reading,* 20, 51, 235.

79 Horatio Alger Jr., "Writing Stories for Boys—IV," *The Writer* 9 (March 1896): 37.

80 Adams, "Fiction in Public Libraries," 334.

81 Porter, *Books and Reading,* 41.

82 Alger, "Writing Stories for Boys," 37.

83 Porter, *Books and Reading*, 47.

84 Thwing, *Reading of Books*, 2.

85 Ibid., 124.

86 Ibid., 121.

87 Scharnhorst and Bales, 70. In light of this fact, it is easy to interpret as homoerotic Alger's claims to have, all his life, "made a close study of boys" as material for his books, and to have a rapport with his readers because "I have a natural liking for boys, which has made it easy for me to win their confidence and become intimately acquainted with them." Alger, "Writing Stories for Boys," 37. However, such sentences are typical of the way the relation between male authors, books, and readers were figured in this period; another writer in the same series of essays proclaims, "I cannot write a book at all until I have actually made the intimate personal acquaintance [of its characters,] so that they will be confidential and tell me how they feel and what they mean to do." William O. Stoddard, "How to Write a Story for Boys— I," *The Writer* 9 (September 1895): 128.

Alger's recent biographers have, with some justification, interpreted his pederasty as a motive for his literary production in general. My interpretation of homosocial erotics in Alger's fiction is closer to Michael Moon's conclusion that the way "his work manifests male homosexuality" is an "encapsulation" of the way "corporate/capitalist America's long-cherished myth" of upward mobility conceals its "male homoerotic foundations." Moon, " 'Gentle Boy,' " 107. What I add to Moon's argument is the claim that Alger places the act of reading itself at this foundation.

88 Scharnhorst and Bales, *Lost Life*, 72–73, 70.

89 Henry James, *Notes of a Son and Brother*, in *Autobiography*, ed. Frederick W. Dupee (Princeton: Princeton University Press, 1956), 401.

90 Review of *In a New World*, by Horatio Alger Jr., *Literary World* 24 (2 December 1893): 422.

Chapter Four

1 Henry James, *The Speech and Manners of American Women*, serialized in *Harper's Bazaar*, November 1906–February 1907, April–July 1907; reprint, in 1 vol., ed. E. S. Riggs (Lancaster, Pa.: Lancaster House Press, 1973).

2 Ibid., 31.

3 Ibid., 27.

4 For an illuminating analysis of James's essays, see Lynn Wardley, "Woman's Voice, Democracy's Body, and *The Bostonians*," *ELH* 56 (Fall 1989): 639–65.

5 James, *Speech and Manners*, 27.

6 Ibid., 68.

7 Ibid., 91.

8 Louisa May Alcott, *Work: A Story of Experience*, ed. Joy Kasson (New York: Penguin, 1994). Subsequent references to this novel will be cited parenthetically in the text.

9 The phrase "representative identities" is adapted from Robert S. Levine, *Martin Delany, Frederick Douglass, and the Politics of Representative Identity* (Chapel Hill: University of North Carolina Press, 1997), but it is also meant to evoke terms from Habermas's *Structural Transformation,* which describes the way the sovereign's "representative publicness" is replaced by a bourgeois publicity whose concomitant form of subjectivity is "oriented to an audience." See Introduction, above, Chapter 5, below, and Jürgen Habermas, *The Structural Transformation of the Public Sphere: An Inquiry into a Category of Bourgeois Society,* trans. Thomas Burger and Frederick Lawrence (Cambridge, Mass.: MIT Press, 1989).

10 Theodore Parker, *Lessons from the World of Matter and the World of Man,* vol. 14 of *The Collected Works of Theodore Parker,* ed. Rufus Leighton (London: Trübner and Company, 1872), 113.

11 By "the psychological novel" Habermas refers to sentimental fiction. However, his focus is not on nineteenth-century American bestsellers by women but on British and German novels of the eighteenth century authored by men.

12 Habermas, *Structural Transformation,* 50.

13 Ibid., 50–51.

14 Ibid., 56.

15 Ibid.

16 David Reynolds has argued persuasively that claims of women's numerical dominance in the reading public, as well as assertions of the statistical preeminence of women's fiction, have been greatly exaggerated. For my purposes here, what matters is the perception that the "mob of scribbling women" was literarily hegemonic. See David S. Reynolds, *Beneath the American Renaissance: The Subversive Imagination in the Ages of Emerson and Melville* (Cambridge, Mass.: Harvard University Press, 1989).

17 Margaret Coxe, *The Young Lady's Companion, and Token of Affection; in a Series of Letters* (1839; Columbus: I. N. Whiting, 1846).

18 Maria Susanna Cummins, *The Lamplighter* (1854; reprint, New Brunswick, N.J.: Rutgers University Press, 1988), 142.

19 Review of *Work: A Story of Experience,* by Louisa May Alcott, *Lakeside Monthly,* September 1873, 246–49, reprinted in *Critical Essays on Louisa May Alcott,* ed. Madeleine B. Stern (Boston: G. K. Hall, 1984), 187–91.

20 Philip Fisher, *Hard Facts: Setting and Form in the American Novel* (New York: Oxford University Press, 1985), 99.

21 Alcott's decision to replace "experiment" with "experience" may be explained by the then quite recent separation of the two terms' meanings. See Raymond Williams, *Keywords: A Vocabulary of Culture and Society* (1976; rev. ed., New York: Oxford University Press, 1983), 126–29, 116. See also my discussions of the concept of experience in the Introduction, above, and in "The Structure of Sentimental Experience," *Yale Journal of Criticism* 12, no. 1 (1999): 146–53.

22 See Introduction.

23 Ibid.

24 The preceding account of mourning as a form of identification with a lost object follows almost precisely Freud's discussion in "Mourning and Melancholia." After describing the features of mourning, Freud remarks that "it is really only because we know so well how to explain it that this attitude does not seem to us pathological." Sigmund Freud, "Mourning and Melancholia," in *General Psychological Theory: Papers on Metapsychology,* ed. Philip Rieff (New York: Collier, 1963), 165.

25 Women's sentimental novels are referred to as female bildungsromans in Nina Baym, *Women's Fiction: A Guide to Novels by and about Women in America, 1820–1870* (Ithaca: Cornell University Press, 1978), x, and Eve Kornfeld and Susan Jackson, "The Female Bildungsroman in Nineteenth-Century America: Parameters of a Vision," *Journal of American Culture* 10 (Winter 1987): 69–75.

26 Nancy Armstrong, *Desire and Domestic Fiction: A Political History of the Novel* (New York: Oxford University Press, 1987), 81.

27 In their analysis of *Work,* Bardes and Gossett argue that by the end of the novel, "Christie has become an independent small businesswoman. Thus Alcott depicts her heroine as having resolved the potential conflict between two of society's most deeply held values, capitalist freedom and female domesticity." Barbara Bardes and Suzanne Gossett, *Declarations of Independence: Women and Political Power in Nineteenth-Century American Fiction* (New Brunswick, N.J.: Rutgers University Press, 1990), 103. At play in Alcott's novel but absent from most analyses of it is the idea that the public sphere is in fact importantly distinct from the economic market. See the Introduction for a discussion of the critical and historical tendency to reduce the public sphere to the market and place it in binary opposition to the private sphere, similarly reduced to the domestic.

28 Gillian Brown, *Domestic Individualism: Imagining Self in Nineteenth-Century America* (Berkeley: University of California Press, 1990).

29 Elizabeth Stuart Phelps, *The Gates Ajar* (1868; reprint, Cambridge, Mass.: Harvard University Press, 1964), xvi.

30 Elizabeth Barnes traces a history of novels by men that make this connection, from William Hill Brown's *The Power of Sympathy* to Herman Melville's *Pierre.* See her *States of Sympathy: Seduction and Democracy in the American Novel* (New York: Columbia University Press, 1997), 19–39.

31 Michel Foucault, *The History of Sexuality,* vol. 1, *An Introduction,* trans. Robert Hurley (New York: Vintage, 1980), 109. Karen Sánchez-Eppler makes a similar point about the representation of incest in temperance narratives, arguing that "the incest discernible in the plots of these stories proves ambiguous; it serves both as the most extreme mark of familial disintegration and as the mechanism best able to produce family order and happiness." "Temperance in the Bed of a Child: Incest and Social Order in Nineteenth-Century America," *American Quarterly* 47, no. 1 (March 1995): 1–33.

32 In an article dealing with Alcott's first novel, *Moods,* Alfred Habegger notes the recurrence of incestuous plots in sentimental fiction and in Alcott's adult writings in particular. See "Precocious Incest: First Novels by Louisa May Alcott and Henry James," *Massachusetts Review* 26 (1985): 233–61.

33 One could describe many of Alcott's sensational tales in much the same terms, though in them the ambiguity is far more explicit and often unnerving. See, for instance, the marriage that concludes "Behind a Mask; or, A Woman's Power," in *Behind a Mask: The Unknown Thrillers of Louisa May Alcott,* ed. Madeleine Stern (New York: William Morrow, 1975), 3–104. Interestingly, a version of the Carrol chapter appeared as a sensation narrative in *Frank Leslie's Chimney Corner* in late 1865 and early 1866. See Louisa May Alcott, "A Nurse's Story," in *Freaks of Genius: Unknown Thrillers of Louisa May Alcott,* ed. Daniel Shealy (New York: Greenwood Press, 1991), 29–114, and Glenn Hendler, "A Nurse's Story," in *The Louisa May Alcott Encyclopedia,* ed. Gregory Eiselein and Anne K. Phillips (New York: Greenwood Press, forthcoming).

34 The most prominent precedent for this assertion of an uncomfortable affinity between sympathy and incest is certainly William Hill Brown's *The Power of Sympathy* (New York: Penguin, 1996). As Cathy Davidson puts it, "The power of sympathy, in this text, runs head first into its own powerlessness in the face of overpowering incestuous desire." *Revolution and the Word: The Rise of the Novel in America* (New York: Oxford University Press, 1986), 136.

35 One narrative thread of *Work* not especially typical of sentimentalism, but still raising the specter of incest, is the one in which Christie assumes that Letty, for whom David has been mourning, was David's lover, who either died or betrayed him. When David comes to Christie to reveal not only that Letty has unexpectedly returned, but that she is in fact Christie's old friend Rachel, he is bewildered by her response: "[H]er voice was sharp with reproachful anguish, as she cried: 'O, David, David, anything but that!'" He realizes what she has thought, and "his own [face] grew white with indignant repudiation of the thought that daunted her; but he only said with the stern brevity of truth: 'Letty is my sister'" (265). David's white face and "indignant repudiation" are due to Christie's misconception, which forces him to think, momentarily, of the possibility of incest.

36 Louisa May Alcott, *An Old-Fashioned Girl* (1870; reprint, Akron: Saalfield Publishing Company, 1928), 85–86.

37 Ibid., 87.

38 Karen Halttunen, *Confidence Men and Painted Women: A Study of Middle-Class Culture, 1830–1870* (New Haven: Yale University Press, 1982), 185.

39 Alcott, *Old-Fashioned Girl,* 29.

40 Ibid., 31.

41 Ibid., 29.

42 Louisa May Alcott, *Jack and Jill: A Village Story* (1880; reprint, Garden City, N.J.: Nelson Doubleday, 1956), 148.

43 Elizabeth Lennox Keyser, *Whispers in the Dark: The Fiction of Louisa May Alcott* (Knoxville: University of Tennessee Press, 1993), 110; Alcott, *Work*, 37. The character of Mr. Power is based upon Alcott's memories of Theodore Parker, the minister who defined sympathy as the ability to communicate "great power of feeling." In Cheney's memoir of Alcott, Alcott says bluntly, "Mr. Power is Mr. Parker." Louisa May Alcott, *Life, Letters and Journals*, ed. Ednah D. Cheney (Boston: Roberts Brothers, 1889), 220.

44 Lauren Berlant, *The Queen of America Goes to Washington City: Essays on Sex and Citizenship* (Durham, N.C.: Duke University Press, 1997).

45 Habermas, *Structural Transformation*, 49.

46 Ibid., 48.

47 Ibid., 49.

48 Madeleine Stern's biography of Alcott includes one amusing anecdote in which the formation of the Alcott children's characters was explicitly represented as being performed for an audience. Margaret Fuller arrived at the family home in Concord announcing that she had come "to see Mr. Alcott's model children." At that moment Louisa and one of her sisters entered Fuller's view, roughhousing wildly and collapsing on top of one another. "Waving her hand dramatically, [their] Mother announced, 'Here are the model children, Miss Fuller.'" Madeleine Stern, *Louisa May Alcott* (Norman: University of Oklahoma Press, 1950), 24.

49 Joel Myerson, Daniel Shealy, and Madeleine B. Stern, eds., *The Journals of Louisa May Alcott* (Boston: Little, Brown, 1989), 47.

50 Richard H. Brodhead, *Cultures of Letters: Scenes of Reading and Writing in Nineteenth-Century America* (Chicago: University of Chicago Press, 1993), 74. Brodhead remarks that "the maternal tutelary mode" is absent from Alcott's early work and that only with the March novels does she emphasize the "edificatory and moralizing" function of writing. However, I would suggest that what remains consistent across her writing—early and late, moralistic and sensationalistic—is an emphasis on the performative character of sympathy. Polly's pedagogy of emotionality is one example of that performativity, but one could certainly read Jean Muir's act in "Behind a Mask" as another version of the same thing, however different its intentions might be.

51 Quoted in Martha Saxton, *Louisa May: A Modern Biography of Louisa May Alcott* (Boston: Houghton Mifflin, 1977), 305–6.

52 For an analysis of Stowe's comment emphasizing the incipient class divisions implicit in the distinction between "dangerous" and "domestic" fiction, see Brodhead, *Cultures of Letters*, 104–5.

53 Its first publication in book form was by Roberts Brothers in June 1873, in both the

United States and England. The serial had run under the title *Work; or Christie's Experiment;* the subtitle changed to *A Story of Experience* with its appearance as a book. Twenty thousand copies were printed in 1873, and Alcott registers in her journal for July of that year a payment of $5,000 from Roberts Brothers for the book. See Glenn Hendler, *"Work: A Story of Experience,"* in Eiselein and Phillips, *Louisa May Alcott Encyclopedia.*

54 Alcott's narration leaves us in no doubt that she is uninterested in breaking down some distinctions, notably those of ethnicity. In one of several gratuitous anti-Irish slurs in the novel, she describes a speaker who inspires her listeners "to rush to the State-house *en-masse,* and demand the ballot before one-half of them were quite clear what it meant, and the other half were as unfit for it as any ignorant Patrick bribed with a dollar and a sup of whiskey" (331).

55 See Chapter 2.

56 Mary P. Ryan, *Women in Public: Between Banners and Ballots, 1825–1880* (Baltimore: Johns Hopkins University Press, 1990), 53–54.

57 Ibid., 55.

58 Ibid., 55–56.

59 Alcott describes her experience as a servant in "How I Went Out into Service: A Story," *The Independent* 26 (June 4, 1874).

60 On the salon in the American context, see David S. Shields, *Civil Tongues and Polite Letters in British America* (Chapel Hill: University of North Carolina Press, 1997), 99–140. See also Dena Goodman, *The Republic of Letters: A Cultural History of the French Enlightenment* (Ithaca: Cornell University Press, 1994).

61 Shields, *Civil Tongues,* 100, 119–20.

62 See Introduction, above.

63 Ryan, *Women in Public,* 55. One could speculate that Alcott's idea of a salon derived in part from her youth in transcendentalist circles, and especially from her personal knowledge of Margaret Fuller, whose "Conversations" were certainly in the salon tradition. Joan Hedrick's biography of Harriet Beecher Stowe details that author's lifelong involvement in literary clubs, from the Semi-Colons in Cincinnati in the 1830s to the Andover Pic Nic club in the 1860s. Hedrick describes one meeting of the Pic Nic club that included a tableau of Madame Pompadour's eighteenth-century salon and concludes, "When the American parlor imitated the salon of the mistress of King Louis XV, it had truly entered its decadence." Joan Hedrick, *Harriet Beecher Stowe: A Life* (New York: Oxford University Press, 1994), 82–88, 298–99. Quotation is on 299.

64 It is suggestive as well that Alcott published a sentimental novel with an image of institution building at the beginning of the period Estelle Freedman has identified as the era of "female institution building," when a formerly privatized women's culture emerged into explicitly public prominence with the founding of women's colleges, settlement houses, women's clubs, and other social and political organizations.

Estelle Freedman, "Separatism as Strategy: Female Institution Building and American Feminism, 1870–1930," *Feminist Studies* 5 (Fall 1979): 512–29.

65 Stern, *Louisa May Alcott*, 244.

Chapter Five

1 There are several connections between Alcott and James, including a personal acquaintance. See Ednah D. Cheney, *Louisa May Alcott* (New York: Chelsea House, 1980), 165. Alfred Habegger has argued that *The Bostonians* was influenced by James's knowledge of Alcott's family, calling it "a kind of refutation of Alcott's most deeply rooted fantasy." Habegger describes this "fantasy" in psychobiographical terms as a reconciliation of her "naturally lurid color with her stern Concord integrity." Alfred Habegger, *Gender, Fantasy, and Realism in American Literature* (New York: Columbia University Press, 1982), 239.

2 Henry James, *The Bostonians* (1886; reprint, New York: Penguin, 1986), 55–57. Subsequent references to this novel are to this edition and will be cited parenthetically in the text.

3 Theodore Parker, "The Public Function of Woman" (1853), in *Sins and Safeguards of Society,* ed. Samuel B. Stewart (Boston: American Unitarian Association, n.d.), 178.

4 James, *Bostonians,* 230–31; Louisa May Alcott, *Work: A Story of Experience,* ed. Joy Kasson (New York: Penguin, 1994), 342.

5 Richard Sennett cites Carlyle's satirical depiction of "the dandiacal body" in *Sartor Resartus,* as well as the Comte d'Orsay and Beau Brummell, in *The Fall of Public Man* (New York: Knopf, 1976; New York: Norton, 1992), 150–94.

6 Ellen Moers and others have associated the Regency dandy with revolutionary political activity, but few if any critics have made similar claims about American dandies. See Ellen Moers, *The Dandy: Brummell to Beerbohm* (Lincoln: University of Nebraska Press, 1960), 12.

7 See James Walton, "A Mechanic's Tragedy: Reality in *The Princess Casamassima,*" *English Studies Collections,* ser. 1, no. 8 (1976), 1–20.

8 These novels' implicit theorization of publicity is ably analyzed through a Habermasian lens in Richard Salmon, *Henry James and the Culture of Publicity* (Cambridge: Cambridge University Press, 1997).

9 See Lauren Berlant, "The Female Complaint," *Social Text* 19/20 (Fall 1988): 237–59.

10 See, for instance, Jonathan Freedman, *Professions of Taste: Henry James, British Aestheticism, and Commodity Culture* (Stanford: Stanford University Press, 1990), and Michael Anesko, *"Friction with the Market": Henry James and the Profession of Authorship* (New York: Oxford University Press, 1986).

11 Sara Willis Eldredge Farrington would have been Fern's legal name at that time, Eldredge being the patronymic of the husband who had left her a widow in 1846, and Samuel P. Farrington being the man whom she had married in 1849 and then left in 1851; they were divorced in 1853. In 1856, at forty-four, she married the thirty-three-

year-old James Parton, a prominent biographer of Horace Greeley and Aaron Burr, among others, who had once worked for her brother at the *Home Journal.* Joyce Warren notes that "the name Fanny Fern had gradually become her own in private as well as in public life. Her husband called her Fanny, her friends wrote to her as Fanny Fern Parton, and she signed her letters Fanny Fern." Joyce Warren, introduction to *Ruth Hall and Other Writings,* by Fanny Fern (New Brunswick, N.J.: Rutgers University Press, 1986), xix. I will refer to her as Fanny Fern throughout this chapter.

12 Fanny Fern, "Apollo Hyacinth," *Musical World and Times,* June 18, 1853, reprinted in *Ruth Hall and Other Writings,* 259–60.

13 The name "Apollo" has historic associations with dandyism. Ellen Moers mentions an early dandy named Thomas "Apollo" Raikes and that Carlyle called D'Orsay "this Phoebus Apollo of Dandyism." Moers, *The Dandy,* 43, 191.

14 All quotations from Fern, "Apollo Hyacinth," 259–60.

15 Fanny Fern, "Have We Any Men Among Us?" *Musical World and Times,* September 24, 1853, reprinted in *Ruth Hall and Other Writings,* 262–63.

16 Quoted in Thomas N. Baker, *Sentiment and Celebrity: Nathaniel Parker Willis and the Trials of Literary Fame* (New York: Oxford University Press, 1999), 55, 97.

17 Oliver Wendell Holmes, *A Mortal Antipathy: First Opening of the New Portfolio* (Boston: Houghton, Mifflin, 1892), 4.

18 Fanny Fern, *Ruth Hall* (1855), reprinted in *Ruth Hall and Other Writings,* 14, 16. Subsequent references to this novel will be cited parenthetically in the text.

19 Fern here attributes to Hyacinth a model of personality and publicity similar to that of a contemporaneous sensationalist like George Lippard, in whose novels the domestic sphere, though sentimentalized, is a space for planning conspiracies for later public consumption as often as it is the authenticating ground for moral public action that it is in domestic ideology. See, for instance, *The Quaker City; or, The Monks of Monk Hall. A Romance of Philadelphia Life, Mystery, and Crime* (1845), ed. David S. Reynolds (Amherst: University of Massachusetts Press, 1995), and *New York: Its Upper Ten and Lower Million* (1853; reprint, New York: Irvington Publishers, 1993).

20 Lauren Berlant, "The Female Woman: Fanny Fern and the Form of Sentiment," in *The Culture of Sentiment: Race, Gender, and Sentimentality in Nineteenth-Century America,* ed. Shirley Samuels (New York: Oxford University Press, 1992), 265–81.

21 Baker, *Sentiment and Celebrity,* 4–5. Baker even ventures to say that Willis "was also probably the first American to use the new term, celebrity, in print" (8). Most of my information about Willis's life is drawn from Baker's invaluable semibiographical study. To a much smaller degree I also draw upon Cortland P. Auser, *Nathaniel P. Willis* (New York: Twayne, 1969), as well as Henry A. Beers, *Nathaniel Parker Willis* (Boston: Houghton Mifflin, 1885).

22 Baker, *Sentiment and Celebrity,* 8.

23 Ibid.

24 Quoted in ibid., 39.

25 Sandra Tomc, "An Idle Industry: Nathaniel Parker Willis and the Workings of Literary Leisure," *American Quarterly* 49, no. 4 (December 1997): 785. Thanks to Sandra Tomc for sparking my interest in Willis and the dandy figure in general by organizing an American Studies Association panel in which I participated along with Nicola Nixon and Robert K. Martin.

26 Willis was wracked by illness through much of his adult life; his innovation was to present both his sickness and his convalescence as narrative commodities for his readers to consume. See the "Dedicatory Preface" to his collection *The Convalescent,* which opens, "To sickness I have always found I had much reason to be indebted," and in which he dedicates his book to two physicians. Nathaniel Parker Willis, *The Convalescent* (New York: Charles Scribner, 1859), i.

27 Baker, *Sentiment and Celebrity,* 44.

28 Thomas Carlyle, *Sartor Resartus: The Life and Opinions of Herr Teufelsdröckh* (1838; reprint, London: Oxford University Press, 1902), 235.

29 Sennett, *Fall of Public Man,* 153.

30 See Chapter 3.

31 Carlyle, *Sartor Resartus,* 236.

32 Jürgen Habermas, *The Structural Transformation of the Public Sphere: An Inquiry into a Category of Bourgeois Society,* trans. Thomas Burger and Frederick Lawrence (Cambridge, Mass.: MIT Press, 1989), 49.

33 Ibid.

34 The description of Willis's appearance is drawn from Baker, *Sentiment and Celebrity,* 62. In a fascinating reading of Melville's use of the dandy figure, Nicola Nixon points out that the tailor Stultz (or Stultze) "was reputedly the dandy's cherished tailor," but that he had also "become synonymous with empty fashionability." Nixon notes that Selvagee, one of the "lords and noblemen" of the quarterdeck in Melville's *White-Jacket,* " 'sport[s] a coat fashioned by a Stultz' with 'all the intrepid effeminacy of your true dandy.' " Nicola Nixon, "Men and Coats; or, the Politics of the Dandiacal Body in Melville's 'Benito Cereno,' " *PMLA* 114 (May 1999): 364.

35 On the role of the salon in producing and instanciating the bourgeois public sphere, see Chapter 4.

36 Quoted in Baker, *Sentiment and Celebrity,* 70.

37 Quoted in ibid., 74.

38 Quoted in Beers, *Nathaniel Parker Willis,* 187; emphasis in original.

39 Quoted in ibid., 188.

40 Fern's publishers courted such accusations by placing an advertisement denying—and thus publicizing—the charge that Hyacinth was based on Willis. Joyce W. Warren, *Fanny Fern: An Independent Woman* (New Brunswick, N.J.: Rutgers University Press, 1992), 123.

41 Quoted in ibid., 121.

42 Quoted in ibid., 122. "Finikin" and "finical" are connotatively linked to dandyism.

The *Oxford English Dictionary* defines "finicking, finikin" as "[a]ffecting extreme re-finement; dainty, fastidious, mincing; excessively precise in trifles. Also of things: Over-delicately wrought or finished; also, insignificant, paltry, trifling," and "fini-cal" as "[o]f persons, their actions and attributes: Over-nice or particular, affectedly fastidious, excessively punctilious or precise, in speech, dress, manners, methods of work, etc. Also of things: Over-scrupulously finished; excessively or affectedly fine or delicate in workmanship."

43 Quoted in Beers, *Nathaniel Parker Willis*, 122–23.

44 Ibid., 162.

45 Nathaniel Parker Willis, *Paul Fane; or, Parts of a Life Else Untold: A Novel* (New York: Scribner, 1857), 29. Subsequent references to this novel will be cited parenthetically in the text. Willis's novel has been plausibly read as a "forerunner of the 'international' novel" of Henry James. See Auser, *Nathaniel P. Willis*, 101–5.

46 As Baker puts it, "Following his sister's lead, he thus prepared to fight fiction with fiction." Baker, *Sentiment and Celebrity*, 183.

47 *American Heritage Dictionary*, 3d ed. Baker also notes the shifting meaning of the term; see *Sentiment and Celebrity*, 204 n. 27.

48 Paul's representation of "personality" in portraits bears comparison with the career trajectory later in the century of Thomas Eakins, whose later portraits are said to be among the first aimed at "psychological" representation. See David M. Lubin, "Modern Psychological Selfhood in the Art of Thomas Eakins," in *Inventing the Psychological: Toward a Cultural History of Emotional Life in America*, ed. Joel Pfister and Nancy Schnog (New Haven: Yale University Press, 1997), 133–66, and Martin A. Berger, "Sentimental Realism in Thomas Eakins's Late Portraits," in *Sentimental Men: Masculinity and the Politics of Affect in American Culture*, ed. Mary Chapman and Glenn Hendler (Berkeley and Los Angeles: University of California Press, 1999), 244–58.

49 I have been unable to locate any direct connection between this Princess C—— and the Princess Casamassima, or any evidence that James read *Paul Fane* (though James was familiar with some of Willis's writings, as I discuss later in this chapter). These various princesses are also linked in multiple ways to Hyacinths, a link that continues into the work of Constance Fenimore Woolson, a close friend of James. Woolson's story "The Street of the Hyacinth" is about a woman painter who goes to Italy to study and there meets yet another Princess C——. Constance Fenimore Woolson, "The Street of the Hyacinth," in *Women Artists, Women Exiles: "Miss Grief" and Other Stories*, ed. Joan Myers Weimer (New Brunswick, N.J.: Rutgers University Press, 1988), 170–210.

50 I am not sure what to make of the fact that in the opening pages of Sade's *120 Days of Sodom*, three of the characters in the first orgy are named Hyacinthe, Antinoüs, and Fanny. It is also worth mentioning a comment from Wilde's *Picture of Dorian Gray*, where the painter Basil remarks, "What the invention of oil-painting was to the

Venetians, the face of Antinoüs was to late Greek sculpture, and the face of Dorian Gray will some day be to me."

51 Henry James, *Roderick Hudson* (1875; New York: Penguin Books, 1986), 119.

52 Early in *Paul Fane,* the protagonist is described as a "walking dictionary of beautiful things, and will tell you the names of any flowers you may not recognize" (14). Fanny Fern refers disparagingly in her columns to a "dictionary on legs."

53 James, *Roderick Hudson,* 120.

54 James also juxtaposed Willis with women writers in a passage in *A Small Boy and Others* (1913): "There were authors not less, some of them vague and female and in this case, as a rule, glossily ringletted and monumentally breastpinned, but mostly frequent and familiar, after the manner of George Curtis and Parke Godwin and George Ripley and Charles Dana and N. P. Willis and, for brighter lights or those that in our then comparative obscurity almost deceived the norm, Mr. Bryant, Washington Irving and E. A. Poe." Henry James, *A Small Boy and Others,* in *Autobiography,* ed. Frederick W. Dupee (Princeton: Princeton University Press, 1956), 36.

55 Quoted in Leon Edel, *Henry James: The Middle Years, 1882–1895* (Philadelphia: J. B. Lippincott, 1962), 164.

56 Quoted in Marcia Jacobson, *Henry James and the Mass Market* (University: University of Alabama Press, 1983), 2.

57 In this, my analysis complements Dana D. Nelson's arguments about the development of "national/white manhood" in scientific and literary texts from the early republic to the antebellum period. See *National Manhood: Capitalist Citizenship and the Imagined Fraternity of White Men* (Durham, N.C.: Duke University Press, 1998).

58 Henry James, *The Tragic Muse* (1890; New York: Penguin, 1995), 64.

59 Ibid., 63.

60 Ibid., 480, 476.

61 Ibid., 33.

62 Nick's lament that such a choice is not a real alternative also applies to Hyacinth: "[Y]ou've converted me," he says to Nash, "from a representative into an example — that's a shade better." Ibid., 471.

63 Henry James, *The Princess Casamassima* (1886; New York: Penguin, 1986), 114.

64 Ibid., 117.

65 James, *Tragic Muse,* 471.

66 Henry James, *Notes of a Son and Brother,* in *Autobiography,* 400.

67 The full list of names is in Baker, *Sentiment and Celebrity,* 121, part of Baker's detailed and insightful analysis of this incident (115–57).

68 Ibid., 127. As Baker explains, the *Herald*'s editor, James Gordon Bennett, managed to associate Willis with free love, the scandalous novels of George Sand, and Fourierist socialism, among other unlikely sins. Later Bennett added to these charges a reference to Willis's early British scandal, accusing him of "introducing the blessed Blessington creed among the fashionable people of New York." Quoted in ibid., 133.

69 Ibid., 131.

70 Quoted in ibid., 136.

71 Ibid., 215 n. 39.

72 James, *Notes of a Son and Brother*, 401.

73 Ibid., 400.

Chapter Six

1 Mark Twain, "The Dandy Frightening the Squatter" (1852), in *Collected Tales, Sketches, Speeches, and Essays, 1852–1890* (New York: Library of America, 1992), 1–2. The sketch was credited to "S.L.C." A year after writing this story, Clemens went to see Edwin Forrest on stage. See Andrew Hoffman, *Inventing Mark Twain: The Lives of Samuel Langhorne Clemens* (New York: William Morrow, 1997), 38.

2 Twain, "The Dandy," 1.

3 Ibid., 2.

4 See B. P. Shillaber, *Ike Partington: or, The Adventures of a Human Boy and His Friends* (Boston: Lee and Shepard, 1879); B. P. Shillaber, *Mrs. Partington's Knitting-Work; and What Was Done by Her Plaguy Boy Ike: A Web of Many Textures, As Wrought by the Old Lady Herself* (1868; New York, William L. Allison Company, n.d.); George Wilbur Peck, *Peck's Bad Boy and His Pa* (Chicago: Belford, Clarke and Company, 1883) and *Peck's Boss Book* (Chicago: W. B. Conkey, 1884). Further emphasizing the link between Twain and Shillaber is the fact that the last image in *The Adventures of Tom Sawyer* is not a drawing by True Williams, who illustrated the rest of the novel; rather, what appears to be a drawing of Aunt Polly is actually a copy of an illustration by Josiah Wolcott of "Mrs. Partington," from the frontispiece of Shillaber's *The Life and Sayings of Mrs. Partington and Others of the Family* (New York: J. C. Derby, 1854).

5 Two Ned Buntline novels are explicitly mentioned in *Tom Sawyer: Bellamira; or, The Last Days of Callao: An Historical Romance of Peru* (Boston: n.p., [ca. 1847]) and *The Black Avenger of the Spanish Main; or, The Fiend of Blood: A Thrilling Story of the Buccaneer Times* (Boston: F. Gleason, Flag of Our Union Office, 1847). It is also worth noting that Ned Buntline—the pseudonym of Edward Zane Carroll Judson—was credited as one of the instigators of the Astor Place riots that broke out as supporters of Edwin Forrest demonstrated against the acting of his rival William Macready.

6 Thomas Bailey Aldrich, *The Story of a Bad Boy*, vol. 7 of *The Writings of Thomas Bailey Aldrich* (Boston: Houghton Mifflin, 1897); Mark Twain, *The Adventures of Tom Sawyer* (Berkeley: University of California Press, 1980); Charles Dudley Warner, *Being a Boy* (Boston: Houghton, Mifflin, and Company, 1897); William Dean Howells, *A Boy's Town, Described for "Harper's Young People"* (New York: Harper and Brothers, 1904). Despite its title, Twain's 1865 "Story of the Bad Little Boy" is, like "The Story of the Good Little Boy," a straightforward inversion of the conventions of didactic Sunday school fiction and not an early example of the bad-boy genre. See "Story of the Bad Little Boy" and "Story of the Good Little Boy" in *Sketches New*

and Old [ca. 1865], vol. 19 of *The Writings of Mark Twain* (New York: Harper and Brothers, 1875), 54–59, 60–67. For a useful discussion of the bad-boy genre, see Anne Tropp Trensky, "The Bad Boy in Nineteenth-Century American Fiction," *Georgia Review* 27 (Winter 1973): 503–17.

7 Twain, *Adventures of Tom Sawyer,* xvii. Subsequent references to this novel will be made parenthetically in the text.

8 Albert Stone cites a comment from Twain's notebook, written on July 7, 1902: "Write a preface: I have never written a book for boys; I write for grown-ups who have been boys. If the boys read it & like it, perhaps that is testimony that my boys are real, not artificial. If they are real to the grown-ups, that is proof." Stone's conclusion is that "Twain was of two minds about the readers for whom he finally published *The Adventures of Tom Sawyer.*" Albert E. Stone Jr., *The Innocent Eye: Childhood in Mark Twain's Imagination* (New Haven: Yale University Press, 1961), 60.

9 Frederick Anderson, *Mark Twain: The Critical Heritage* (London: Routledge and Kegan Paul, 1971), 65, 72. Each of the reviews of *Tom Sawyer* collected in Anderson's book raises the question of the novel's audience.

10 Steven Mailloux analyzes the contemporary response to *Huck Finn* to demonstrate that that novel as well was taken by most of its readers to be—and thus in an important way *was*—a bad-boy book addressed to children. See Steven Mailloux, *Rhetorical Power* (Ithaca: Cornell University Press, 1989), 100–129.

11 Mark Twain and William Dean Howells, *Mark Twain–Howells Letters: The Correspondence of Samuel L. Clemens and William D. Howells, 1872–1910,* ed. Henry Nash Smith and William M. Gibson, 2 vols. (Cambridge, Mass.: Belknap Press of Harvard University Press, 1960), 90, 91, 112.

12 Howells, *A Boy's Town,* 1.

13 Louis Althusser, *Lenin and Philosophy,* trans. Ben Brewster (New York: Monthly Review Press, 1971), 127–93.

14 Given most of Twain's comments about his readership, I think it is fairly uncontroversial to say that *Tom Sawyer* primarily addresses male readers. As mentioned above, however, Twain claims in the preface that *Tom Sawyer* addresses both sexes, and in any case the question of female responses to texts aimed at male readers is an interesting and important one. For a variety of reasons I have limited the scope of this chapter to the way the interpellations and identifications figured in the bad-boy book constructs and deconstructs masculine identity, thus largely ignoring the question of female readers. One way of thinking about this issue would be to take up a thesis analogous to that advanced by Laura Mulvey and other feminist film theorists in attempts to theorize female spectators of classical Hollywood cinema, to argue that female readers of bad-boy books are masculinized by their identification with a figure like Tom Sawyer. I am reluctant to advance such a claim, however, because, as I argue below, the novels consistently figure their readers' identification with their boy protagonists as including an element of distance from him; the pleasures of identi-

fying with a boy, even for a man, involve a reassertion of difference. This element of distanciation might open up an identificatory position for a female reader—a position that is neither the same as that offered to the male reader nor one that could easily be described as masculinized. See Laura Mulvey, *Visual and Other Pleasures* (Bloomington: Indiana University Press, 1989). I expand on the disjunction between interpellation and identification in the Coda.

15 See Introduction and Chapter 4. Even in the mid- to late nineteenth century, Adam Smith's *Theory of Moral Sentiments* was still an extremely influential account of sympathy. For an illuminating discussion of the influence on Twain's work of Smith and the concept of sympathy, see Gregg Camfield, *Sentimental Twain: Samuel Clemens in the Maze of Moral Philosophy* (Philadelphia: University of Pennsylvania Press, 1994).

16 See Chapter 3. Twain lampooned the conventions of sentimental children's fiction in his 1865 "Story of a Bad Little Boy" and "Story of a Good Little Boy" by reversing the conclusions the stories would have had in "Sunday-school books." The mischievous boy does not die the expected horrific death but instead grows into a prosperous though still quite "wicked" member of the legislature. The good little boy is accidentally blown up by nitroglycerin and thus is denied the conventional deathbed speech he has planned for all his life. See also the mocking appropriation of feminine sentimental writings in *The Adventures of Tom Sawyer*, 156–59. Trensky in "The Bad Boy" and Alfred Habegger in *Gender, Fantasy, and Realism in American Literature* (New York: Columbia University Press, 1982) both read the bad-boy figure as a reaction to sentimentality.

17 For an extended discussion of Tom in these terms, see Elizabeth P. Peck, "Tom Sawyer: Character in Search of an Audience," *American Transcendental Quarterly,* n.s., 2, no. 3 (September 1988): 223–36.

18 The figure of the detective is briefly invoked in *The Adventures of Tom Sawyer,* but only to be mocked. "One of those omniscient and awe-inspiring marvels, a detective, came up from St. Louis" to hunt for Injun Joe, but he departs with no success (174).

19 Howells, *A Boy's Town,* 104.

20 Ibid., 209.

21 Ibid., 209–10.

22 Warner, *Being a Boy,* 50.

23 Alfred Habegger discusses the thematization of boys' "savagery" in *A Boy's Town* in *Gender, Fantasy and Realism,* arguing that "the central idea in *A Boy's Town* . . . is that boyhood in the life of a man corresponds to savagery in the history of the human race" (213).

24 Howells, *A Boy's Town,* 67.

25 Warner, *Being a Boy,* 150.

26 Howells, *A Boy's Town,* 104.

27 The title of the second chapter, "The Right that Pony had to Run Off, from the Way

his Father Acted," seems to imply that both parents are equally responsible for Pony's oppression, but its first sentence dispels any such possibility: "Pony had a right to run off from some of the things that his father had done, but it seemed to him that they were mostly things that his mother had put his father up to, and that his father would not have been half as bad if he had been let alone." William Dean Howells, *The Flight of Pony Baker: A Boy's Town Story* (New York: Harper and Brothers, 1902), 15.

28 Mark Twain, "Huck Finn and Tom Sawyer among the Indians" (1884), in *Huck Finn and Tom Sawyer among the Indians and Other Unfinished Stories* (Berkeley: University of California Press, 1989), 33–81.

29 See Chapter 2.

30 On nineteenth-century norms of masculine individuality, see John G. Cawelti, *Apostles of the Self-Made Man: Changing Concepts of Success in America* (Chicago: University of Chicago Press, 1965), and Karen Halttunen, *Confidence Men and Painted Women: A Study of Middle-Class Culture, 1830–1870* (New Haven: Yale University Press, 1982). Among the most useful social histories of nineteenth-century boyhood and its relation to ideals of manhood are David I. Macleod, *Building Character in the American Boy: The Boy Scouts, YMCA, and Their Forerunners, 1870–1920* (Madison: University of Wisconsin Press, 1983), and Allan Stanley Horlick, *Country Boys and Merchant Princes: The Social Control of Young Men in New York* (Lewisburg, Pa.: Bucknell University Press, 1975).

31 Howells, *A Boy's Town*, 190.

32 Warner, *Being a Boy*, xviii.

33 The composite order is an architectural term designating a Roman capital formed by superimposing an Ionic volute on a Corinthian capital.

34 William Dean Howells, review of *The Story of a Bad Boy*, by Thomas Bailey Aldrich, *Atlantic Monthly*, January 1870, 124.

35 Aldrich, *Story of a Bad Boy*, 3.

36 Howells, *Boy's Town*, 171.

37 For a complex account of the shifting opposition between interiority and external appearance and its role in the construction of both male and female identity, see Halttunen, *Confidence Men*.

38 Elizabeth Peck describes Tom as narcissistic for similar reasons in her "Tom Sawyer," 233.

39 On death fantasies in the sentimental novel, see Chapter 4.

40 For discussions of the debates over the reading of boys and young men, see Horlick, *Country Boys;* Macleod, *Building Character;* Mailloux, *Rhetorical Power;* and Catherine Sheldrick Ross, "Metaphors of Reading," *Journal of Library History* 22 (Spring 1987): 147–63. For some examples of this debate, see *Library Journal* 4, nos. 9–10 (September–October 1879).

41 See Introduction, above.

42 Lionel Trilling, *The Liberal Imagination: Essays on Literature and Society* (1948; re-

print, New York: Harcourt Brace Jovanovich, 1979), 110. The same is true of other Twain stories involving Tom. For instance, in the unfinished tale "Huck Finn and Tom Sawyer among the Indians," Tom blames his mishaps on the misconceptions about Indians he got from reading "Cooper's novels" (50). James Fenimore Cooper was one of Twain's favorite targets for ridicule; see Mark Twain, "Fenimore Cooper's Literary Offenses" in *Great Short Works of Mark Twain*, ed. Justin Kaplan (New York: Harper and Row, 1967), 169–81. Here, as elsewhere in his writings on boys, Twain joins his own critics in claiming that fantastic and unrealistic tales like those of Cooper are capable of taking hold of a boy's mind and influencing his actions.

43 Each of the "lines of action" Walter Blair identifies in *The Adventures of Tom Sawyer*—"the story of Tom and Becky, the story of Tom and Muff Potter, the Jackson's Island episode, and the series of happenings (which might be called the Injun Joe story) leading to the discovery of the treasure"—is more or less directly inspired by Tom's attempt to act out his own version of a narrative he has read, to identify with its hero. Walter Blair, "On the Structure of *Tom Sawyer*," *Modern Philology* 37 (August 1939): 84. All but the first are clearly variations on or parodies of sensational adventure stories and include typical elements such as grave robbing, piracy, running away from home, and the deciphering of a cryptic message. The "love story" is a bit more ambiguous in its literary sources, but Tom's attempt to win Becky's favor by fraudulently claiming a reading prize in Sunday school can easily be seen as an attempt to take on the role of the hero of a "good boy" Sunday school story. See Twain, *Adventures of Tom Sawyer*, 34–36.

44 Howells, *A Boy's Town*, 171. The bookishness of Howells's, Warner's and Twain's boys differentiates them from some of their sources in the popular bad-boy tradition such as B. P. Shillaber's Ike Partington and George Peck's "Bad Boy." The heroes of these books do not refer quite so frequently to literary sources for their activities, although they are, like the later boys, openly scornful of good-boy books. The "savagery" and cruelty represented by the more genteel authors are also quite mild compared to the sadistic antics of heroes like Ike, who at times seem almost inhuman in their indiscriminate attempts to injure or humiliate anyone who crosses their paths with often violent practical jokes. But Howells and Warner, like Aldrich in *The Story of a Bad Boy,* are so intent on proving that a "bad boy" can grow up to be a good man that the acts they characterize as "savage" are rarely more disruptive than lighting fireworks and swimming in a forbidden area.

45 William Dean Howells, review of *The Adventures of Tom Sawyer,* by Mark Twain, *Atlantic Monthly,* May 1876, 621.

46 Howells, *A Boy's Town*, 176–77.

47 Ibid., 177.

48 For discussions of the way this metaphorics was often literalized, see Steven Mailloux, "The Rhetorical Use and Abuse of Fiction: Eating Books in Late Nineteenth-Century America," *Boundary 2* 17, no. 1 (Spring 1990): 133–57, and Ross, "Metaphors

of Reading." Freud sometimes describes identification as incorporation, though the latter term more often designates the infantile, physical model for the later development of the process of identification. See J. Laplanche and J-B. Pontalis, *The Language of Psychoanalysis,* trans. Donald Nicholson-Smith (New York: Norton, 1973), 211–12; Sigmund Freud, *The Interpretation of Dreams* (1900), trans. James Strachey (New York: Avon Books, 1965), 183. The connection between identification and incorporation is developed more fully in Melanie Klein, "On Identification," in *Our Adult World and Other Essays* (New York: Basic Books, 1963), 55–98.

49 Howells, *A Boy's Town,* 181–82.

50 The best work on Comstock's long and complex career is Nicola Beisel, *Imperiled Innocents: Anthony Comstock and Family Reproduction in Victorian America* (Princeton: Princeton University Press, 1997).

51 Of course, Comstock's rage is generally directed against the more sensational forms of boys' literature, for which Howells as well had little affection. But Comstock is quite explicit that no matter how mild or extreme, depictions of immoral acts lead to immoral responses from their readers. Thus the pranks, disrespect for authority, petty theft, and lying in *A Boy's Town,* like the arson, theft, bribery, and escape from jail in Aldrich's *Story of a Bad Boy* (much of which, in both books, remains undiscovered and unpunished) would qualify each book for Comstock's condemnation.

52 This opening paragraph's account of the formation of subjectivity through incorporative identification is no more overtly gendered than Locke's "blank slate" metaphor, on which it is obviously based. It is meant as a description of the lures of all the "traps" the book denounces. However, its metaphorics are most fully developed in Comstock's chapter on bad-boy books, and its consistency with the rhetoric of other denunciations of the genre justifies its use as an example in this context. Anthony Comstock, *Traps for the Young* (1883; New York: Funk and Wagnalls, 1884), ix.

53 In the unfinished 1897 manuscript titled "Tom Sawyer's Conspiracy," Twain develops the equivalence between books and boys in a scene of veiled competition between Tom and Huck over the use of language. In a moment of frustration, Tom says that his brother Sid "was too good for this world, and ought to be translated." Huck, who is narrating, knows the correct definition of the word translated but refrains from correcting Tom. Huck confides to the reader that "I knowed you can translate a book, but you can't translate a boy, becuz translating means turning a thing out of one language into another, and you can't do that with a boy. And besides it has to be a foreign one, and Sid warn't a foreign boy." Mark Twain, "Tom Sawyer's Conspiracy," in *Huck Finn and Tom Sawyer among the Indians,* 153. The humor of the passage derives from the fact that Huck almost accepts the possibility that a boy could be like a book.

54 Comstock, *Traps,* 31.

55 For a somewhat different interpretation of the figure of the gang in the bad-boy book, see Habegger, *Gender, Fantasy, and Realism,* 206–19.

56 Adult men in the late nineteenth century were also searching for escape from the constraints of public masculinity through the rituals of organizations like the Freemasons and the Odd Fellows. For a discussion of the importance of secret societies in the construction of nineteenth-century masculinity, see Mark C. Carnes, *Secret Ritual and Manhood in Victorian America* (New Haven: Yale University Press, 1989).

57 Howells, *A Boy's Town,* 10.

58 Leslie Fiedler, "Come Back to the Raft Ag'in, Huck Honey!" (1948), in *A Fiedler Reader* (New York: Stein and Day, 1977), 3–12.

59 See Sigmund Freud, "On the Sexual Theories of Children" (1908), in *The Sexual Enlightenment of Children,* ed. Philip Rieff (New York: Collier Books, 1963), 25–40.

60 Bernard DeVoto, *Mark Twain at Work* (1942), reprinted in *Mark Twain's America, and Mark Twain at Work* (Boston: Houghton Mifflin, 1967), 12–14.

61 Tom's position in a conventional domestic space is anticipated in an earlier scene in which he mentions that if he ever finds a treasure he will "buy a new drum, and a sure-'nough sword, and a red neck-tie and a bull pup, and get married." This depresses Huck, for "if you get married I'll be more lonesomer than ever." But Tom states authoritatively: "No you won't. You'll come and live with me" (178–79). Like Alger, who refigures the domestic realm as a homosocial space, Twain places a homosocial bond at the center of his utopian image of domesticity. Alger's brief visions of homosocial domesticity seem to exclude marriage, whereas Twain's even briefer vision of married domesticity includes homosociality. On homosociality in Alger, see Michael Moon, " 'The Gentle Boy from the Dangerous Classes': Pederasty, Domesticity, and Capitalism in Horatio Alger," *Representations* 19 (Summer 1987): 87–110.

62 Eve Kosofsky Sedgwick, *Between Men: English Literature and Male Homosocial Desire* (New York: Columbia University Press, 1985).

63 Howells, *A Boy's Town,* 2.

64 Harriet Beecher Stowe, *Uncle Tom's Cabin* (1852; reprint, New York: Norton, 1994), 428.

65 Mark Twain, "Boy's Manuscript" (1868), in *Huck Finn and Tom Sawyer among the Indians,* 17.

66 Ibid., 11.

67 Ibid., 17. The story ends with Billy falling in love again, but this time with a girl many years his senior who is clearly uninterested in him.

68 One possible answer to this question, in the case of *Tom Sawyer,* is that this shift in Tom is the novel's weakness. Some of Twain's critics have claimed that, as readers, they lose interest in Tom at the end, even charging that Tom betrays Huck by convincing him to resubmit to the Widow Douglas's care. Others, agreeing with the premise that Tom becomes less attractive at the end of the novel, argue that Twain deliberately ironizes Tom's character, especially his tendency to subordinate reality to what he has read in books. This interpretation makes the end of *Tom Sawyer* consis-

tent with that of *Huckleberry Finn,* in which Tom's insistence that Jim's escape from slavery be "by the book" results in Jim's humiliation and pain.

To sustain either of these interpretations, however, it would be necessary to re-conceive the entirety of *The Adventures of Tom Sawyer* as ironic, for all the traits sati-rized at the end of *Huckleberry Finn* exist in Tom from the beginning of the earlier book. From the start, the "literary furnishings" of Tom's mind determine his actions, and he is willing to cause pain to others in order to make things come out "by the book," as, for instance, when he delays the boys' return from Jackson's Island de-spite his awareness of Aunt Polly's sorrow and Joe Harper's homesickness. And the same letter to Howells in which Twain insists that the book "is *not* a boy's book, at all" records his decision to refuse to narrate Tom's ascension to manhood as based precisely in a desire to avoid arousing this distaste in the reader. "If I went on, now, & took him into manhood, he would just be like all the one-horse men in litera-ture & the reader would conceive a hearty contempt for him" (Twain and Howells, *Letters,* 91).

69 Warner, *Being a Boy,* 69.

70 Aldrich, *Story of a Bad Boy,* 4–5.

71 As we saw in Chapter 4, marriage was only one of the forms of affective connection valorized by the sentimental novel for women. But by the 1870s it was both a com-monplace and a source of ridicule that sentimental novels had to end in the heroine's marriage. Louisa May Alcott strongly felt the constraints of this convention even in her children's fiction, responding to letters from the mostly female readers of *Little Women* by insisting, "I won't marry Jo off to Laurie for anybody." Of course, she did ultimately "marry Jo off," though not to Laurie, thus underscoring the perception that marriage was the mandatory conclusion for feminine fiction.

Coda

1 Louis Althusser, *Lenin and Philosophy,* trans. Ben Brewster (New York: Monthly Re-view Press, 1971), 174.

2 Mark Twain, "Boy's Manuscript" (1868, in *Huck Finn and Tom Sawyer among the Indi-ans and Other Unfinished Stories* (Berkeley: University of California Press, 1989), 16. All errors in spelling and punctuation are from the original.

3 Gender and sexuality, of course, are not issues Althusser addresses in much detail, although in the section on interpellation in his essay on ideology he does remark on the way the family interpellates an expected baby as a "sexual subject." After briefly gesturing to Freudian (and implicitly Lacanian) theories of sexual identity, Althusser concludes by "leav[ing] this point, too, on one side." Althusser, *Lenin and Philosophy,* 176.

4 Ibid., 180.

5 Fuss's claim comes at the beginning of a chapter on "Frantz Fanon and the Politics of

Identification," where she argues that identification's history is "a colonial history." Diana Fuss, *Identification Papers* (New York: Routledge, 1995), 141.

6 For a marvelously nuanced account of these debates, see Carla Kaplan, *The Erotics of Talk: Women's Writing and Feminist Paradigms* (New York: Oxford University Press, 1996).

7 Theodore Parker, *Lessons from the World of Matter and the World of Man,* vol. 14 of *The Collected Works of Theodore Parker,* ed. Rufus Leighton (London: Trübner and Company, 1872), 108–9.

8 See Kaplan, *Erotics of Talk,* 144–63, and Ann Cvetkovich, *Mixed Feelings: Feminism, Mass Culture, and Victorian Sensationalism* (New Brunswick, N.J.: Rutgers University Press, 1992), 1–6.

INDEX

Howells, William Dean, 25, 115, 116, 197; *A Boy's Town*, 23, 185, 186, 190, 192, 193, 194, 198, 199, 205–6; *The Flight of Pony Baker*, 191; review of *Tom Sawyer*, 198

Musical World and Times, 153
Mystery, 57

National Emigration Convention of
Colored People, 55, 58
Nationalism, 59, 62, 65, 81, 161, 175, 176;
American, 50, 71, 76; black, 53, 62, 63,
76, 236 (n. 3)
Nationality, 46, 50, 55, 62, 64, 68, 72, 87;
and sentiment, 61, 136, 163, 174–75,
177
Negro Convention movement, 15, 16, 53,
56–58, 62, 92
Negt, Oscar, 16
Nelson, Dana, 8
New World, 30
New York Aurora, 30
New York Crystal Font, 48
New York Enquirer, 156
New York Herald, 181
New York Mirror, 158, 160, 162
New York Observer, 38
New York Washingtonian and Organ, 30
New York Times, 14, 161, 186
Noble, Marianne, 9
Nord, David Paul, 95
North Star, 57
Novels, 48–49, 162, 176, 212; as com-
modity, 14; dime, 84; theory of, 16,
48–49

O'Connell, Daniel, 160
Olmsted, Frederick Law, 83, 84, 85, 89,
96
Optic, Oliver, 97
Ouida, 86

Pan-Africanism, 53, 236 (n. 3)
Parker, Theodore, 3, 12, 115, 138, 148, 218,
222 (n. 12), 253 (n. 43)

Penn, Arthur: *The Home Library*, 104
Performance, 148–49; of identity, 158,
165–69, 182, 184; of sympathy, 129,
154–55. *See also* Theatricality
"Personal," 116, 117, 141, 147, 148. 151,
152, 155, 161
Personality, 25, 145, 147, 149, 151, 157,
159, 166, 169, 172, 189
Phelps, Elizabeth Stuart, 136; *The Gates
Ajar*, 126
Politics of affect, 8, 12, 16, 118, 147,
218–19
Porter, Noah: *Books and Reading*, 102–5,
245–46 (n. 49)
Postfeminism, 113
"Principle of negativity," 18
Print, 16, 18, 46, 95, 149, 150, 156
Prohibitionists, 44
Projection, 205–7, 215
Protestant Episcopal Quarterly Review, 161
Public: opinion of, 2, 13, 149; political,
22, 44, 56, 117, 146, 151, 212; reading,
22, 76, 118, 146, 186
Public sphere: access to, 18–19; black,
53, 57, 58, 60; and civil society, 13; cultural, 44, 83; versus domestic sphere;
83, 155; Habermas defines, 12–14;
intimate, 132; literary, 117, 212; versus
market; 83–91, 93, 104; versus personal
sphere, 161; versus private sphere, 155;
women in, 113–14, 137–40

Quarterly Journal, 160

Ramée, Marie Louisa de la, 86
Rational-critical debate, 13, 15, 21, 46, 47
Reading clubs, 13
Reid-Pharr, Robert, 241 (n. 60)
Renan, Ernest, 61
"Representative publicness," 12–13, 58
Republicanism, 31–32, 94, 95, 212